Interior Architecture Now

Published in 2007
by Laurence King Publishing Ltd
4th Floor
361–373 City Road
London EC1V 1LR
e-mail: enquiries@laurenceking.co.uk
www.laurenceking.co.uk

Text © 2007 Laurence King
Publishing Ltd
This book was designed and
produced by Laurence King
Publishing Ltd

A catalogue record for this book is
available from the British Library

ISBN-13: 978-1-85669-520-6
ISBN-10: 1-85669-520-4

Project managed by Lara Maiklem
Design by SMITH, Karl Shanahan

Printed in China

Author's Acknowledgements

I would like to thank all the architects and designers featured in this book for their time
and patience in answering my questions and for supplying all the material necessary for
publication. I would like to express my gratitude to my editor Lara Maiklem for her hard
work, support and unerring eye for detail; to my copy editor Ramona Lamport for trying
to tackle all my split infinitives; and to the designer of the book, Karl Shanahan, who must
surely want to kill me by now. At Laurence King, I would like to thank Sheila Smith in the
Production Department and our Editorial Director Philip Cooper for keeping all on track.
I would also like to show my appreciation to Laura Willis and Lori Taylor for their
marketing and publicity expertise and for the hours they will spend promoting the book.

Interior Architecture Now is dedicated to my son Willoughby Oliver Hudson Werner.

Interior Architecture Now

Jennifer Hudson

LAURENCE KING

Contents

Introduction

In the following pages I have sought to bring together 55 of the most interesting people and practices designing interiors today – from the well known and long established to the young and experimental. With the relatively restricted extent of the book and given the fact that I wanted to allocate the majority of entries the same coverage (comprehensively illustrated with examples showing the diverse nature of the work), it is unavoidably a personal selection with inescapable omissions and surprise features. *Interior Architecture Now* does not set out to be a comprehensive survey; it seeks to highlight the scope and variety of the interiors in which we conduct our lives, as well as the range of approaches the architects and designers have taken to achieve these cutting-edge spaces. Indeed, what struck me when I was interviewing the people featured was that, although common threads were apparent ('the need to take a holistic, multi-disciplinary approach', 'methodology having a more significant role to play than style', 'influence and inspiration being more likely to be found in life experience, the commonplace, unrelated disciplines and different cultures than in the work of individuals and movements', 'the importance of site, cultural context and client' and 'the pre-eminence of space over form', etc.), when I came to writing the features, not once, in essence, did I have to repeat myself.

All 55 individuals and practices have unique ways of working. Even though many stated that they wanted their interiors to speak for themselves and improve the quality of life of those using them, the results – whether they be the minimalist lines of John Pawson, the neo-baroque extravaganzas of Fabio Novembre or the ground-breaking office spaces of Clive Wilkinson – are all staggeringly different.

Interiors intimately affect our lives. The spaces where we live, shop, eat, are educated and entertained, surround us; the scale is smaller and we are physically close to them. Interior architecture has a link to psychology, the architect/designer being able to manipulate emotions through the narratives and forms used to create environments. As well as appealing to our conscious sense of aesthetics and physiological requirements, interiors inspire and communicate, speaking to us subconsciously in their harnessing of memory, ritual, metaphor and association to engage the user on intellectual and emotional levels. Our lives are shaped by the spaces we occupy. At its best, interior architecture has the capability of creating new and progressive behaviour patterns as well as new languages for living.

Interiors offer an important starting point for any space-design career. Architectural projects are long, laborious and time-consuming. Adapting more readily to the spirit of the time and with a limited shelf-life, interiors can be small, quick and fun, lending themselves to research and experimentation with materials and design ideas. Interiors, especially retail and restaurant/club environments, offer the opportunity for innovation and imagination to be given free rein. Yet it is a serious discipline controlled by strict adherence to codes and programmatic functioning, and in collaboration with engineers, contractors and builders. Although artistic, it is not art, and of utmost importance are commercial viability, the needs of the end user, and the role of the client who knows best about his or her business and preferences. In most instances clients are invited to work closely with the architect/designer to arrive at a solution which is a studied symbiosis of pragmatic necessity, their own identity and the architect/designer's experience and aesthetic expression.

The people and practices in this book come from varying backgrounds. The majority are trained as architects, some are industrial designers who have moved on to the design of interiors, and a few are autodidacts who, through apprenticeship, have gone on to found their own interior-design companies. Very few were actually trained as interior architects or interior designers. Whatever their background, their work is concerned with space and volume: the architectonic elements of the inside of a building rather than the merely decorative.

Interior Architecture Now is not about cosmetic plastic surgery but about complete organ transplant. The individuals and companies featured are not only concerned with surface and appearance – the ephemeral, frail and convertible – but through their work they control shape, space, services and identity to reflect the new needs and innumerable faces of twenty-first-century society.

To reflect the fact that the content of the book is primarily concerned with the intelligent programming of interior space and the architectural as well as the design opportunities this presents, I have chosen the title *Interior Architecture Now* rather than *Interior Design Today*. Although this might be considered the splitting of terminological hairs, because of the proliferation today of decorators, stylists and hobbyists calling themselves designers, the word 'design', when used in association with interiors, connotes a surface application concerned with decorative elements as opposed to a rigorous investigation of space, form, issues and ideas. On the other hand, interior architecture could be understood as 'just a simple layout', whereas design gives the impression of something more conceptual and 'exciting', allowing for human interaction.

It is an unfortunate confusion of terms made more acute because of the international scope of this book, and some countries use 'interior design' while others use 'interior architecture' – and let us not forget three-dimensional design, spatial design and the many other terminologies now being adopted by colleges. Regardless, all these titles refer to a similar discipline that is quite apart from decoration. For the purpose of this book I find 'interior architecture' is more inclusive in that it concerns the cross-disciplinary nature of design, bringing together the skills required to investigate interior design within the wider context of architecture.

A decade ago it was embarrassing for architects to be involved in the design of interiors, but attitudes have changed. Again and again in the case studies featured, the point is made that energy and stimulation is gained from the blurring of boundaries between creative disciplines; influences are sought in all kinds of fields, from product and graphic design to media, film and art. A more Italian approach is being adopted, which traditionally made no distinction between disciplines. In Italy it is common for architects to undertake design projects and therefore to inject a spatial vision and quality into them; interiors merge into architecture and vice versa. Today there is an intimate relationship between product design, interior design and architecture – the thought process is more holistic, with structure becoming a part of surface decoration, and the architect's role being one of involvement from the macro to the very smallest detail: from spatial flow, form and three-dimensionality to skin, surface, materiality, and the use of colour and light.

The roles and methodologies of the architect and the interior designer are shifting as our social, economic and political world mutates. Architecture, interior architecture and interior design are now disciplines, together with graphic, product and landscape design, whose focus is to solve the problems of an evolving society needing to be housed, entertained and prepared for a better future. This book is just the tip of the iceberg – a taster to whet the appetite – illustrating as it does the many ways individuals are approaching the opportunities which this loss of dogma has liberated.

Practical notes: all measurements are in metric, followed by the imperial equivalent (rounded to the nearest whole number) in parentheses. Although the majority of the illustrations are interiors, the occasional exterior has been included where necessary to give a better understanding of the space within. Iconic works of particular interior architects have been featured, although the majority of the illustrations are from the turn of the century onwards. The features are organized alphabetically by practice or individual; where a company is eponymous it is listed under the name of the architect.

3deluxe

With work ranging from graphic identities through media installations to architecture, 3deluxe conceives every project it works on holistically, using its full expertise base. Two of the original partners, Dieter Brell and Nikolaus Schweiger were previously involved in furniture and interior design, but together with co-founders graphic designers Andreas and Stephan Lauhoff, they established the basis for their diversified team. 'We treat graphic design like architecture and architecture like graphic design.' Every time their office grows (they now employ 20 people), their aim is to expand their range of disciplines, knowledge and skills. They call themselves a group of designers rather than pigeon-holing themselves, and their band includes architects, interior designers, graphic designers, media designers, product designers and artists. They believe that to reflect adequately the culture of today, each task requires creative diversity and cross-disciplinary thinking rather than separation and categorization, and this is reflected in the work they produce.

Since founding their company in 1992 in Wiesbaden, Germany they have gained international recognition for their computer-generated organically shaped forms, their strong graphics (which serve as an interface between two- and three-dimensionality), and their experimental interior designs. They have also coined the phrase 'genetic architecture' to describe a series of multipurpose in- and outdoor environments, the latest being the 2006 FIFA World Cup Football Globe. As architects and interior designers, 3deluxe creates global and sometimes gigantic presentations for companies such as MTV, Volkswagen and Mercedes Benz, as well as being invited to take part in art festivals. The company's interiors mix the real and the virtual. Partly based on multimedia technology, partly on the built environment, interactive installations encourage visitors to explore their surroundings playfully and individually. 3deluxe believes that these stylistic elements cause a positive over-stimulation of senses which is intended to lead to a new and holistic perception of the environment. 'We do not design the space itself but the experience of the people spending time there.' For this reason most of the firm's interiors include relaxation furniture to encourage the users to slow down, unwind and open themselves up to the event they are enjoying.

All 3deluxe's built schemes explore new technology and employ flexible, apparently weightless materials as well as atmospheric cyber lighting. The projects are futuristic, other-worldly and bionic.

The group believe that its most important projects are those in which members were able to create not only the design but also the content: for example the 'Neue Räume' ('New Spaces') (Frankfurt Fair, 1996), exhibition designs such as 'Scape for the Expo' (Hannover, 2000) and 'Cyberhelvetia' for Expo 2002 (Biel), or alternatively the CocoonClub in Frankfurt (2004), all of which deal with youth culture, new media and the digital expansion of materiality.

(Top and below) **CocoonClub, Frankfurt (2004)** The venue comprises a club and two restaurants, combining architectural, multimedia and graphic elements. Described as a three-dimensional interface, the clubbers actively participate in creating the moment. Based on the anatomy of a cell, the division between the frenetic dance floor and quieter outer areas is created by a perforated 'membrane wall' penetrated by 13 capsule-shaped glazed micro-rooms.

(Top)

**'Cyberhelvetia',
Swiss Confederation
Exhibition Expo (2002)**

The glass 'pool' in the middle of the exhibition space replaces the original swimming pool. The 'pool' is filled with virtual water which is enriched digitally by the visitors both present or via the Internet with imaginative life-forms. The interaction between real and virtual creates atmospheric images on the 'pool's' surface, giving the impression of a living organism being formed.

(Below)

**Autostadt atmosphere
1 – VW Autostadt
International
Automobile Exhibition
IAA, Frankfurt (2001)**

The brief was to create an atmospheric interpretation of the corporate philosophy of Autostadt Wolfsberg. 3deluxe's concept focused on addressing visitors' emotional perception. A white gauze membrane covering a textile structure with a complex network of organically shaped segments defines the space, allowing exterior and interior to be seen in relation to one another.

3deluxe draws inspiration from many sources but one of the main influences for them is nature, 'We are fascinated by the principles of nature, especially by the idea that objects created by man could adopt the abilities of living organisms.'

Both CocoonClub and 'Cyberhelvetia' are examples of interior-design projects which have a 'biological' derivation. CocoonClub is a nightlife complex which comprises a techno club and two concept restaurants. The idea is based on cell metabolism, with the various nightclub activities – eating, drinking, talking, lounging and dancing – being allocated different areas analogous to the organelles of a cell. The main dance floor is the interior of the cell, with the DJ pulpit as the nucleus, and the whole is surrounded by a 'membrane wall' which people can pass through in both directions: a constant osmotic exchange of guests. 'The Cyber-helvetia Pavilion' is a virtual swimming pool where visitors can go 'swimming' without the need for water. The pool is replaced by a mysterious glowing glass cube which is surrounded by loungers. The 'water' is constantly changing as a result of data received from a weather station on the roof which animates the glass. Like the lake outside, it changes its appearance during the course of the day. Additionally, Internet messages create atmospheric images of natural life-forms on the surface of the pool. Nature and technology are amalgamated into a novel and fascinating experience of space.

When asked what 3deluxe aims to achieve in its interiors, the company replied, 'Functionally designed spaces are important, but there are already enough of them. We want to create spaces you can usually only dream of. We like to inspire and sensitize people with our work. To achieve that goal we could have become painters or actors but we set our heart on designing real spaces. The enhancement of real space by artificial and imaginary components still is unexploited terrain. That excites us.'

(Above)
Mobile Exhibition Pavilion for Mercedes Benz (2005–07) The exhibition promotes Mercedes research into eco-friendly propulsion concepts. The pavilion is constructed from anodized aluminium tubing while the interior, which showcases a 360° projection screen, is influenced by cool lighting and streamlined aesthetics, with surfaces – wool felt, white leather and foam – looking and feeling warm to the touch. This hard/soft dialogue cites the material language of automobile construction.

(Top)
Silk Restaurant, CocoonClub, Frankfurt (2004) Food and drink are served on white leather beds in a fuchsia-infused ethereal space. The experience was conceived to 'raise eating and drinking to the status of an artistically staged ceremony reminiscent of ancient Rome'.

(Below)
Interactive Game Stations, 2006 FIFA World Cup Football Globe The football-like globe was designed by André Heller and travelled to the 12 German FIFA World Cup host cities. Visitors to the pavilion can focus on football in an emotional and playful way. 3deluxe created the interiors. An interactive 360° projection captures in real time the enthusiasm felt for soccer by visitors and people all over the world.

(Top and below right)
Visionscape, Hannover, Expo 2000 Visionscape rose to a height of 2km (1.23 miles) above the trade-fair complex and was conceived as a reaction to the topical architectural discourse on computer-generated, immaterial spaces. The 'vision' was the construction itself, and the 'scape' a multi-layered perception area housing a series of events and interactive installations. The architectural design was based on a genetic concept, with softly shaped structures giving material form to the fluid framework of virtual space.

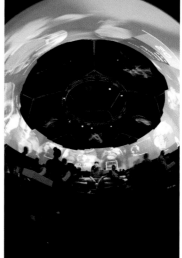

Boris Zeisser and Maartje Lammers, partners in life as well as work, both studied architecture at the University of Delft, the Netherlands, where interior design did not feature strongly in the curriculum. However, since founding their company, 24-HArchitecture, on 01.01.01, most media attention has been given to their interiors. To date, they have been involved in projects of varying scales, among them the Ichthus Academy in Rotterdam, the hotel lobby for Ashlee House in London, an exhibition design for Romantic paintings in the Kunsthal in Rotterdam, the Dragspelhuset (accordion house) in Övre Gla, Sweden, and social housing projects in Nieuw Vennep and Hoofddorp.

Both Zeisser and Lammers have collaborated with some of the leading architects in the Netherlands. Lammers started out in the offices of OMA and later worked for Mecanoo, where she was involved in the split of the company, joining one of the partners, Erick van Egeraat, in his newly formed practice EEA. Zeisser also worked for EEA, so it's not surprising that an association with the most flamboyant and baroque Dutch architect has been a great influence and is evident in the expressive, unique, visually rich interiors of 24-H Architecture.

One of the biggest inspirations for the duo is nature. They travel to extreme destinations to source unusual materials and exotic shapes: the volcanoes and lava flows of Iceland; the rocks and rich colours of the Canyon de Chelly in the southwest corner of the US; and the far north of Scandinavia, where they spent time with the Sami tribe and witnessed their primitive use of reindeer skins and ice. These elements, or an abstract representation of them, are introduced into the work of 24-H, stamping a personality and warmth onto rigorously conceived tectonic spaces which ensures that their interiors not only function well but tell stories, and are unexpected and surprising. Building up a strong character is of paramount importance to the partnership.

They work in themes which can be seen in varying proportions and combinations in all their work: their buildings and interiors all have the capacity to adapt in response to the changing needs and conditions of the user. 'Buildings should evolve through a lifetime, a season or 24 hours,' states Lammers on the theme of 'evolution'. Each space is rich in detail which has a humanizing effect. Zeisser and Lammers are not interested in the grand statement but in the personal: 'sensibility'. Their designs are sympathetic to locale and take into consideration environmental issues and sustainable-building technologies; 'landshape'; and finally what they refer to as 'event', which is the most abstract of the themes and refers to the flexibility in the design of a building or interior so that when it is occupied it can easily mutate in ways unforeseen by the architect.

24-H considers the summerhouse in Övre Gla, Sweden, and the Ichthus Academy in Rotterdam as most clearly reflecting its partners' goals as architects. They started work on the former while

(Top)
Ichthus Academy, Rotterdam (2002)
A basket-weave structure of plywood ribs and beech strips containing three meeting rooms snakes its way through the centre of the space and separates the communal areas from the offices.

(Below)
Ichthus Academy
Digital prints depicting colourful natural imagery, blown up almost to the point of abstraction, wrap the tilted, ribbon-like outer walls of the four classroom clusters.

(Above left)
'Masters of Dutch Romance' exhibition, Rotterdam (2005) The design follows the trend of the Romantic movement away from the formality of classicism to the freedom of spirit associated with nature. The 'Living Room' space with chandelier and benches represents the former.

(Above right)
'Masters of Dutch Romance' The rock-like stairs with branch handrails represent the primeval forces of nature.

(Below)
Ashlee House, London (2003) A semi-transparent sheath adorned with images of London wraps around the original masonry of the reception area of this student hostel. A service hatch links the communal areas to the office.

(Far right)
Ashlee House The opaque polyester skin allows light to shine spectrally through images of Victorian street lanterns, lending the space a surrealistic atmosphere by night.

they were establishing their own practice, and to them it has become the physical manifestation of their design philosophy. The biomorphic house blends into its setting and can literally adjust itself to its environment depending on weather conditions, season or number of occupants. It extends and contracts by means of a series of pulleys and a retracting steel frame mounted on roller-bearings. The interiors are a visual feast of tactile and sinuous walls lined with silver-birch laths and coated in reindeer skins. The furniture is modern and the lighting is powered by solar panels.

The Ichthus Academy redefines what has come to be expected from an academic institution. Gone are the boring series of dull classrooms, which have been replaced by a space that seems to live and breath. A variety of shapes, surfaces and colours immediately hits the eye, the linear space transformed and united by a sinuous, fish-like structure of plywood ribs and beech strips that contains a series of meeting rooms, and which tapers off, turning into a comfortable bench where students can gather and socialize. Luminous walls covered in distorted digital imagery taken from nature define the classroom areas.

The work of 24-H Architecture is outspoken and avant-garde and, as such, invites very varied criticism. 'We would like to keep inventing and renewing ourselves: spaces, materials and atmospheres. If people are surprised every time they enter our designs, we are happy!'

(Overleaf)
Dragspelhuset, Övre Gla, Sweden (2004) The cave-like interiors of the retractable extension of Zeisser and Lammer's summerhouse are lined with reindeer fur, inspired by the Sami culture of northern Scandinavia.

Harry Allen

Harry Allen does not like to be called an interior architect, preferring to describe himself as an interior designer. 'Very often I am mistakenly referred to as an architect and it makes me nervous – I am always quick to correct. I have respect for the architectural profession. I am actually an industrial designer, working on products, packaging, furniture and lighting. My interiors, however, are very architectural. I am interested in building, not in surface decoration.' Working in New York (his studio, apartment and recently opened showroom are located in the East Village) where most of the design being carried out is interior (as opposed to exterior) building, he frequently finds himself competing with architects. 'Traditionally an architect would build an interior framework and the "decorator" would then be employed to fit and furnish it. Today structure is regarded as an integral part of decoration. There is a greater freedom to work in a multidisciplinary way.'

Allen studied political science before undertaking a postgraduate degree in industrial design at the Pratt Institute in New York. He says that he will never be 'the hot-shot draughtsman', but what he does bring to his work is an overall appreciation of culture and context. His major influences come from outside the sphere of design, and in particular from the art world, as artists are permitted a much more conceptual and pure vision: qualities which he strives to bring to his own design work.

After graduation Allen worked for Prescriptive Cosmetics, designing counters and point-of-purchase displays. This early experience taught him a lot about retail design, and his first commission after setting up his own studio in 1993 was the showroom on Greene Street for the design entrepreneur and guru, Murray Moss. This is still, undoubtedly, the interior for which Allen is best known, although at the time he confesses to being very naïve. In 1994 Murray Moss was selling European contemporary design pieces largely ignored by the American market. He wanted a fresh approach for his store. Arranged by association rather than category, often displayed alongside *objets d'art* and presented using the language of art galleries or museums, Allen's concept was an innovative departure in design

(Left)
Bedford House, New York State (2006) Allen describes his renovation of a 1840s country retreat in Bedford, formerly a single room schoolhouse, as 'contextual innovation'. Keeping in mind the idea of material and colour envelopment, the kitchen – including the floor, cabinetry, counter tops, wainscoting and stainless steel appliances – are all a uniform grey.

(Right)
Dragonfly Selects, Taiwan (1998) To match the jewellery on sale, the interior is simple, modern and unfussy. Experimenting with the innovative use of materials, Allen has used acoustical foam on the ceiling to diffuse light, rubberized gym flooring to prevent damage to dropped goods, and fibre optics in perforated panels above the showcases.

(Right)
Hushush basic clothing outlets, 100 locations throughout Asia (concept: 2000) Awarded as the result of a paid competition, the brief was open but stressed creativity. Pairing each material with a designated category (illustrated here: stainless steel for cosmetics, plywood for the store's café and cash desks), Allen created a highly functional and clear coding system.

retailing. The resultant natural, white interior was an exercise in clarity against which every product could be seen, desired and, ultimately, purchased. 'I trained as a product designer and you can really see that in some of my first projects – like Moss, where all I did was design white furniture and put it in a white space. I really knew very little about how to finish an interior at that point. But it all seemed to work, and maybe my innocence provided a fresh perspective.'

Now, with a string of widely published interiors to his name, including successful retail projects such as the Los Angeles Supreme skateboard apparel shop, the Dragonfly Selects jewellery store in Taiwan, the Hushush family clothing stores in Japan, More (the expansion of Moss), the SX137 restaurant/nightclub in New York, offices for *Metropolis* magazine and the Guggenheim Museum, and a variety of residential interiors, he is concerned that his experience could have a detrimental effect on his work. 'Now that I know all the rules, I worry that my work will begin to look like everything else. I am constantly trying to dumb myself down and approach things from a naïve perspective. My most recent project

in Bedford illustrates this. Here I'm going back to basics, creating humble detailing and building in a very direct way. Ironically, it is both difficult and expensive as I'm breaking with convention.'

Allen is a collaborative designer, working closely with a client. 'I like feedback. I like learning … from my clients. I am very open to ideas, and look at the whole process as a dialogue.' Consequently his style varies from commission to commission. However, forced to define reoccurring elements, he lists: clean geometrical lines built on a process of refinement and simplification; the use of new and surprising materials or humble materials transformed by meticulous craftsmanship; a seamless blending of art, furnishings, form and function; innovation and narrative.

Goals for the future include working on large-scale projects with bigger budgets, a move towards more residential schemes and the renovation and revitalization of buildings. 'There is so much potential there and I hate the fact that we just build and build when there are so many derelict buildings already in existence with history to contribute to the design process.'

(Top)

Moss, New York (original design 1994, expansion 1999) Carrying on with the original white aesthetic of the original, the products are now behind glass, but majestically displayed in pivoting cases, dioramas and walls of beautiful shelving.

(Below left)

Union Store, Los Angeles (2006) Long famed for its high-end street wear, the owner of Union approached Allen to use his rigid systematic aesthetic and materials expertise to complete the renovation of the LA-based store. The focal point is a huge wooden box, reminiscent of a packing crate, which houses the cash and wrap, storage area and changing rooms. The structure forms a mezzanine level for the display of Japanese brand 'A Bathing Ape', creating a store within a store.

(Below right)

Sovereign lobby, New York (2002) Allen's face-lift of an Upper East Side apartment building refers to both contemporary modernity and the international-style architecture of the building. Rationalization of the floor plan exposed clean lines that lay beneath years of piecemeal renovation.

Harry Allen

(Left)
**Supreme skateboard
shop, Los Angeles
(2004)** An internationally
recognized brand looked
to rejuvenate rather than
reinvent itself in its LA
outlet. Humble materials
(concrete, galvanized steel,
composite decking) are
raised to a higher status
by their precise usage.
A giant skateboard bowl
is suspended from the
ceiling and is illuminated by
fluorescent halos of light.

(Right)
SX137, New York (2000)
The brief was to design
a restaurant/bar/lounge.
Taking a cue from the low
rent and highly creative
neighbourhood, the
project was low-budget
but highly conceptual.
The brief was taken
literally and the space
is delineated into three
distinct areas marked
by varying sophisti-
cated applications of
simple materials.

Ron Arad

Ron Arad's experimentation with form, process and material has put him at the forefront of contemporary design. Born in Tel Aviv in 1951, he arrived in London in 1973. Coming from a cultured and creative background, both his parents are important artists, Arad explains 'I had an extraordinary affinity to draw, to paint and to make things. There was no struggle involved; they were normal activities for me.' He studied fine art at the Bezalel Academy, but left after a year – as a self-confessed hippy he was enticed by the 'exoticism' of London, which was emerging from the peace-and-love generation of the 1960s into the anti-establishment, youth-fuelled, aggressive punk rock years.

He studied architecture at the Architectural Association under Peter Cook of Archigram fame, the deconstructivist Bernard Tschumi, and architect Rem Koolhaas whose work is as much about ideas and social commentary as it is about buildings. 'The AA at that time was more exciting and experimental than the Slade or the Royal College. Zaha Hadid and Nigel Coates were a couple of years ahead of me. It was more like an art school in those days.'

He graduated in 1979 and spent a brief period in a small architectural practice in Hampstead: 'It didn't take me long to realize that I didn't want to work for anyone. One lunchtime out of sheer boredom I walked out and I didn't go back. I went to a scrapyard behind the Roundhouse and started work on my first Rover car seat. That turned me into a furniture designer.'

In 1981 Arad founded his own company, 'One Off', producing individual pieces and ready-made items, followed two years later by the opening of his own showroom in Covent Garden. Iconic pieces such as the Rover 200 car seat mounted on Kee-Klamp scaffolding and the concrete stereo have become iconic, capturing as they did the *Zeitgeist* of the early 1980s with its streetwise DIY aesthetic, individualism and ruggedness set against a background of urban degeneration and disaffected youth. Arad, however, is very keen to point out that his work was not punk; it shared a certain rebelliousness and disregard for the rules, but it was not angry: 'I'm a privileged person. I had nothing to rail against, I'm the product of an expensive education. I've always been interested in ready-made in art, in the poetic licence of Dadaism. I just expanded that into things I could do. I was lucky to be in the right place at the right time and with the right sort of audience. If you think about it, London was a design desert at that time so I had to invent my own profession. Thank God for that. If I had moved to Milan I would have probably joined in with everyone else, which is something I'm not good at. I don't follow rules; I much prefer to invent my own.'

Teaching himself to weld and beat steel, his series of volumetric chairs brought him international recognition. In the late 1980s he collaborated with Vitra to create the Well-Tempered Chair, the profile of which resembled an overstuffed armchair but which relied on its softness and spring

(Right)
Belgo Noord Restaurant & Bar, Chalk Farm, London (1994) The brief was to build a permanent roof over a courtyard while still allowing natural light into an existing restaurant, and also to open up the space to include a bar servicing stand-up and sit-down customers. The support structure for the new glass roof was used to provide shade and reflect light for the seating area below. Massive but very thin plywood beams act like horizontal *brise-soleil*.

(Top and below)
Belgo Centraal, Covent Garden, London (1995) Housed in the basement of a former nineteenth-century warehouse, this subterranean spectacle retains an industrial aesthetic with wrought iron pillars, vaulted ceiling and exposed brick work. The restaurant is accessed via an illuminated metal bridge, which affords glimpses down into the kitchen and seated areas below. The customer descends in a former goods lift, which is now fully glazed.

(Far right)
New Tel Aviv Opera, Israel (1994) Ron Arad Associates won the commission to design the public spaces by limited competition and the work progressed alongside the project of Yacov Rechter, architect of the building. The space is inhabited by a series of autonomous structures/buildings, each performing a different function. The bronze wall of the bookshop is in direct contrast to the foyer's concrete volumes

from the properties of tempered steel. Collaborations with Moroso, Kartell and Driade followed, and by the turn of the decade he was a well-established figure on the European design scene.

Ron Arad Associates was formed in 1989 and One Off was incorporated into the company in 1993. Today the practice is involved in mass-manufactured products, gallery pieces, interior design and architecture. Whether designing a vase or an apartment block, his work is always technologically advanced, experimental, consistently inventive and challenging.

Although Arad is known more for his industrial design work, that is about to change. Since graduating from the AA his architectural projects have been consistent. His first interior was for the Tel Aviv Opera House in 1994, for which he designed a series of autonomous curved forms within the foyer. Commissions for retail and restaurant spaces followed, including the Belgo restaurants in London and the Y's Store for Yohji Yamamoto in Tokyo. In 2002 Arad took part in a group exhibition in Milan which showcased hypothetical hotel interiors. Such was the success of his concept that hotel commissions flooded in, including a floor in the much publicized Puerta América designer showcase hotel; the Arad signature hotel

in Rimini for which he has designed everything from the layout to the numbers on the doors of the guest rooms; the Swarovski hotel in Wattens (2004–) with its multifaceted exterior; and the Upperworld Hotel (2003–), which will sit at the top of the much-awaited restoration of Battersea Power Station. In addition to hotels, he is working on the Magis headquarters in Treviso, The Holon Design Museum in Israel, an apartment block in Tel Aviv and a 10.5-metre (34.5-foot) public sculpture in Cor-ten steel in the centre of Jerusalem.

In common with most architects in the book, Arad does not consider that he has a specific style but rather an approach or a quality which gets him noticed. However, he is known for his curvilinear structures, and when I pointed this out, not wanting to be typecast stylistically he said that it was not a conscious decision, but if he did use curved lines then he worked with the full gamut right down to the shortest curve – the straight line. A typical Arad reply.

When asked what he thought made clients select him over the competition he replied: 'Because we're fantastic. Because we have freedom of mind. We're not a good-taste option or a safe bet. It takes an adventurous person to choose us.'

(Top)
Y's Store, Roppongi Hills, Tokyo (2003) The 570 sq m (6,135 sq ft) area is divided by three large structural columns which Arad has masked by surrounding them with aluminium 'turntables' which pirouette, transforming the space constantly and creating an illusion of lightness and movement. The ceiling and floor appear to be held together by four ever-changing sculptural elements. The loops are used as hanging rails for Y's clothes, and can be transformed into wide shelves using customized 'plug-in' units.

(Below)
7th Floor, Hotel Puerta América, Madrid, (2005) The hotel comprises 14 floors, each conceived by a different designer. In Arad's rooms, sinuous, rounded shapes prevail. A curved continuous wall, white in some and bright-red in others, acts as a divider and separates the different uses of the space: first the entry, then the bed, then the bathrooms, the sink and the toilet, each usage revealing itself bit by bit.

(Right)
Hotel Duomo, Rimini, Italy (2006) The bronze of the exterior meanders its way into the building, forming the back wall of the bar and uniting exterior and interior. The bar is a large island with sinuous-shaped cut-outs for patrons to eat and drink at. The top is formed in bronze and the sides finished in mirror-polished stainless steel, which creates distorted reflections and highlights the activity of the bar.

(Overleaf)
Hotel Duomo
The entrance to the hotel is through giant pinball-flipper-like doors which frame the reception desk, which becomes the focal point of the hotel. The desk is a stainless-steel ring, which leans dramatically against a polished steel column.

Antoni Arola

The interior and industrial designer Antoni Arola was born in Tarragona, Spain in 1960. He studied design at the Eina School of Design in Barcelona. He worked for a period in the studio of Liévore and Pensi where Arola inherited, what he refers to as Liévore's 'secrets of design'. 'He [Lievore] used tiny drawings to find gestures that were not in the head. He worked with his heart as well as his head.' However, it was one of Arola's encounters at the nightclub Zeleste, which he frequented as a student, that was to become formative. A chance meeting with physicist Pep Sants led to him joining Sants' newly formed agency, Associate Designers, as head of projects where he stayed for four years, designing trains, buses and urban furniture.

'When I left, I had learned not only about Liévore's secret world but also about marketing, large projects and management. I had all that was necessary to go it on my own.' Arola opened his own practice in 1994.

Arola is well known for his ethereal and quirky lighting designs, which he has produced for Santa & Cole, Metalarte and BD Ediciones de Diseño; the Nimba lamp launching him to national fame in 1997. He is a versatile designer, his portfolio including furniture design, interior architecture and even perfume-making. 'I think titles are irrelevant; the important thing is finding solutions for the challenges with which one is faced, not the titles we have.' Despite his reticence to be defined, he received

(Right)
Oven, Barcelona (2002)
The multifunctional space is situated in a former warehouse in the Poblenou suburb of Barcelona. The distribution and atmosphere of the space are evocative of a domestic aesthetic brought to an urban scale. The restaurant is laid out on various levels. A glass-enclosed kitchen, suggesting an oversized oven, offers soundless visual entertainment.

(Left)
Royalty shoe shop, Barcelona (2002)
Commercial strategy eliminated a traditional shop-window display, inviting the public to walk straight in. The interior is lined with Plexiglas walls printed with shoe-brand logos.

(Left)
Vinoteca Torres wine shop, restaurant and bar (2005) This concept store is situated in a shopping centre a short drive from Barcelona. The design encompasses a store, tapas bar and restaurant, and is evocative of a wine cellar. Light is allowed to pick out strategic corners.

the National Design Prize for his interior-architecture in 2003.

He quotes classical references as his influences (for example, art nouveau, and the works of such pioneers as Eames, Van de Rohe and Jacobsen), but it is probably his love for travel and primitive cultures which has been his major source of inspiration. 'When you travel, you end up finding something you didn't know you were looking for. In Africa everything is dependent on something else. Even the language, the meaning of words, is redefined according to context. Life isn't very concrete. It's this unfinished air, this fragment of freedom which is reflected in my work.'

Arola looks on himself as an artist/ designer or an artist of design, and relies on serendipity for most of his concepts. He does not seek to surprise but is surprised himself by chance meetings and juxtapositions. 'Things always occur to me when I feel free, calm or nervous, and with the studio full of *objets trouvé*. I'm more spontaneous than technical.'

His studio comprises six people who develop his ideas, and he works closely as a team with Jordi Tamayo, Sylvain Carlet, Sandra Müller and Franck Fontana. The spaces and objects they create speak of a hands-on aesthetic; they are at once spontaneous, warm and natural while displaying sobriety, a high quality of finish and a sound knowledge of design and tectonics. 'We approach every job differently. There is a kind of magic in the evolution of ideas, which in the execution and navigation of the projects, with their plans, models, simulations and detailing, become a reality. But there are also surprises. If we had to formulate the process in which we work it would be magic – development of the magic – final results – surprises!'

Estudi Arola's first important interior design commission was the Restaurante Mos in 1998, followed by the Cacao Sampaka chocolate shop which won

(Above right)
Fourth Edition of the Innoval Space at the Biennial Barcelona Foodstuff and Drinks Show (2004) The concept was to re-create a banquet set-up. The tables are covered in starched cloths with foodstuffs enclosed in glass cases. Screens projecting images group different food types and are suspended at varying angles, which seem to defy gravity.

(Above left)
Cacao Sampaka chocolate shop and restaurant concept, Barcelona, Madrid and Valencia (2000) A warm, ethnic-inspired ambience envelops a space distributed in three specific zones: sales area, cafeteria and workshop. The use of wood offers a play of tones from dark to light, symbolizing dark and white chocolate.

(Top)
La Caixa offices, pilot scheme Sant Andreu de la Barca, Barcelona (2006) The design emphasis is on creating spaces for privacy as well as the creation of custom-made furniture to suit the specific needs of the employees.

(Below)
Santa & Cole Stand at the Light+Building Fair, Frankfurt (2006) The project was built entirely from raw construction materials. The exterior resembles a large packing case while the interior is divided into four functional areas. The meeting room has a wall made from a mesh of adjustable square slabs, which recall Arola's new hanging-lamp 'Cubrik', showcased in the same year.

the FAD prize in 2000, but the interior which made Arola's name was The Oven, which he completed in 2002. An undefined space (part bar and restaurant, part gallery and concert hall), it added a vibrant locale to Barcelona's night-life: comfort and naturalness replacing the studied sophistication, which was the norm for bar design in the city at that time. The project resulted in an unusual collaboration among several artists, including architect Minos Digenis and graphic designer Pablo Martín. They designed it together, with Arola overseeing everything from the interior architecture to the seating and, of course, the lighting.

Subsequent schemes include The Royalty shoe shop, Vinoteca Torres wine shop, restaurant and bar, and the La Caixa offices, as well as trade stands for Santa & Cole and for Innoval.

'My ultimate ambition is to get clients whose priority is culture before finance; and if I can't get them I will have to become my own client.'

(Above)
Sixth Edition of the Innoval Space at the Biennial Barcelona Foodstuff and Drinks Show (2006) An array of transparent multicoloured laminates are suspended from the ceiling with some superimposed over others to create a kaleidoscope of backlit colours.

AV62

AV62 was founded in 1994 by Toño Foraster and Victoria Garriga, both of whom studied architecture at the ETSAB (Barcelona School of Architecture). They have collaborated with architect Enriqué Poblet, industrial designer Josep Llusca, interior designer Rafael Carreras, and on several projects and competitions over a two-year period at the offices of Enric Miralles, gaining experience in all disciplines. Their practice works across the board, with equal importance being placed on new-build schemes and the design of retail, commercial and restaurant spaces.

When jokingly asked which architects they would like to invite to inspect their work, or to help them collaboratively, their reply is revealing, as they consider the professions and expertise which go into creating a holistic interior more important then peer recognition. 'I think it would be more interesting to invite people who work in other industries: a spatial anthropologist, an artist specializing in fine art, a graphic designer, a professor of aesthetics, an event/exhibition organizer, a cultural manager, a sincere politician (if that's possible), a sociologist, psychologists and builders.'

Although it is often demanded of an architect, Foraster and Garriga wish that being associated with a signature style was not an important issue as 'being branded can only be limiting'. However, forced to quantify what would make a client choose their work above the competition, they list clarity, both in terms of construction and spatial sequencing; a quest for

freshness and airiness; a search for that which can be dismantled and reconstituted; and the ability to relieve architecture and people from self-imposed restrictions.

Although active in both architecture and interiors, they consider both disciplines to be one and the same rather than overlapping. 'Architecture can be viewed from inside out or outside in, but the main issue is not what we look at or touch; it is rather who is doing the looking or touching. Architecture informs the way we live; it adds a material extension of how man exists in the world. If we were made to separate the two we prefer to be thought of as interior architects rather than designers as it is a much broader and complex concept and speaks of protection of the body and of intimacy rather than the superficial connotations connected to design or decoration.'

AV62's first projects were for a retail establishment and an exhibition design, both concerned with the endeavour to build a new and defined concept in an existing space. 'Surely this has made our architecture projects go, virtually unconsciously, from inside out, but inversely it is important to remember that the containing building should never forget the contents it will be hosting. These contents are ultimately not furniture or graphics, not textile nor light, but the people that occupy them: the fragile nucleus of any architectural project.'

This preoccupation with the human element over the stylistic means that major inspirational sources for Foraster and

(Top)
Ovni restaurant, Barcelona (2002) The aim was to design an attractive restaurant for people who want to eat healthily, do not have a lot of time and do not want to spend a lot of money. All the design decisions hold on to this concept and the resultant space is fresh, easy and contemporary.

(Below)
VIPS, Barcelona (2006) In re-branding of a very popular and commercially successful chain of Spanish restaurants, AV62 has revived and revised the perfectly finished, washable and durable industrial materials popular in restaurants in 1950s America. Colours and graphics have been adopted from the chain's original logo.

(Above).
Girona 62, Barcelona (2000) AV62's office is located in a former textile warehouse. The work space is dominated by a unique large iron table divided by two light graphic panels. All storage is placed against the perimeter walls.

Garriga are architects who may have incidentally conceived iconic masterpieces: Arne Jacobsen, Le Corbusier, Louis Kahn, Eames, Asplund and Miralles to name a few, but who have also responded either with enthusiasm or pessimism to the constraints and requirements of their times. Of equal importance to Foraster and Garriga are the unrepeatable traditional buildings, which appeal to collective memory and which have been fundamental in the building up of the duo's reference archive, for example – architectural statements associated with cult or faith, such as the Cordoba Mosque, which speaks of relationships, nurturing and care as well as the importance of interaction and interdependence.

The partners' biggest success is always their latest project, as this necessarily is the culmination of their design approach and is most consistent with how they are feeling at the time. However, a scheme which remains significant to them is the Sant Boi de Llobregat library, which in terms of scale and media coverage has been instrumental for their professional projection. 'In this public building we were given the opportunity of developing everything from the construction to the furnishings, graphic design and signage.' In terms of interior architecture, the Bilbao-Express travel agencies, and the KIN and Ovni restaurants have been important benchmarks.

AV62 places great importance on working closely and collaboratively with the client. At every stage concept, development and construction, shared ideas and ways of seeing bring new aspects and decisive factors to the scheme.

'Our goal is to create architectural objects which are best able to contribute to the enhancement of people's lives.'

(Abobe)
Bilbao Express 1, Bilbao (2002) The travel agency is situated in a very good business location in Bilbao. The space acts as a window showcasing a series of graphic elements and furniture design as well as an image façade. The concept was easily repeatable in the chain of agencies AV62 was subsequently commissioned to design.

(Left)
Apartment, Casco Viejo, Bilbao (2002) Housed in an eighteenth-century building, a large part of the project was the demolition and consolidation of the existing, emphasizing the series of interventions which have taken place in the space throughout its history while leaving the structure of wooden beams and iron pillars visible and free.

(Top left)
Kin Sushi Bar, Barcelona (1999) Contemporary design and tradition mix in this two-storied Japanese restaurant. Natural materials combine with plastics in a clear and rational way, while huge photos of Sumo wrestlers dominate the space.

(Bottom left)
Bruch 59, Barcelona (1997) The aim was to leave the traces time had left on the space while rendering it habitable. All things handmade (wood, joinery, plaster ceilings) were conserved and then contemporary elements such as kitchen, bathroom, furnishings and graphic elements were added.

(Right)
Antonio Miro, Bilbao (2000) To reflect the designer Antonio Miro's style which combines up-to-date fashion with expert quality, AV62's interior, using bleached wood and minimal lines, transmits the idea of the contemporary leavened by nostalgia for a lost past.

Christian Biecher

Christian Biecher studied at the Paris Belleville School of Architecture under the direction of Chilean modernist Henri Ciriani. The concept behind his dissertation, entitled 'Architectural Flow' remains as prominent in his current approach, both to his built projects and his interiors, as it did to his theory on architecture when he graduated in 1988. The flow to which he refers is the rhythmical pacing of a space which an architect sets up by his use of shape, colour, texture and light. It is a theme which was reinforced in the publication of Gilles Deleuze's *Le Pli,* which Biecher quotes as one of the influences introducing him to the complexity of shapes. This, too, explored the notion of movement and form: the way a fold can be at once continuous and discontinuous, revealing space as a whole from one viewpoint and a series of parts from another. While still studying, Biecher met Bernard Tschumi, later becoming his assistant and working on the famous follies in the Parc de la Villette, Paris. This introduction to the renowned 'deconstructivist' architect was pivotal and led to Biecher investigating the possibility of 'exploding' an entity, watching the complexity of shapes reform into something new and inspirational.

It is this experimentation and the quest to provide a narrative through form and fluidity, to soften straight and minimal lines by the use of light and material, and to cut space and volume with colour, which lie at the base of his work today.

Biecher's agency, which he founded in 1992, is interdisciplinary. Interviewed by *Frame* magazine for its 50th-edition special issue, he says, 'The funny thing is that in Japan, where I've been working on my fourth building, I am perceived as an architect. In Europe, probably because of some store or restaurant that made a big impression, I'm considered an interior designer. And in America I'm a furniture designer because of my successful collaboration for Bernhardt.'

His introduction to interiors came through his furniture design. He started to create customized furniture for some of his first buildings, such as the public library in Carcassonne and a factory in Strasbourg. His first interior project was Le Petit Café, which resulted from the client having seen furniture pieces in a group show called 'Global Techno' in 1996. The project which made his name was the Korova restaurant in Paris, since when major interior schemes have included Issey Miyake's offices in Tokyo; the Tur building in Tokyo; the Video Lounge at the library of the Pavillion de D'Arsenal; the Paris Tourist Office; the Pierre Hermé patisserie, Paris; and the Harvey Nichols stores in Hong Kong and Dublin. In contrast to his architectural projects, Biecher's interiors allow him the opportunity to give free reign to his artistic sensitivity, encouraging his boldness in the use of colours and the organization of volumes.

Colour is both functional and emotional for Biecher. Le Petit Café is bright yellow, a departure from the norm at a time when black, white and various degrees of grey were the fashion. He uses colours which he imagines will make people happy.

(Right)
Paris Tourist Office (2004) A good example of Biecher's use of primary colours, light and complex shapes to define a space. To reflect the kaleidoscopic, multi-cultural heritage of the city, the concept was close to the idea of a puzzle or a mosaic. The basic form is that of the trapezoid, with the floor and ceiling arranged in blue, red, yellow, black and white geometric patterns.

(Left)
Video Lounge at the library of the Pavillion de L'Arsenal, Paris (2002) Because this is a place for watching films, Biecher maintained that the interior had to be red – the colour of cinema. Vibrant PVC flooring, curved red neon tubes and polycarbonate 'booths' provide the unit with an assertive identity.

(Right)
Pierre Hermé patisserie, Paris (2004) Biecher looks on the work of the master-*pâtissier*, Pierre Hermé, as a blend of precise technique mixed with the *esprit* of childhood (the domain of all things sweet). His interior is a simple, rectangular space, defined by granite floor and walls; a mix of jubilant, pastel-coloured displays set against austere white.

(Far right)
Caisse des Depots et Consignations, Paris (1999) The refurbishment of a 15,000 sq m (161, 000 sq ft) building which houses the banking division of the oldest French financial institution, the lobby has a ceiling clad with hand-blown glass panels, lacquered green. The offices are designed in monochromatic yellows and greens with attention paid to light and rhythm in the circulation spaces.

'People always react to colour, which can actually rivet them to the spot.' His early works were dominated by bright hues, while later he played with subtler shades. His next stage was a series of interiors which used tone upon tone, followed by spaces which blended colour and light in such a way that the light altered the colour. Biecher is now back to using primaries: 'I'm more into form than concept, and I want shapes to be beautiful. I tend to be rigid in terms of line and design, and tender when it comes to colour. A good friend of mine has told me that my style is elegant and arrogant. More seriously, I guess I design shapes which are clear, dynamic and graphic with a personal use of colour and light.'

Biecher is a self-declared enemy of nostalgia and professes to a disbelief of people who want to be retrogressive in their surroundings. 'I could never live in an environment that refers only to the past. I want to live in a modern era. I want to be happy to live in the twenty-first century.' He draws much of his inspiration from cutting-edge technology, urban night-life and electronic music.

'My goals are to design spaces and shapes which please the people as much as they please me. In being pleased and surprised I hope to affect their lives for five minutes or more and share with them a vision of the world that is founded on hope and confidence more than fear and reminiscence.'

Christian Biecher

(Top far left)
Fourth-floor restaurant, Harvey Nichols store, Hong Kong (2005) Two silver screens in silver mesh delineate the long sides of the restaurant. Coloured surfaces on the floor and ceiling, surrounded by LED lighting rails, add rhythm to the interior. At night the colours get stronger and the lights softer – a combination of Chinese colours and European sharp and sleek shapes.

(Top left)
Harvey Nichols store, Dublin (2005) Biecher dreamt of a space that would be less neutral than regular retail spaces. Taking what he considered to be images of England (country gardens, the Sex Pistols, David Hicks' textiles and luxury cars), he created a provocative but subtle environment, with the themes he had selected evident in screens, carpets and motifs.

(Below left)
Issey Miyake office, Tokyo (2000) Minimal lines mark the architecture of an office building whose interior is characterized by the interplay of light and matter.

(Right)
Tur Building, Tokyo (2001) This is a good example of Biecher's use of texture and contrasting surfaces, skins and layers.

Block Architecture

Block Architecture searches for inspiration in the dynamics of the urban environment, in the commonplace and in the utilitarian. It admires generic objects, spaces and furniture for their directness of purpose and inherent beauty, free of all stylistic artifice. Its work is an architecture of reference and shared experience, and its approach a remanipulation of these banal signifiers into something new, inspirational and unexpected. 'We produce work that is uniquely guided by the context that generates it. I would also say that we tend to draw from and recontextualize recognizable and everyday references, making what we do accessible to clients that are architecturally aware and clients that aren't. Our design philosophy probably has an underlying essence. This can be described as a form of resonant composition or referential collage. To put it simply, we use what we know to generate what we don't expect.'

Block's interiors are created in a filmic way using art, photography and graphics as associated imagery to build a narrative which plays on the psychological associations of the client and end use. Each project is unique and is the result of a completely different set of circumstances and, as such, Block does not have one signature style – although its overall aim is to generate work that is engaging, playful and curious rather than work that is overtly self-conscious of its material or stylistic qualities.

Zoe Smith and Graeme Williamson studied architecture at Strathclyde University in Glasgow before moving to London, Smith spending a period at the University of London before joining Williamson at the Bartlett School of Architecture. Their educational background plays a big part in the approach they take to their work, and to design generally. The years spent in Glasgow inspired an emphasis on political and social radicalism in architectural practice, while the Bartlett introduced the duo to the more experimental peripheries of architectural research and modes of representations. During that time they worked largely on speculative objects, apparatus, drawings and texts. Williamson comments: 'Ironically for an architecture school, I never actually designed a building while I was there and, to a certain degree, that may have formed the basis of continual experimentation for our practice. Education is still an intrinsic part of what we do, as we are both currently teaching Diploma in Architecture at the Bartlett.'

Smith and Williamson founded their own company, 24/7, in 1997 before changing the name a few years later to Block, the building unit which is the most basic form of architectural representation. Their first break was the design of multimedia and advertising company Tomato's studio and exhibition space in Soho's Lexington Street, but it was the completion of the Grand Central bar in London in 2000 which probably established their name as a practice producing interior work. The bar is located on a busy junction and is housed in a former bank. The client wanted an interior which would generate dynamism

(Right)
Market Place bar/ restaurant, London (2002) The client wanted the interior to be warm and cosy, and to appeal to a broad cross-section of users. Block employed a Swiss-chalet aesthetic to evoke a sense of escapism, of a rural environment in an urban setting.

into what was a very static space. In response, Block used light, movement and electricity as building elements. Employing time-lapse photography of traffic flow, walls were constructed, which were suggestive of headlights and tail-lights in strips of white and red Perspex laminated together and lit from behind. The context of the exterior is brought into the interior, resulting in a space which captures the movement of the city.

Subsequent schemes, including the Market Place bar, London; The Social Club, London; the Hussein Chalayan outlet, Tokyo; the Tree House apartment, London; the Broome Street loft, New York; and the modernization of Oxford's Museum of Modern Art have earned Block numerous awards and nominations, including Blueprint's Interior Designer of the Year in 2005. Not without

controversy, this accolade caused considerable debate at the time as none of the three short-listed were interior designers (the other two were Rei Kawakubo, creative visionary behind Comme des Garçon, and architect Ferhan Azman). 'Essentially as sub-species we design things, be they objects, spaces, exhibitions, furniture, lighting, buildings, whatever. Having said that, we are architects and have never considered ourselves anything else. We will always refer to the output of our office as architecture in its broadest sense – that is, contributing to the physical and tactile nature of our manufactured or generated environment. Titles for us are in the end fairly meaningless as long as the work itself is engaging, experiential and open-ended … Our aim is to produce work that challenges or provokes a reflexive response, a conversation or exchange.'

(Left)
Treehouse apartment, London (2000) Inspired by the top-floor location of the flat, and to keep the space as open as possible, Block created a 'treehouse' in the form of a cantilevered bed platform. The wood lining is slatted and allows visual penetration through the space. At night the platform and the kitchen unit glow, cutting lines of light across the walls.

(Left)
Hussein Chalayan, Tokyo (2004) The womenswear department was visualized as an olive grove. The entrance ramp is finished in a backgammon pattern of ceramic tiles. Full-height blackboards with handwritten text describe Chalayan's approach to each fashion season.

(Top right)
The Klinik hair salon, London (1998) A pure, clinical and utilitarian design which refers to materials and furnishings found in hospital interiors and waiting rooms. The interior introduces a new kind of experience such as the CCTV cameras which allow customers to see the backs of their heads on TV monitors.

(Below right)
ICA bar, London (1999) This space explores the relationship between the borrowed and the made by using found materials deployed out of their expected context. A backlit billboard is made from cellbond (a lightweight aluminium honeycomb core with GRP lining normally used in aircrafts), and white fire-clay urinal slabs form the fronts and sides of the bar itself.

Giorgio Borruso

Giorgio Borruso's international reputation as the designer of innovative and phantasmagorical retail interiors which breathe new life into long-established brands such as Fila and Fornarina, has been expediential since he arrived in Los Angeles from his native Palermo, Italy, at the turn of the millennium. Such is his popularity that he now has more work than he can handle, with commissions throughout America, Europe, South America and Asia. Borruso has been the recipient of a string of major prizes, culminating in the 2006 SADI Best New Retail Design Award for the Snaidero showroom in Los Angeles, and his life and work have formed the subject of a TV documentary aired recently in the States.

Borruso studied architecture in Palermo and travelled widely throughout Europe before moving to California at the invitation of UCLA as visiting scholar. 'I feel lucky to have been born in southern Italy with its colours, textures, light, art and architecture, all of which have had a profound effect on my sense of aesthetics, but I always had the desire to explore different cultures. When I first came to Los Angeles I didn't like it, but then it all began to make sense. It's a conglomerate of different experiences with such a sense of space that I felt I could breathe for the first time. Italy is beautiful yet claustrophobic; you are forced to be flexible because the opportunities are lacking but here there is so much energy and an interest in experimentation that it seems anything is possible. I can fully develop my research into how materials can be

worked and adapted, using the latest in technology to create new structures. I can push my clients to do things they hadn't considered.'

Although Borruso is presently undertaking more new-build projects, the majority of his work concerns interiors. He sees no real distinction between architecture and interior architecture. Coming from Italy where the tradition is to give equal importance to all aspects of design, and where the blurring of disciplines is more established, he approaches his work methodologically, whether creating a piece of furniture or light fitting for one of his stores, a complex architectural form, or the building itself. He considers that it is this ability to adapt from the micro to the macro and vice versa that has played a major part in his success: 'In America everyone is a specialist working with all kinds of experts. Of course all architecture is a collaborative process, dependent on teamwork – we are not artists and need codes, contractors and consultants – but where I'm different is that I try to do everything, or rather be in control of the whole process down to the smallest detail. If you have mastery of the detail you have mastery of the whole.'

Borruso always looks on an interior in terms of space and volume. Whether he is working within an existing building or constructing the exterior himself, the most important factor for him is context; how his work fits into the urban space or with nature, how the elements within an interior can act as tools to add to the general movement of space, or how he

(Top left)
Miss Sixty, Aventura, Florida (2004) Simple geometric forms echo the Panton style of the 1960s. Curves emerge and amplify across floor and ceiling, dividing the area in two, demarcated by the use of opposite colours and textures: one red but cold to the touch, the other pearly white but warmer and softer.

(Below left)
The Paul Frank Store, South Coast Plaza, California (2004) Glazing the entire exterior allows the interior to become the façade. Within, the area is divided; the right side to reflect the chaotic, eclectic nature of the client – products and artefacts are randomly displayed on a Douglas Fir wall which can be used for skateboarding – while the left side has more geometry, control and precision with movable and adjustable display elements.

(Right)
Miss Sixty, South Coast Plaza, California (2002) The cocoon dressing rooms address the age-old mystery of shadow play. Constructed of ultra-light aluminium circles wrapped in an elastic translucent fabric, the users can be seen as indistinct silhouettes.

the paul frank store

Giorgio Borruso

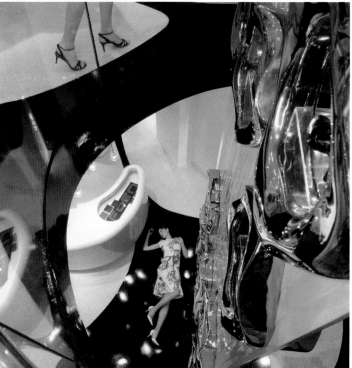

can manipulate the minds of the end user, through architectural form, to undergo an experiential journey of discovery. You will never see a directional sign in one of Borruso's stores.

Borruso approaches each project differently; as he works for market competitors he cannot afford to have a signature style. He feels passionately for every commission he undertakes. 'It's almost like falling in love. I dream of my projects at night and wake up thinking about them in the morning. No two obsessions can be the same. I'm not arrogant, but if I don't have that moment of infatuation with a project at the beginning I don't take it on.'

He is often quoted as the designer of organic, free-flowing surreal spaces, but if there are perceived similarities they are accidental rather than contrived. Every-thing in a Borruso interior is there for a reason: 'I don't like to think of style; I think there is a strong difference in each of my commissions. There is definitely a

shared approach. I conceive an interior cinematically, as a narrative to be experi-enced. Pictures of my work don't tell the whole story; you have to immerse yourself to fully understand. Each visit will reveal something new, some hidden detail. The curves are not just decorative, they have a meaning – the Snaidero ribbons unite the space, the curve forming an optical illusion to make the space look bigger; the organic shapes in Fila allude to the concept of speed and movement; and the 'eyes' in Fornarina have a shape best suited to display the product. My architecture is strong but it serves to complement the product – never to overshadow it. Architecture is about communication. If a user can't engage with the brand or the product, then the architect has failed.'

(Top)
Fila, New York (2005)
The store has an elegance, lightness and grace based on the concept of movement. The custom-made furniture stretches like muscles about to sprint. Curvilinear strips speed across the ceiling. The centre of the space is dominated by two ellipsoidal metallic elements which envelop the existing columns and appear to descend in search of an anchor.

(Below)
Snaidero, Los Angeles (2005) Borruso has again glazed the façade so that the interior is clearly visible from the street, the architectonic form within becoming a building within a building. The seven strips merge and recede into the showroom, uniting the varying styles of kitchen on display. The line continues and curves around, creating an office space which appears to want to spill back out onto the street.

Cassandra Complex

Cassandra Fahey studied interior design, and then architecture, at The Royal Melbourne Institute of Technology (RMIT), graduating in 1997 and 1999, respectively. She is currently undertaking a masters in architecture. She founded her own company, Cassandra Complex, during the last year of her undergraduate training.

The majority of Fahey's work is new build but, because of her training in both disciplines, all her projects to date have a strong interior quality. Fahey is influenced by the works of Carlo Scarpa who, in buildings such as Banca Popolare, Verona and Tomba Brion, shows how exterior and interior should merge into one consistent whole. Fahey comments: 'The best architecture starts with the world and ends at the toothpaste holder. It's holistic. For me the design of interior spaces is an artistic process. The interior is the canvas. I became preoccupied with working up interiors through my love of art and creative thinking via architects, such as Scarpa, who showed me the potential of space as a way of describing the world.'

Ironically, the scheme with which Fahey is most proud is an interior, The Chameleon. A former candy factory built in 1910, it was taken over decades later by Davey's Automative Electrical Company which emblazoned the red-brick exterior with its name. The 91 cm (3 ft) -high letters still remain today and are historically preserved. Unable to change the exterior, Fahey intervened with an inner façade which glimmers behind the original. From the street it is possible to view the luminous, curving, candy-red wall set several feet behind the second-floor windows and be reminded of 'the great big lollies they once made in the sweet factory here'. In light of Fahey's holistic approach to her profession, however, it is not surprising that this is her favourite project. 'Chameleon is architecture in an interior. I designed a building within a building whereby the interior of the warehouse is the landscape and the big red object is the building. It is an interior manipulator.'

Cassandra Complex (a six-person architectural company) has built up a reputation in Australia for being fresh and experimental. The youthful team draws on a diverse range of academic and professional backgrounds and demonstrates a contemporary understanding of the world. The Sam Newman House caused a stir in the media when it was completed in 2000. By plastering the face of Pamela Anderson across its exterior it spoke in an accessible language of public icons. The aim of the practice is to extend architectural expression into a wider public realm by developing awareness and proffering new ideas, engaging the viewer on many levels. 'The quality of our work lies not only in sheer, naked creativity and uniqueness, but in the story. My training taught me to look around and *see* – to look not only at the architecture which surrounds us but at everything. I am always interested in going further. It's not about style – that's hideously boring. The work is about the client, the world and anything relevant. I think the smart clients can see that in our work but they have to

(Top)
Violin House, Melbourne, Australia (2006) The design of the Violin House was inspired by the client's parental home, which was created by Alistair Knox, who was strongly influenced by Frank Lloyd Wright. Fahey has used clerestory windows and recycled Jarrah as references to this heritage, adding her own idiosyncratic quirks, which she refers to as 'a bit of techno, a bit of silliness, a bit of colour and a bit of hearty beef'. The kitchen adjoins the central sunken music space.

(Below)
The Smith Great Aussie House, Port Philip Bay, Australia (2006) The main space is coloured to match the surrounding countryside. Origami-like, the ceiling uses complex joinery and detail to bedazzling effect. Large windows in the lounge and kitchen offer views to the horizon, which are captured on mirrored surfaces that bring the exterior into the interior.

Cassandra Complex

(Top left)
BHP Billiton Platypusary, Healesville Sanctuary, Victoria (2005) Fahey's inspirations vary. At the moment she is concerned with human connection to nature. The platypusary avoids faux naturalism. Its form is based on the platypus egg.

(Below left)
BHP Billiton Platypusary
The tripartite exoskeleton supports an internal, radial, scaly skin of gold-leaf panels. The sun is filtered through, casting shadows on the ground and into the pools which are lined with 20 million toy marbles. Each reflects the entire space.

be brave, too, because what they will get has never been seen before – they can't pick it off the shelf. This is good for some and bad for most.'

It is not surprising therefore that all her work is markedly different, from the graphic quality of the Newman House to the rich, oriental references in the Husk outlet or the curvaceous gold pipes in the Platypusary (a building to shelter a breeding programme for platypuses).

The company has a wide range of experience ranging from small residential to commercial interiors, retail and restaurant design, medium-scale residential and commercial architecture through to medium-scale institutional, commercial, academic and government projects. As well as the Newman house and The Chameleon, notable projects include: the Smith Great Aussie house, Black

Rock, Victoria; the Violin House, Brighton, Victoria; the BHP Billiton Platypusary, Healesville, Victoria; the Husk Collins Street lifestyle and clothing outlet, Melbourne; the New Gold Mountain bar, Melbourne (due for completion after going to print), and the Pavilions for New Architecture at the Monash Museum of Modern Art.

Cassandra Fahey's visions for the future are not trifling. She would like to design a house for Woody Allen and 'I would like a commission like the Sydney Opera House. Everytime I go there I cry. Jørn Utzon knew stuff that most people will never know. He is communicating the most important thing that an architect can communicate: that can never be spoken. I try and do this with my projects. This is and has always been my goal.'

(Above)
The Chameleon, north Melbourne (2003) The architect's own apartment is a building within a building. The bathroom can be viewed through a slice of the glowing red internal extension.

(Left)

Husk Collins Street, Melbourne (2004)
Husk encourages ethical clothing manufacture, sourcing it from around the world. Housed in a former nineteenth-century apothecary, Fahey's interiors are mind-altering, offering infinite reflections and many Persian references, which allude to the fact that Husk's products come from exotic countries.

(Top)

Newman house, St Kilda West, Victoria (2000)
Fahey used a palette of 'jelly bean' colours: pinks, aquas, oranges, purples and yellows ('We're drawn to things we enjoyed as children, the glossy and plastic things we want to put in our mouths'), contrasting these 'edible' colours with modernist materials like concrete, corrugated steel cladding, steel frames and louvres.

(Below)

Newman house Exterior. Set in a street of 'post-modern' anonymous terraced houses, The Newman House façade is manufactured from laminated glass, digital film and an aluminium flat-plate grid frame. Varying light, reflections, shadows, direction and distance contribute to the depth and density of the image.

Johnson Chou

After graduating from University of Waterloo School of Architecture, one of Canada's pre-eminent architecture institutions, Johnson Chou worked for a number of architectural firms including Arthur Erickson before the recession of the early 1990s forced him to make a career move. With his life/business partner Patricia Christie he opened a fine-art gallery, focusing primarily on the design and film industry. He designed his own gallery spaces which garnered such acclaim that he had the confidence to found his own practice in Toronto in 1999.

Although a self-declared modernist, to describe Chou's work as minimalist would be too facile an approach to refer to a body of work, which undoubtedly elemental and pared down in style, and using a catalogue of materials associated with the reductivist school, is nevertheless much more eclectic in concept. Describing his design philosophy, Chou notes five conceptual streams that are currently informing his interiors, only one of which is 'architectural reduction or search for the elemental': the others are 'narrative', the 'articulation of the complex within the simple', 'transformational poetics' and 'programmatic invention'.

Chou lists as one of his major successes the fact that while at university he was lucky enough to develop ideas which he still finds compelling enough today to adapt to his architectural practice. His university thesis was a criticism of architecture, its central theme focusing on the need for buildings and spaces to engage the viewer on many levels.

Utilizing narrative as a means of creating intensified forms of metaphor and ritual, the thesis examined narrative structures in Chinese gardens (Chou is Taiwanese by birth) as well as Russian constructivist art, film theory and set design.

All Chou's work has in common a theatricality, or rather a filmic quality. He approaches each space with a storyboard, creating a narrative – what he refers to as an 'architectural promenade' – in which form and detail are imbued with metaphoric content. His prime motivation is to engage the viewer or participant on an intellectual, emotional and physiological level of experience. His interiors appear to be straightforward but belie the complexity of technique and reference which underpin them – a paradoxical relationship that he applies equally to form as well as function.

His interiors are performance. His subtle, cinematographic control of lighting is used to dematerialize form. Shifting planes of light seem to emanate from nowhere, the luminescence creating ephemeral and translucent spaces. Space, light and form are developed by transformation by being cantilevered, swivelled, occluded, slid or suspended. 'I have always been fascinated with objects and space that transform, and mutable sculptural forms that are inflected by function – buildings and spaces that can convert, spaces animated by the fascination and beauty of movement.'

The Yolles Residence, completed in 2001, is probably the most publicized of Chou's works, and one in which he was

(Top)
Grip Limited offices, Toronto (2006) The brief from this witty advertisement company was to create a space that would reflect its work, foster creativity, and address the notions of play and indoor/outdoor. Chou created a series of informal meeting places offering various spatial experiences and metaphoric readings, using forms, textures and surfaces which manifested the concept of recreation, combining them with materials which blurred the interior with the exterior.

(Below)
Yolles Residence, Toronto (2001) This is housed in a converted warehouse in downtown Toronto. All non-structural walls were removed, including the one dividing the public and private areas which was replaced by an 8m (25ft) sandblasted glass screen. Layered with sliding partitions of varying dimensions, views through the rooms change as the panels move, transforming and revealing one area as they conceal another.

(Left)
11a Baldwin Avenue, Toronto (2004) The client's former childhood home had fallen into disrepair. Maximizing a restricted site, the brief was to create an elegant, open and minimal living space. Based on the notion of the telescope, Chou ordered the circulation spaces to frame views of various Toronto landmarks. This appropriation of the exterior creates an illusion of infinity within the interior.

(Right)
Blowfish restaurant and sake bar, Toronto (2003) Inspired by the notion of fusion cuisine, the space was conceived as a dialectic of Eastern and Western forms, materials, textures and iconography. The bar is defined, and the dining area is enclosed, by a fine metal 'curtain' based on the Japanese *shoji* screen which creates a dialogue between the visible and the obscure and captures nuances of daylight.

(Far right)
TNTblu, denim boutique, Toronto (2002) The long, narrow space has white epoxy floors and glossy surfaces which are 'painted' by light cast through coloured gels. The space is articulated by a cantilevered cash desk and denim bar which is suspended from the ceiling. The dressing rooms are designed as capsules: a fluid form which transforms as the doors open and close.

able to assimilate the various conceptual preoccupations outlined above. 'The project is emblematic of our studio's work: that is, conceptual complexity and clarity realized through economy of gesture and "transformation".'

Chou is adamant that his main inspirations are his clients. 'While there is a consistency in our aesthetic and the ideas we pursue, our work is constantly inflected and tested by our clients. The narrative, or story, we create is essentially inspired by the client. The concept for the Yolles Residence was influenced by the concluding words in the brief: "think penitentiary".'

This Chou interpreted as a need for the client not to live as a convict but in spaces that were contemplative, with a minimum of distractions, using simple, massive materials spare of detailing and without any overt decorative embellishments. He removed all non-structural walls,

replacing the division between public and private spaces with an 8m (25ft) sandblasted glass screen, layered with sliding partitions which afford varying views through the rooms as the panels move. The largest of these is a 5m (15ft) stainless-steel section which separates the bedroom and bathroom from the living area. Inspired by the 'panopticon' – a prison type that allows the warden to view all the prisoners from a single position – the design amplifies the voyeuristic pleasures of surveillance; when closed, the panel has a 25cm (10in) strip of clear glass through which the bather can be spied upon from the living room. The bathing area is like a stage set where one enacts the self-conscious performance of both watching and being watched. Light is added to the interior as a whole to lend a sculptural, other-wordly quality, to re-define space and create atmosphere.

(Left)

Womb, Toronto Interior Design Show (2002) Designed as four rooms in one – work, office, meditation, base – the concept recognizes the need for our refuge to fulfil a variety of needs. The space transforms as necessary, with furniture and cabinetry that appear and disappear into walls and floors at a touch of a button.

(Top right)

TNTWOMAN, Toronto (2000) The boutique is defined by translucent glass screens spaced 3m (10ft) apart to create four individual rooms. With dramatic lighting, white walls and acid-etched glass screens, the space is serene and ethereal. Transforming mirror/tables, which can pivot from the horizontal to the vertical, animate the shop according to desired use.

(Below right)

Vizio Eyewear and Photogallery, Toronto (1999) The dual purpose of eyewear boutique and photography gallery is combined. The concept of the space is based on the mechanistic characteristics of glasses frames with elements that slide, tilt and pivot. Two service desks are suspended longitudinally from the ceiling. For receptions they are drawn to either side of the gallery, expanding the space.

Antonio Citterio

Antonio Citterio has earned a reputation for his uncompromising design; his self-coined term for this is 'proto-rationalism'. Citterio's approach, whether designing a piece of furniture or the interior of a boutique hotel, starts by examining the thought process behind the function and the spatial integrity. Citterio graduated in architecture from the Politecnico of Milan in 1976 and was greatly inspired by the modern movement with its adage of 'Less is More'. His work today is still concerned with rationality, functionalism and the philosophy of living with comfort and practicality.

He feels that it is as important that the profession is concerned with 'ingenious architects, capable of expressing and conveying emotion' as in a more constant approach which strips a design back to its basics and investigates it through prototypical research which necessarily involves a component of standardization. 'I want to convey my approach to contemporary architecture through the concept of the golden section expressed in a precise artistic language. The image consists of an abstract geometric shape with an indistinct border, arranged horizontally in accordance with strict rules of proportion to express nothing other than the complete internal cohesion of the shape itself; in other words, structure shorn of all expressive intentions.'

Although trained as an architect, Citterio first made his name as a furniture designer, and by the end of the 1990s his list of clients included many leading European design-orientated manufacturers including Kartell, Vitra, Artemide, Flexform, Olivetti, Moroso and most importantly B&B Italia (he is currently the latter's highest-profile designer and sits on its board of directors). Italy at that time was unique in Europe in that no courses in interior design were on offer. For Citterio this background is fundamental to how he works. 'The nature of my approach – reflected by the work of my practice – lies in the intimate relationship between product design, interior design and architecture.' His assistant jokes that, with an individual floor devoted seperately to architecture, interiors and products, even the design layout of his own studio reflects this plurality.

Despite his prolific output, designing for design's sake is something that Citterio cannot comprehend. Aesthetics are not enough; there has to be a technological development or a good reason for an

(Right)
Edel Music headquarters, Hamburg (2002) Interior. The transparency of the ground floor, which houses the reception, restaurant, bar and auditorium, indicates the public character of the interior. The concept of the design is based on the idea of the 'campus' where young people have the chance to meet employees of the company and communicate with visitors from all over the world.

(Below)
Exterior, Edel Music
The lower two levels of this five-storied structure sit comfortably on their podium, while the three upper levels cantilever over the polder and overlook the River Elbe.

(Right)
Hotel Bulgari, Milan (2005) Exterior. Dating from the 1950s, Citterio's refurbishment in white marble expresses refinement and lightness in contrast to the massive neighbouring stone buildings. The eighteenth-century part of the façade was fully restored.

(Far right)
Hotel Bulgari Interior. Careful design has been applied to every single detail: from door handles to the whole façade, from all furniture to desk accessories, and from architecture to drinking glasses and fabric. The use of black granite and Burmese teak in the communal areas creates an elegant, though informal, environment.

object, and a clarity of tectonics or social need which makes an interior useable: 'For me, undertaking an interior consists of studying the relationship between the space and the function that such space is intended to have – what I would refer to as interior architecture. At the moment in which this relationship is resolved the project is complete. I am proud of projects that work. An environment is fully serviceable when the users – those who live in it and animate it – become aware and feel the properties and quality of the scheme.'

After graduation Citterio established a design partnership with Paolo Nava and worked with architect Vittorio Gregotti on the restoration of the Brera Art Gallery in Milan. In 1987 he went into practice with his wife, the American architect Terry Dwan, with whom he completed such prominent buildings as the commercial and administrative complex in Seregno, Italy; offices for Espirt in Amsterdam, Antwerp and Milan; a production plant for Vitra in Nuremberg, Germany; the Massimo de Carlo gallery in Milan; and private residences in Japan and Europe. Today he works under his own name, Antonio Citterio and Partners, and is known for the interiors and furniture he creates for fashion-design labels: the

Valentino flagship in Milan; boutiques for Cerruti in New York, and Emanuel Ungaro in Paris; a flagship store for Stefanel in Milan; a Fausto Santini boutique in Düsseldorf, and a De Beers outlet in London. Recent projects number the Bulgari Hotel in Milan, the B&B Italia store in London and a private residence in Sardinia.

In common with so many of the people and practices featured in this book, Citterio does not feel that he has a particular style, each project being governed by an unique set of circumstances. Yet his interiors share a pared-down clarity, superb craftsmanship, and a subtle use of colour highlighted by vivid accents. He works closely with his clients, whom he says select him for the quality of his designs which extends to the smallest detail, for his choice of materials, and for his knowledge of the construction process.

'The relationship with the client is of fundamental importance. From this interaction a concept for a project is defined, then my sketches are developed in increasing detail by my collaborators until all that is superfluous has been extracted and there is nothing missing any longer. I do simple architecture because I've always done it – I can't change now.'

(Top)
**Enzo degli Angiuoni
headquarters, Lecco,
Italy (2002)** Interior. The
design of the interstitial
part aimed at combining
all the elements by a single
approach. Glass-panelled
hallways lend openness
to spaces like the meeting
room and world library.

(Below)
**Enzo degli Angiuoni
headquarters** Exterior.
The original building,
which houses this textile
company, is dated with
a complex profile. The
new warehouse annex
(in black) was later
acquired. The project
was to link the two
by connecting indoor
passageways on the
ground floor and a
research and planning
department on the
first floor.

Antonio Citterio

(Top)
Private seaside residence, Sardinia (2004) Interior. Here the spaces are kept simple. Apart from the kitchen and bathroom that are finished in earth colours, the floors and walls throughout are white, which extenuates the light and shadow play created by the deep openings in the façade. The sloping shapes of the splays open up views to the sea or garden which, accordingly, become an integral part of the interior design. The walls are finished in a lime and pulverized marble mix, flatteringly hand-finished with a stainless-steel spatula to add texture.

(Below)
Private seaside residence Exterior. Building on the shore is no longer allowed. To reduce the presence of architecture on the beach the ground floor was coated with granite-hewn rocks, so that the building merges with the garden.

Claesson Koivisto Rune

The Swedish design trio Ola Rune, Mårten Claesson and Eero Koivisto founded their multidisciplinary design studio in 1993, a bold move as at that point they hadn't even received their architecture diplomas from Konstfack, the national school of art and design in Stockholm where they had met in the course of their studies.

If you are not familiar with CKR's architecture (although with the completion of the much publicized Sfera Building in Japan that would be surprising), you will be aware of their furniture design. Working either as a group or individually, they have collaborated not only with native manufacturers such as Asplund, David Design, Swedese and Offecct, but also with major international companies, probably most significantly Cappellini, for whom they conceived the Pebbles chair – a new seating typology consisting of one 9m (6.6ft) upholstered disc with a second smaller one 'hovering' above.

According to the group, however, the product designs are a means to an end, 'compared to architectural work, which is our trip, it's more like a hobby ... It provides us with the stability we need to maintain our philosophy. If necessary, we can spend more time and lose money on an interior design or architecture project, and get it up to standard.'

CKR's first interior design commission of any note was the flagship McDonald's outlet in Stockholm. A departure from the usual plastic, bright and garish spaces we normally associate with the brand, CKR's interior is a perfect example of Scandinavian modernism,

with blond wood-panelled booths and, as you would expect, stylish seating. Since that time the firm has worked in many typologies, from corporate and commercial to leisure and residential, with projects including the Swedish ambassador's residence in Berlin, the headquarters of Sony Music in Stockholm, refurbishment of the famous Operakällaren restaurant in the historic Royal Opera House in Stockholm with a contrasting new bar in the glass veranda, as well as various private apartments and houses.

Having benefited greatly from the renewed interest in Swedish design that has developed over the last few years, CKR is, however, at pains to point out that its partners do not consider their work as strictly adhering to a rigorous Scandinavian minimalist tradition. 'Modernism is

(Left)
Private apartment, town house for Kjell Nordström, Stockholm (2005) The original building was an early twentieth-century neoclassical apartment block. CKR stripped down the walls, carefully leaving and restoring original floors, windows and radiators. All wood is oak.

(Right)
Villa Råman, Baldringe, Sweden (2000) The villa is in a former country school building. The calm and openness of the surrounding manmade farm landscape is reflected in the spacious interior. The kitchen is open to the dining area. The minimalist white aesthetic is warmed by accents of colour.

our extraction – that's where we acquired our personal taste and style. But we're not modernists.' Certainly all CKR interiors are uncluttered; there are a lot of white walls, natural materials and open stream-lined spaces but, more importantly for the trio, each project shares a carefully studied use of daylight, a natural 'fluidity', and the creation of living environments, which can adapt to clients' way of life.

Living in a Nordic country, where the sun shines only for a couple of hours a day in winter, the band endeavour to bring as much natural light into a building as possible, hence the use of white, or a cool palette, warmed by accents of bright colour, as well as sensuous woods or furnishings. A mixture of matt and gloss surface materials are used on the walls. Floors are pale and bleached, and joints are hidden away behind varying finishes, the interior being given what almost amounts to an inner skin.

Although CKR does not view its work as sculptural (as interior architects they are primarily concerned with solving prob-lems of function), the company's approach is very much in this vein. Internal walls

are cut through to allow daylight to penetrate, and there have been increasing experiments with glass. Glazing is used not only for its transparency but also for its reflective qualities, translucent panels for their materiality, and coloured glass for its ability to accentuate and shade. The result is a complex composition of semi-closed open space. The trio design their interiors as a fluid sequencing, one room leading to another with as little division as possible, allowing the user to experience light and acoustics in a seamless experience as they move through the building.

Structure, space, light and composition are used to create feeling. It's probably what most separates CKR's work from the modernist Scandinavian tradition. When asked what qualities would make a client select their work above the rest, they replied, 'A passionate standpoint to create emotionally charged environ-ments, yet leaving room for different kinds of people, actions, and objects in the finished space.' Using a modernist style language CKR manages to animate and humanize interiors.

(Left)
Sony Music, Stockholm (1999) The offices are housed in an old building, three floors of which were previously used as a church. The key to the project is the articulated staircase. The open space with two mezzanines works both horizontally and vertically. When moving between floors, lines of vision open and close.

(Top)
Swedish ambassador's residence, Berlin (1999) The remodelling of an old villa was carried out by Arkitekt Magasinet. The residence is used for informal meetings with the ambassador. CKR's brief was to create interiors which were modern but not trendy. The colour scheme (soft blue, grey and cappuccino) refer to Swedish minerals. All furniture and fittings are Swedish and contemporary.

(Below left)
Private residence for Markus and Kajsa Mostrom, Nacka, Sweden (2003) The house forms a geometric volume where the interior is as important as the exterior – a box with a series of openings. A grid was superimposed onto the space, creating a basic room structure. Each room has one of its sides glazed, allowing a dialogue between interior and exterior while also allowing light to flood the building. The bathroom window is on the top of the box, with daylight entering through the ceiling.

(Below right)
Private apartment, town house for Kjell Nordström, Stockholm (2005) The upstairs bathroom contains a bathtub designed by CKR for Boffi, which is raised to afford views of Stockholm harbour.

Concrete

The company was founded in 1997 by Rob Wagemans, Erik van Dillen (who is currently only involved as a creative consultant), and Gilian Schrofer (who left in 2004 to form his own practice). It is multidisciplinary and is involved not only with interior architecture but also urban planning, architecture and product design. 'Concrete does not believe in disciplines! So for us there are no borders. Why does an architect stop after the façade and the rough spaces? Why should someone else take over? Why does the façade come after the interior spaces? We base our creativity on an ability to look across every discipline. We try to make a total concept on every level of design.'

Wagemans studied architecture in Utrecht and Amsterdam but was not impressed by his education, which he found to be limiting – surrounded as he was by people, mainly his teachers, who only looked towards architecture for their inspiration – 'the history of architecture, the future of architecture, the technique of architecture'. He felt alien in an environment that didn't take a more holistic approach, which ignored the influences of movies, fashion and art. It was this period which started him on the road to designing spaces that he refers to as 'architecture on the inside'; a month spent at the Bauhaus in Dessau reinforced his approach.

Concrete is probably best known for the Supperclub restaurant and nightclub which originated in Amsterdam and has now expanded to include venues in Rome and San Francisco, as well as a floating version, 'Supperclub Cruise'. The brainchild of a group of artists headed by Bert van der Laden, the collective envisaged a whole new dining experience, a meeting place for a clientele of unconventional artists, writers, musicians, advertisers, fashion designers and assorted progressive kindred spirits. Using dramatic and mood-changing lighting effects, video installations and rooms dominated by single colours and ambiance, Concrete created environments where people could escape reality, an experimental and sensuous series of spaces where you recline to eat on huge mattresses, where all the senses are stimulated and anything seems possible. In 2004 Supperclub Cruise won the Lensvelt de Architect Interior Prize, the jury's statement concluding, 'The winning design gives shape to an experience that fits in seamlessly with the night-life of the current age. This makes the Supperclub Cruise into an icon of the contemporary interior design.'

The Supperclub interiors are a manifesto for Concrete's approach to creating space. Their aim is to seduce people. They take as their starting point the fact that on entering an interior you feel, hear and feel things without really realizing it. It's this subconscious seduction that is built on. Concrete believe that a visitor should be constantly surprised and find new things every time they return. The company's work is always experiential with a touch of the absurd and relies on the dynamic of the user to give it meaning: 'We do not only work with height and width but with "time" as well. We design "event" spaces which develop only when touched by people.'

(Top)
La Chambre Obscure, Supperclub, Amsterdam (1999) The space is lined with faux-leather cushions with a centrally placed nut to attach handcuffs. Sixteen TV screens embedded into the ceiling add colour, each showing a part of a specially commissioned pornographic movie – a kinetic, erotic mosaic. The space can be cleared of beds for dancing.

(Below)
Hotel Überfluss, Bremen (2005) *Überfluss* means 'abundance', and Concrete took this as a reference for the interiors of Kastens and Siemann's hotel. Classic elements were given a modern twist in shape, material or manufacturing process. The reception desk is an 8m (26.25ft) long 'baroque' table finished in black piano lacquer. A chrome box underneath stores everything away neatly.

Concrete

(Left)

Nomads Restaurant, Amsterdam (2001) This is a different kind of eating experience. All guests arrive at the same time, are welcomed in the bar, eat the same menu and are entertained until 3.00am. The aesthetic is '1001 nights' created by a palette of red, brown and gold, and the use of Arabian scripts on mirrors and walls. Beds are employed in the dining area and each niche is separated by metal curtains.

(Top right)

Supperclub, San Francisco (2005) The latest venue, La Salle Neige, has a centrally placed bar and kitchen so the kitchen staff can become DJs for the evening. Beds are placed around the edges of the space. The floor is resin and corresponds in colour to the room. The colour of the light can be changed to give mood-altering experiences.

(Below right)

Laundry Industry, London (2000) The shop consists of three elements: concrete, steel and light. The light can be constantly altered to adapt to seasonal collections. The floor is tilted at an angle of 4°, playing with the customers' sense of balance.

Clients number only those that are willing to take a risk. They shy away from narrow-mindedness: 'A "Concrete customer" should have guts, should be enterprising, should want to break with conventions, and has no fear. Fear is our only opponent. We believe [that] in today's society, fear is everybody's largest enemy.'

The approach is analytical and concrete works closely with clients, asking many questions until they have built up an idea of the customer's passions and ambitions which they can then reinterpret through their own vision into a solid surrounding that will work commercially. They look on the process as a mathematical one, that once the equation has been grasped then the answer is simple and only one solution will be left. It's this conceptual stage that they enjoy the most.

I asked Rob Wagemans what he considered to be his greatest success, and the answer was surprising. It wasn't any of his built works – not Supperclub, nor the central hall of the Van Gogh Museum, not Nomads, Envy Delicacies, Laundry Industry, the Hotel Überfluss nor the Centraal Museum in Utrecht – but something much more personal: his own company. 'Creating an office where there is humour, where there is discussion and where every problem gets such a nice solution, and of course a team of multi-talented people who are not afraid to cross any boundary … hopefully this will stay the project of which I'm most proud for very many years to come.'

(Far left)

Central Hall, Van Gogh Museum, Amsterdam (2005) The concept was to provide a space which would attract the young to come to meet and drink on Friday evenings. By projecting a painting by Van Gogh on the wall, filming the lobby at the same time and superimposing this over the painting, visitors appear to inhabit the artist's world.

(Left)

Van Baarenzaal exhibition, Centraal Museum, Utrecht (1999) The museum is modern, the van Baarenzaal family's collection classic. Concrete's brief was to link the conservative and the progressive. They used glass cabinets which have the dual effect of showing the front and back of the paintings, as well as providing an unimpeded view throughout the space.

(Top)

Envy Delicacies, Amsterdam (2005) The aesthetic combines sleek minimalism with living-room-style comfort. Although a restaurant not a shop, the concept is based on a rural, family-run Italian delicatessen where customers shop but also join the owner to sample the produce over a glass of wine. One wall is formed by 26 refrigerators showcasing wines and food.

(Below)

Rituals, Amsterdam (2000) The company specializes in home and body-care products. The store is open and transparent, the interior entirely visible through the façade window. All products are linked with water and all materials refer to this element. Bamboo is used on walls and floors.

Matali Crasset

There is nothing understated about Matali Crasset from her severe, androgynous appearance and distinctive Joan d'Arc logo, to her use of acid colours in her interiors (frequently lime green, 'the colour of energy', and chartreuse). 'Colour is life. Why should cheerful spaces be reserved for children?'

Born in 1965 to a farming family in the tiny village of Normée, in the Champagne region of France, she studied marketing at the École Nationale Superièure de Création Industrielle in Paris where her eyes were opened to the world of design. Transferring courses to industrial design, she graduated in 1991 and worked for the designer Denis Santachiara in Milan, followed by five years with Philippe Starck, first in his own studio and then for Thomson Multimedia electronics group – and ever since has suffered the double-edged sword of being labelled a 'Starck baby'. She opened her own practice in 1998 and today works across a wide range of disciplines, including furniture and electronic design, and architecture. Her most significant interiors include the HI hotel in Nice, a futuristic pigeon loft in the Caudry Leisure Park, the Lieu Commun shop in Paris, the restaurant Végétable (also in Paris), the annexe of the BHV store created specifically for the youth of a Parisian suburb, and the temporary accommodation of a regional museum in Den Bosch, Holland.

Crasset looks on her upbringing as both a handicap and liberator: a handicap as she came to culture later in life, but also a liberator as it meant she approached her design work without preconceived notions of the decorative arts or French 'good taste'. Her parents taught her the simple, natural pleasures of life, and it's this simplicity which, she maintains, has given her the freedom to approach her work in a fresh and innovative way. An early example of this *liberté* was the seating system she designed for Edra in 1998, which consisted of a collection of poufs made from the cheap checked plastic bags usually used for laundry, which she fitted together modularly – a concept which came to her from childhood games building structures from bales of hay.

Similarly, the result of a childhood roaming the countryside and climbing trees, the pigeon loft for the Beauvois Pigeon Fanciers' Association is a giant brightly coloured mushroom on the outside with an interior consisting of a branching arboreal structure made from chrome metal. 'I like to use reflections of everyday life in my designs: common experiences, childhood events, basic human reactions which I rework and inject into spaces that radiate a universally recognizable feeling.'

When asked to describe her work, Crasset uses adjectives such as 'hospitality', 'homeliness', 'generosity', 'fluidity'. She thinks less in terms of interior architecture and more in proposing new ways of living through her designs. Her furniture designs speak not of luxury and elegance but of questioning domestic rites and inhabiting space. Her famous 'Hospitality Column' is certainly a guest bed but also creates its own environment by unfurling to provide

(Top)
The BHV Belle Epine, Paris (2005) The annexe to the BHV store is entirely dedicated to youth, and proposes four different arenas of exchange and expression: action, movement, escape and fashion. The Café Yelo forms an encampment around a central column designed as an informal area to meet and listen to music. For greater privacy, large tables with bench seats are set in octagonal metal structures wrapped in woven fabric.

(Below left and right)
Capsule pigeon loft, Caudry leisure park (2003) The loft was conceived to attract a new generation to the dying hobby of breeding carrier pigeons. The brief stated the loft should combine aesthetic appeal, functionality and a pedagogic dimension. The capsule is made from resin. The chrome metal mast is reminiscent of a tree.

(Top left)
Infinite Interior F.L.A.T. for the 1st Architectural Biennial in Beijing (2004) The sofa allows one to go from a relaxed position to an active one.

(Below left)
Infinite Interior F.L.A.T. The installation was designed to question our preconceived notions of living spaces. The rooms are defined by contemporary structures and question codes of use. The bed is linked with a workplace

(Right)
Vert Anis restaurant, Annecy (2005) The interior is based around a 'cross' formed by the wooden bar which continues into the main dining area where it becomes the head table (illustrated), and a metal frame housing a vinyl graphic wallpaper designed by Crasset for Habitat's vinyl range.

a 'guest room' within a room, complete with integral lamp and alarm clock. Similarly, her interiors do not present a *fait accompli* but rather through examining our living environment, suggest solutions which are not fully conceived and controlled but which, on the contrary, form adaptable spaces, open to experimentation.

The 38-room HI hotel (the interior-design project of which Crasset is most proud) offers nine room types, nine ways of living in a given area: monospace, up and down, strata, digital, happy day, technocorner, indoor terrace, white and white, and rendezvous. The hotel takes the visitor on a voyage of discovery to choose the ambiance they find most agreeable. It is a concept which is a departure from the usual luxury hotel

and is diametrically opposed to the idea of areas dominated by interior decoration. The guest is not trapped by one décor but is the recipient of a host of stimuli and life experiences.

From her early days working with Starck, Crasset learned the valuable lesson of being able to manage several complex jobs at the same time. 'This was an important period in my development as a designer.' When asked what she considers her career goals, she replies, 'What I value the most is my autonomy: to be able to work on a tea towel or a museum with the same degree of spontaneity.' And her approach to design? 'My approach is still to research new typologies which also address the fundamental needs of mobility and freedom, and to enable people to use objects and spaces in their own way.'

(Top)
Lieu Commun shop, Paris (2005) Established by Eric Morand and Laurent Garnier's label F Communications, the stylist Ron Orb and Matali Crasset, the space is a commercial platform for all three. Conccived as an environment in which all the separate creations converse together, the interior is opened up and allowed to breathe by using light natural wood and a sky-blue colour scheme.

(Bottom)
Vegetable restaurant, Paris (2005) To reflect chef Alain Passard's passion for nature and biodiversity (all vegetables served in the restaurant come from his own garden), Crasset has created a unique and ephemeral interior reminiscent of a greenhouse repleat with 'cold frames'.

(Far right)
The HI Hotel's Happy Bar, Nice (2003) Crasset's signature use of lime green and cerise is present in the double-height bar and restaurant area. The slatted enclosure in birch plywood evokes the basket of a hot-air balloon.

Eldridge Smerin

Nick Eldridge and Piers Smerin founded their practice in 1998 after meeting at John McAslan and Partners, where they were both partners. They studied at the Architectural Association and Royal College of Art, respectively, and gained experience early in their careers while working in the offices of exceptional architects like Norman Foster and Zaha Hadid at a time when even the more junior members of staff worked directly with the principals. Today their company employs between eight to ten personnel, a size which they prefer to maintain as it is big enough to allow them to take on substantial projects while still being small enough for them to be able to pick and choose their commissions. They only select individuals or companies they know they will get along with and who will share their vision.

Their first major commission was The Lawns, a family house in the Highgate Conservation Area in London, for Frances and John Sorrell, which won awards from both the RIBA and the Civic Trust, and was short-listed for the Stirling Prize. From the start, their reputation as cutting-edge domestic architects was sealed with a series of commissions for new houses on similarly sensitive sites. However, their first residential scheme remains for them their greatest success as it still encapsulates their attitude to design in many ways: challenging the planning restrictions of building in an historic area, transforming an existing structure into something new, and fusing the design of the interior with the exterior.

Although usually responsible for both the building and interior of a project, they do not like to label what they do, preferring to use the more amorphous term of 'designer' or 'design'. 'To be honest we are not much concerned with how our work is described or classified. Design is either good or bad, successful or unsuccessful, irrespective of where it originated, what was intended by it, or how it has been classified.' The duo prides itself on the ability of being able to work on all aspects of a project, from the shell to the furniture.

This overall approach has built the partnership a reputation for producing

(Right)
BT Cellnet/O2 Centre, London (2001) The space occupies one of the historic Ealing film studios. The interior intervention was minimal, acting as a backdrop for a series of finely engineered mobile structures housing meeting rooms and development facilities. The architects collaborated with theatrical lighting and sound specialists to create unique and programmable *son et luminèire*.

(Left)
The Lawns, Highgate, London (2000) The new accommodation wraps largely glazed extensions around the core of the original 1950s house, doubling the footprint. The brief included all aspects of design, from the organization of space to the provision of custom-designed furniture.

intelligent and memorable solutions in response to varied clients' briefs, often within tightly constrained budgets.

They work across a range of typologies from workspace and retail to educational and residential design, collaborating with landscape architects, fine artists, lighting designers, and graphic and identity designers, which they believe enriches the project while still resulting in a coherent whole. Notable schemes include a number of commercial projects, including the radical new research and development headquarters for BT Cellnet/O2, Ealing Studios, London; the headquarters for E. Oppenheimer and Sons of De Beers, Hatton Garden, London; Prisma's headquarters at Centre Point, London; an entire floor devoted to youth fashion 'Spirit' and technology in the Birmingham Selfridges; and the interior and landscape of the Villa Moda department store for Sheikh Majed Al-Sabah, Kuwait. More

recent projects include the redesign of the Design Council's workspace in Bow Street, London; a Performing Arts Centre for a school in north London; and the new Business and Intellectual Property Centre at the British Library.

Eldridge and Smerin do not consider they have a particular design style, preferring the site, client or intended users of a building to dictate the look of the finished project, making each example distinctive and unique. However, what all their work has in common is timelessness being measured, well conceived and constructed. The organization of the spaces is simple and clear, and there is a strong attention to the innovative use of materials as well as detailing. They are sleek and engineered, with strong lines and exude a calmness and restraint which belies their complexity. They could be called minimalist, but it's an enriched form of paring down.

(Above)
Technology department on the 'Spirit' floor, Selfridges, Birmingham (2003) Swayed by an earlier project (BT Cellnet), Vittorio Radice (former chief executive of Selfridges) selected the architects despite their lack of previous retail experience. An out of character, trendy environment was the result. The space is inspired by the boxes, which contain electrical products with cardboard exteriors and foam interiors. The tactile nature of the materials and the choice of unifying green is the antithesis of conventional, sterile electrical departments.

Eldridge and Smerin agree that the greatest influence on their career has been their association with the Sorrells, not only because the couple took a risk employing unknown architects for the ground-breaking design of their home, but also because they share the architects' desire to promote good design within schools. The Sorrell Foundation, set up in 2001-02, promotes designers in a range of disciplines to undertake projects with schools to prove to the government that design does make a difference.

Eldridge and Smerin's goals for the future are to continue to do more work in the schools' sector and to become involved in mainstream mass housing, an area where most developers still offer unimaginative housing on the exterior and internal spaces which are poorly considered and unresponsive to the needs of contemporary life.

(Top left)
Design Council, London (2004) To answer the client's request for a long-term space solution and new ways of working as a multidisciplinary team, the architects designed bespoke worktables and mobile screen systems incorporating whiteboards and pin boards. The structures act as room dividers and also house the council's collection of design publications, known as the 'Knowledge Centre'.

(Below left)
The Shed, Private Members Club, London (2006) Playing on the idea of sheds, the architects have created spaces where the users can shut themselves away, propagate ideas, catch up or simply while away the hours. The interiors have been stripped back to the concrete of the original Havana Bank. Refined by new architectural elements and customized furniture, the old and new are linked by polished flooring and discrete lighting.

(Right)
Pilgrim's Lane, Hampstead, London (2003) An extension and refurbishment of a Victorian town house. The annexe between old and new is created by a full-height glazed volume containing a main staircase constructed entirely from glass, which allows light to penetrate into the heart of the house.

Fantastic Design Works Incorporated

When asked what distinguishes his design style, Katsunori Suzuki, who founded his own company Fantastic Design Works Incorporated in April 2001, replies 'playful, spirited and freewheeling thinking'.

His route to interior design was not the usual one. He studied art at the Kyoto Seika University of Art, but his first love was clubbing – the culture, clientele and design of the many discos and nightclubs which sprang up throughout Japan during the late 1980s. An effect of the bubble economy, which saw a massive expansion of disposable wealth during a relatively short period, Japanese youth emerged from their cloistered, traditional upbringing to play all night in these newly opened nightspots, where each entrepreneur vied with the next to attract this enthusiastic clientele with ever more outrageous interior designs. It was a period which saw Tokyo gain an unrivalled reputation for being at the very forefront of the international design scene. Even after the bubble burst during the 1990s, design has thrived with large international companies employing the services of world-renowned architects and designers to add their signature style to cutting-edge buildings and interiors.

Suzuki was at first primarily interested in the business side of the nightclub industry, but a trip to New York while still a student, where he spent most of his evenings and nights in the many themed bars and restaurants, inspired him to return to Japan and seek employment with MD, famed for its design of nightclubs. He spent the following ten years gaining the technical expertise and contacts to enable him to work independently.

Fantastic Design Works Incorporated is mainly concerned with the design of discos, clubs, bars and restaurants, giving Suzuki the opportunity to liberate his imagination in full-scale interior projects which share a theatricality and inventiveness, springing from his love of films (from the sci-fi greats *2001: A Space Odyssey* and *Blade Runner*, to Tarantino's masterpiece, *Pulp Fiction*), the aesthetics as well as musicality of such bands as the Sex Pistols, The Doors and Marilyn Manson, and the combination of image and narrative found in the comic books of Tezuka Osamu and Go Nagai. 'When I analyze my work, I often compare it to rock music: the guitar equates to the finishing of a restaurant, the drum to the facilities, and the vocals to the food and drink. The musical introduction is the signboard at the entrance, and the base is the rhythmic experience of time spent in one of my interiors.'

Although they are aesthetically otherworldly, and somewhat 'off-the-wall', all of Suzuki's designs are carefully planned. They are executed using orthodox methods – sketches, models and computer-generated designs – in close collaboration with the client and keeping the needs of the end user in sight. 'I am a cooperator and co-worker for my clients' success in commercial terms. What I aim to do is to make their plans more exciting and delightful. One of my favourite projects is J-Pop, Taiwan, because I, as an oriental, realized a space in which I managed to get across a feeling of subculture, which

(Right)
Vampire Café, Tokyo (2001) Paying homage to the themed bars and restaurants Suzuki experienced in New York, this small restaurant takes horror movies as its starting point. It is divided into six areas: 'Altar', a raised area between two columns; 'Victim', a dining area for couples; 'Coffin', a private dining area decorated with a cross; 'Black', another private room; 'Blood', the arterial red corridors; and 'Cross', the reception area.

(Left)
Euro Dining and Bar Marvellous, Tokyo (2001) This bar, which targets an older clientele, was completed (from design to construction) in just 24 days and adopts a mid-century aesthetic.

(Top right)
J-Pop Café, Tokyo (2002) This futuristic bio-morphic bar and restaurant has spectacular views over Tokyo's harbour. The space is mainly constructed from gypsum and hemp fibres: at once durable but readily adaptable to the curvaceous, organic shapes of the walls. Mainly white, they are continually washed by ever-changing hues generated by the computer-controlled LED lighting system.

(Below left)
Zaru, Tokyo (2002) The design of this canteen-come-winery (*zaru* means prodigious drinker in Japanese) was based on the sci-fi cinematography of *Blade Runner*. Huge ventilation fans are made into decorative features which emerge at night from their daily concealment in the walls. The chandeliers are constructed from plastic wine glasses and 1,570 colours, controlled by computer, pan the futuristic space.

(Below right)
J-Pop Café, Taiwan (2003) The close collaboration between Suzuki and the client had a great influence on the project. The concept is based on the sub-culture of manga and otaku, as well as the classical graphics found in the Japanese tattoo and the kimono print.

was as important for my client, a Japanese music video producer, as it was for me. This scheme followed on from the J-Pop Café, Tokyo, which was seized on by the media, bringing me international recognition which is great as it embodies 100 per cent my "fantastic" dream.'

The café is located in the Odaiba district on Tokyo's waterfront, an area which, during the bubble, was earmarked for expansion as a sub-centre of the city. Although many of the plans were scrapped during the ensuing recession, the district remains important as a media centre. J-Pop is part of Tokyo's Joypolis video arcade, and attracts trendy Tokyo-ites to eat, drink and watch promotional pop.

The initial concept was the sci-fi aesthetic which sprang up from the 1960s anti-modernist design trend, which re-appraised the art-nouveau; however, Suzuki layered this with his own personal homage to bio-design, adopting forms found in nature and

coining the expression 'bio-future'. 'The forms at the micro level of nature in themselves do not have a futuristic sense about them, but I think that bio-design that occurs from an emulation of them clearly holds a futuristic element about it. Nowadays buildings are constructed from concrete, iron, steel and wood. I imagined a future in which bio-technology would enable material from trees or plants to be used as a building material. Thinking of the way that ivy grows, creeping over walls, I envisaged a space where a tree and plants had grown over the years, metamorphosing to create an ornamental setting, while also serving a function.'

Suzuki's goal for the future is to take his unique design approach into areas not normally touched by design: 'I would like to design something that is usually out of a designer's sight – a gas station, for example. My gas station design will become a global standard. That is my dream.'

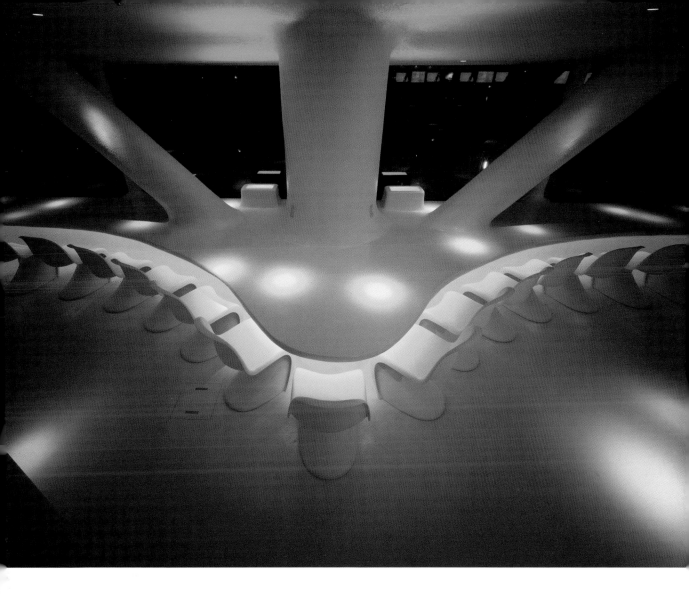

(Top left)
Bar Taketori – 100 stories, Tokyo (2005)
Part of the Fantasy Story Complex which comprises the Blue Lounge, The Wizard of the Opera, and Pork Dish, the main influence of this bar was the famous Taketori *monogatari* tale which recounts the story of a girl born from bamboo. The interiors are full of reference to the fairy tale, with decorative works in bamboo and floating seats placed in a carp pool.

(Below left)
The Wizard of the Opera, Tokyo (2005)
Part of the Fantasy Story Complex, the main theme of this restaurant is the musical *The Phantom of the Opera*, with the restaurant and bar reflecting its dark but romantic atmosphere.

(Top right)
Alice in the Country of Labyrinth, Tokyo (2003)
The concept is based on *Alice in Wonderland* and uses the mix of gothic and prepubescent sexiness which is popular in Japan. Various rooms reflect the surreal world of the novel. The long glass table is a reference to the Mad Hatter's tea party.

(Below right)
Alux restaurant, Tokyo 2006 Alux is a chic restaurant, comprising bar, lounge and dining room, and is situated in an area of Tokyo that is famous for its hip and fashionable inhabitants. It's name derives from 'All Luxury'. The wall decoration is made of plaster and is washed by ever-changing light effects – it was inspired by the famous Hong Kong actress, Kelly Chen.

Gabellini Sheppard Associates

Michael Gabellini was born in 1958 in Verz Cruz, Pennsylvania, the home town of the Knoll furniture factory. Being the son of an interior designer and living a few miles from the factory engendered within him a fascination for design from an early age. He entered the Rhode Island School of Design (RISD) in 1976, originally to study environmental sculpture but soon found that his real interests lay in architecture. He graduated with a degree in fine art in 1980 and a B.Arch. the following year. His main inspirations come from the art world and ancient civilizations. 'I began to develop my own design sensibility through an interest in contemporary art as well as architectural history. I was fascinated with the work of the California Light Artists James Turrell and Robert Irwin, for example, and sculptors such as Brancusi and Serra. As a student I also drew inspiration from an opportunity to study Etruscan art, and the culture and architecture of ancient Roman baths. Our projects have always been a kind of investigation of ancient culture and the way you can use things that predated you in a correct rather than a superficial way. Today I work with space and light in ways that interest me as an artist and with archaeological references for which I have great respect.'

After graduating from RISD, Gabellini travelled in Europe, taking classes at the Architectural Association, London, and

(Left)
Salvatore Ferragamo Boutique, Venice (2001) The large arched windows of the former palazzo frame views into the shop's interiors, where understated furnishings and classic proportions blend with the rich historical context. Sliding nickel silver chain-mail panels with integrated ambient lighting act as theatrical scrims, defining the window displays and offering various degrees of translucency into the shop.

(Right)
Jil Sander, London (2002) The blending of new and old is a frequent feature in the 87 Jil Sander outlets Gabellini has designed to date. In London, the boutique is situated in an early Georgian building. Freestanding mirrors, made from lead-free spectacle-quality glass that colour corrects light, reflect contemporary clothing and eighteenth-century plasterwork.

(Above left)
Nicole Farhi Boutique, New York (1999) The shop, which includes a restaurant is housed on three levels of a 1901 landmark building. The entrance bridge in water-white glass and walnut spans a 8m (26ft) high atrium. The women's wear section is suspended between this and a second atrium to the rear. The restaurant is below.

spending time in Rome where he became interested in ancient civilizations, in stone carving and the works of the Arte Povera artists, whose simple use of light and material appealed greatly to his sensibilities. His professional career began in a traditional way, working in the offices of the major American architectural practice, Kohn, Pedersen & Fox, specialists in modern skyscrapers. He also worked on a freelance basis with interior designer Jay Smith. In 1984 they designed an outlet for the fashion designer Linda Dresner. The *New York* magazine ran a feature contrasting it to the Diane Von Furstenberg outlet, a postmodern extravaganza by Michael Graves.

It was a departure at the time and this early project set the seal on a signature design aesthetic which has now earned Gabellini the international reputation of being an architect of elegant, serene, pared-down spaces carved by light and with a simplicity which belies their technical complexity. 'Our clients are attracted to the way we balance a sense of purity with warmth and comfort. Influenced

by modern masters Neutra, Barragan and Schindler, we look at space holistically from the inside out. We focus on the structural as well as surface elements to meet a client's programmatic needs. Spatial clarity, attention to detail, a discerning use of materials and colour as well as a sensitivity to the dynamic quality of light come to mind as distinguishing ideals of our work.'

Gabellini founded his own company, Gabellini Sheppard Associates in 1991, specializing in the design of commercial, residential and contemporary art spaces, as well as products. The interdisciplinary practice now employs 30 staff working closely with artisans, craft experts and specialists in numerous fields. Gabellini credits partners Kimberly Sheppard and Daniel Garbowit as instrumental to the firm's success. The studio is chiefly known for its work with fashion designers, notably Jil Sander. Since the ground-breaking outlet (which launched the practice headlong into the world of designer and fashion environments)

(Above right)
Coleen B. Rosenblat showroom, office and atelier, Hamburg (1999) The concept was for an elemental design, which would complement the refinement of craft in handmade jewellery. The materials used are imperial plaster, Spanish limestone, translucent optical glass and wenge wood. Light has been used atmospherically and, despite heavy security, the space remains open and inviting.

(Right)
Top of the Rock, Rockefeller Center, New York (2005) Blending contemporary forms with references to the art deco of the original 1933 building, the six-level project celebrates the center's narrative between old and new, ground and sky, and site and city. The triple-height atrium is dominated by a crystal sculpture designed by Gabellini Sheppard in collaboration with Swarovski.

(Right)
View through the Weather Room to the 67th level Grand Viewing Room The Weather Room is a triple-height space of chapel-like proportions. Natural light floods through restored windows onto three colours of honed terrazzo, radiating from the centre to the perimeter grey to pale beige that renders the floor in relation to the incoming daylight. The Viewing Room showcases the Swarovski Crystal Geode Wall, which celebrates the *Zeitgeist* of art deco: the experimentation with geometry, surfaces and new production technology.

(Far right top)
West Village Apartment, New York (1987) One of Gabellini's first residential projects, it still represents a physical manifestation of his design philosophy. An environment of functional simplicity is conceived spatially as two white volumes connected by a white marble stair. Light is treated as a rich, temporal and transforming element of the spare, contemplative space.

(Far right below)
Giorgio Armani Retail Centre (Spazio Armani), Milan (2000) Conceived as a multi-use complex, the space brings together the various collections associated with the Armani brand as well as a bookstore, café, florist and Nobu restaurant. The commercial components are designed around a cruciform 'street' plan and are softly lit by translucent ceiling panels over the atrium, which is animated by coloured walls.

opened in Paris in 1993, it has designed 87 outlets for her worldwide. Other much-publicized projects include the Nicole Farhi flagship store in New York; the Armani Centre in Milan; the Salvatore Ferragamo boutique concept with stores in Venice and New York; the glowing red Ultimo Boutique in San Francisco; New York art galleries for Marian Goodman and Anthony Grant; commissions for the Guggenheim Museum and the Cooper Hewitt National Design Museum; the competition-winning design for the redevelopment of the medieval Piazza Isolo in Verona; custom furniture lines for Nakashima, B&B Italia and Cappellini (Gabellini's Davide Cenci boutique in Rome is home to 100 specially designed pieces); and the restoration of the panoramic observation decks on the Rockefeller Center. 'Top of the Rock was a great challenge … Carving out new interiors for New York's grand, public living room allowed us to revitalize the building's urban legacy and public profile.'

It is no accident that Gabellini refers to this public building in domestic terms. His retail interiors are peppered with references to residential spaces. 'We have an understanding of interior space that is more about the home environment than the overtly commercial; the human element is important to us. We believe good design can enhance daily experiences such as lounging, bathing, shopping, travelling or viewing art. Our interior environments are set up as theatres or backdrops for the unfolding of these activities, heightening perception and sensorial pleasure.'

Since the Hotel Q in fashionable West Berlin hit the design media in 2005, Graft, the international design firm with offices in Los Angeles, Berlin and Beijing, has quickly built up a reputation for being one of the most exciting and innovative practices around.

The partners, Wolfram Putz, Thomas Willemeit and Lars Krückeberg, met during their studies at the Braunschweig Technical University, Germany, sharing not only their interest in architecture but also their love of a cappella singing and choral music. Influenced by Kings College, Cambridge, they founded their own choir, 'Acantus', and toured the States. Architectural scholarships from Braunschweig Technical University allowed them to stay in America, where they took masters at the Southern Californian Institute of Architecture (Willemeit returning to Germany to work for a period in the office of Daniel Libeskind) before founding their own company in 1998.

Harmonized singing is one of Graft's greatest influences, as it taught the partners (they were later joined by Gregor Hoheisel, who runs their Chinese office, and Christoph Korner, an occasional collaborator and jazz musician) how to listen and feel unspoken communication, and to work as a team, never allowing one 'voice' to rise above another. They look on it as a 'glue which binds us together'. At the start of a project the group meet either physically or, as they are based in different countries, by frequent media conferencing to 'kick around ideas until

Graft

one of us scores a goal'. Being more interested in the unknown than the known, this period to them is the most exciting; the moment of enlightenment, Putz maintains, is almost erotic in its intensity. They use a multitude of media from hand-sketching and computer-generated diagrams to modelling – printing off and altering, refining and adding until the idea is encapsulated. 'It's like a Dadaist session. We like serendipity and intentionally search for misunderstanding; passing the concept back and forth allows it to mutate slowly like a game of Chinese whispers.'

The definition of 'graft' is various – medical transplants, cheating, hard work – but it's the horticultural meaning of the word which is the main reason it was adopted by the practice. In the late nineteenth century, the North American

(Right)
The studio of Brad Pitt, Los Angeles (2003)
A contemporary fusion of traditional Japanese proportions and Western golden section creates a new design language delineating live/work areas A fold-up service wall contains desktop, shelves and studio equipment.

(Left)
Fix restaurant, Bellagio hotel, Las Vegas (2004)
The supernatural glowing ceiling plane is constructed from panels of padouk and acts as a façade for the restaurant interior, guiding diners into the space.

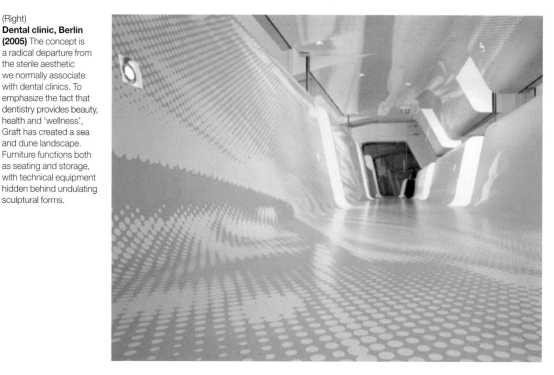

parasite Phylloxera Vastarix decimated the vineyards of Europe. The native vines of the Occident were without protection and it was only by grafting the aristocratic scion onto the wild, resistant root of the New World that a robust hybrid was created.

With feet firmly planted in Europe, America and China, Graft sees itself as a cultural nomad with an ambiguity of identity which arises from being at once native but also a guest in its adoptive countries. 'In LA we're these crazy German guys and in Berlin we are not accepted into the Berlin architecture mafia – we're cowboys. We've got the American virus.' They have 'grafted' their strongly empirical training in the Bauhaus school onto influences gained from working in the States, from their Hollywood clients to cinematography, and their long-standing association with art critic and curator David Hickey, who taught them to be fresh and direct, and to ignore the limitation of a pure academic background.

Although Graft doesn't like to be associated with any one style, its work (a studio-cum-guesthouse for Brad Pitt –

who has become an honorary member of the team, collaborating on the concept for an hotel in the desert near Palm Springs; the now famous Hotel Q; the Fix restaurant in the Bellagio Hotel; live/work spaces in Berlin; the Gleimstrasse loft, a dental practice in Kurfürstendamm, Berlin; various exhibitions, including the 'Beaux Monde: Towards a Redeemed Cosmopolitism' at SITE Santa Fe and trade fair designs, the most recent being for NBC Universal Television Networks), shares a biomorphic fluidity with the use of natural materials and smooth surfaces that lend a feeling of warmth.

Graft conceives interiors not as a series of static architectural spaces but as narratives – a cinemagraphic story-board that helps the team to define a new way of thinking. This perception facilitates a holistic, sensual, thoughtful approach which makes the practice's designs emotional as well as rational. Wolfram Putz, however, was keen to point out that projects in the pipeline – a villa in Majorca and an hotel in Georgia, Russia – will be a departure as both share a crisp and sleek aesthetic.

(Top)
Hotel Q, Berlin (2004) The reception area is a sculptural landscape of red linoleum planes which flow over floors and walls and form seating, the reception desk and the bar.

(Below left)
Hotel Q The screen wall divides the bar from the lounge which has been given a beach aesthetic, complete with recliners and sand.

(Below right)
Hotel Q The bed incorporates a bath and slate dressing table.

(Top)
The Gleimstrasse loft, Berlin (2004) Living and working, openness and intimacy, Graft has used the same fluidity of form as in the Hotel Q. Bathroom, hallway and toilets are hidden behind white biomorphic-shaped walls.

(Below)
Sci-Fi Booth 2005, San Diego A convention booth to represent Sci-Fi brand at the Comic-Con International 2005, this was a departure from traditional exhibit design in which space is defined through classical architectonic expression of wall, floor and ceiling. Here these elements have been grafted onto a continuous organic figure, a free-standing autonomous fibreglass object with integrated multimedia.

Graven Images

Ross Hunter and Janice Kirkpatrick trained at the Glasgow School of Art and the Mackintosh School of Architecture, Scotland graduating in architecture and graphic design, respectively. They met following Kirkpatrick's MA in design when they collaborated on a series of furniture products and went on to found their Glasgow-based practice, Graven Images, in 1986. Employing 30 core staff from different backgrounds (architects, interior designers, graphic and exhibition designers), and calling in experts from academia to film makers when necessary, they look upon themselves as a cross-disciplinary rather than a multidisciplinary group.

Their work ranges from brands and furniture to bars and clubs, workplaces, streetscapes and packaging, but whether they are working on the new design of Glasgow's *Herald* newspaper (early 1990s), the exhibition which accompanied Tony Blair's visit to Shanghai in 1998, or the interiors of the Radisson Hotel in Edinburgh, their work transcends barriers of expertise. 'A cross-disciplinary company goes for a blurring at the edges, and architecture is just one of many design disciplines. Designing a building is the same as designing a chair, a poster or a helicopter, but with different skills involved. The important part is the thinking. If you can conceive it, you can design it.'

Their Scottish heritage is very important to them. When they first set up their studio they were criticized for not doing so in London, or the design Mecca, Milan. This was a constant source of annoyance for them and they set out to prove their detractors wrong.

The late 1980s and early 1990s was an exciting time for Scotland in general and Glasgow in particular (1990 was the city's year as European City of Culture), yet for many, Scottish identity was still based on outdated regional stereotypes. Graven Images wanted to change all that and to build up a new contemporary design language for Scotland, as well as to bring wealth to their country, which they felt would be the result if businesses adopted a more open-minded attitude to architecture and interior design.

Glasgow remains Scotland's most cosmopolitan centre, with the largest population of designers, architects and artists outside London. It's a city involved with creative thinking and creative doing. Glaswegian culture is rich and complex, which Graven Images believes influences its design processes and gives its work a different perspective from London-based companies. Glasgow was a city which was involved in generating industrial products and wealth. Although that prosperity has gone, the relationship the city has with continental Europe remains – links that are evident in Graven Images work, a synergy of local and international.

Their interiors, mainly located in Scotland, include exhibitions, installations, bars, hotels, offices and restaurants. They are most proud of the refurbishments of the Radisson hotels both in Edinburgh and Glasgow, the Tramway Club (a much-published early project), The Living Room nightclub and restaurant,

(Left)
Collage Bar, Radisson SAS Hotel, Glasgow (2003) A palette of cream-coloured stone was used alongside glass and stainless steel to create a cool, elegant and comfortable environment.

(Above top)
Radisson SAS Hotel, Edinburgh (2005) The hotel is located in a '70s neo-gothic building. The brief was to keep the sense of the original while bringing the interiors into the twenty-first century. All materials and finishes were sourced in Scotland.

(Above below)
Tinderbox, Islington, London (1999) Following their earlier success with the Tinderbox in Glasgow (1998), GI was again asked to develop and design the brand package, as well as the interior for Matthew Algie and VGF Catering. The space includes a coffee bar and retail outlet for specialized coffee-making equipment.

(Above)
BBC Scottish headquarters, Glasgow (2007) The building by David Chipperfield contains the whole programme-making and broadcast process in a simple glass box overlooking the River Clyde. Graven Images has unified the space around a red sandstone 'street', which rises through the interior, connecting the reception with the fifth-floor restaurant, and is surrounded by formal workspaces (nationally grown wood in the monolithic benches were custom designed by the architects). The concept was to encourage interaction, collaboration, flexibility and creativity, and goes far beyond the concept of 'break-out' areas.

the Collage Bar in The Radisson Glasgow, and the BBC's Scottish headquarters as well as less media-friendly schemes such as their series of children's residential homes.

The starting point for each project begins with a strong understanding of space and architecture rather than surface and decoration. Hunter and Kirkpatrick then go on to look at the human factors (how the spaces will be used), and finally they choose a palette of materials and finishes – a process they believe many designers get the wrong way round, putting too much emphasis on finish rather than tectonics. The duo work closely with their clients to build up an idea of their real needs so that they can respond with solutions that work from a commercial as well as a practical point of view.

Their work is serious and considered but not without a certain sense of playfulness and theatricality, and they are not frightened of colour and texture.

Design for them is the process of ordering creativity and giving a concrete form to an evolution of ideas. It is not about decorating but about being in control. 'As designers we understand the vision and values of a company and then crystallize these into objects and architecture.' They adopt a pragmatic attitude to their work, producing interiors which offer architectural solutions for everyday problems but at the same time create environments which appeal to the senses.

As important as their built work is Hunter and Kirkpatrick's desire to demystify and politicize design. They lecture globally and have campaigned to get design into the school curriculum, into business and onto the UK and Scottish political agendas. The practice was involved in the Glasgow Design Festival, in the city's bid for City of Architecture and Design, and in the creation of The Lighthouse – Scotland's centre for architecture, design and the city.

(Top)
Sub Club, Glasgow (2002) This well-known bohemian musical venue dates from the mid-1980s but was destroyed by fire in 1999. Graven Image's refurbishment strips back to basics. Bars, perimeter booths and dance floor were fused with the old existing steel and brickwork creating a balance of old and new.

(Below)
The Living Room, Glasgow (1993) This had an enormous impact on Glasgow when it first opened. The concept was to create an 'un-designed' space as a critique on the 'cool' bars of the moment. The architects used traditional Scottish materials: harling (wet dash), corrugated iron and slate, making features of the cast-iron fireplace, candles and archangel statue.

Eva Jiricna

Since founding her architectural studio in 1984 Eva Jiricna has been showered with accolades. She is a Royal Designer for Industry, a Commander of the British Empire for Services to Interior Design, she has been elected a Royal Academician by the Royal Academy of Arts, and has been inducted in the American Hall of Fame. In 2003 she was made president of London's Architectural Association. Not bad for a young Czech woman who arrived in London in early 1968 and who, a few months later, following the Warsaw Pact's invasion of Czechoslovakia to overthrow the liberalizing Dubcek regime, was to become an exile for the next 21 years.

Coming from a communist-controlled country, and having been educated in the strict modernist school of Czech functionalism, the experience was liberating. She entered the world of the swinging '60s and quickly built up connections with the young British architects of the time: Richard Rogers, James Stirling, Norman Foster, Peter Cook and the futuristic Archigram Group.

Jiricna was born in 1939 in Zlin, a town built for Tomas Bata, whose shoe-manufacturing empire had made him one of the richest industrialists in Czechoslovakia. Her father worked as an architect for the Bata shoe company, along with other representatives of the Czech avant-garde and the town became famous for its modernist architecture. Following in her father's footsteps, Jiricna studied architecture and urban planning at the Technical University in Prague, qualifying in 1962 as an engineering architect. She continued her postgraduate studies at the Academy of Fine Arts, moving to London in 1968 on a six-month placement with the GLC.

She brought with her to London the humanistic traditions of the avant-garde: the responsibility of an architect to the profession, the importance of self-expression, the belief that a building without an integral interior concept is unthinkable, a love of technology, and the determination to create a better world in architectural terms.

Her break came when she was employed by Luc de Soissons on the Brighton Marina scheme which, due to the oil crisis, was never completed. Here she was given the opportunity of creating engineering feats – floating platforms and reclamation projects – as well as developing a nautical design language which can still be seen in her work today.

Of seminal importance to her career, however, was her meeting with Joseph Ettegui in the early 1980s, and the redesign of his small London flat. 'I was full of enthusiasm to do the job from beginning to end. To my astonishment that little project was published in every single existing architectural/interior design magazine. Peter Davey, then the editor of the *Architectural Review*, said that the total area of published pages would have covered the footprint of the apartment several times.' It was a turning point for Jiricna. From this point she has been labelled an interior designer: a mixed blessing. 'I guess my biggest successes are my interiors but my biggest setback is the fact that people forget I can design buildings as well.'

(Top and below)
'Modernism: Designing a New World', exhibition, Victoria and Albert Museum, London 2006
The heyday of the modernist movement lasted only 25 years from 1914–39, yet greatly influenced central European art, architecture and design. 'It was a pleasure for me to work on this project and be re-introduced to these inspired individuals.' The space was designed to reflect the speed of construction during that time; the 'scaffolding' towers displaying key objects, which describe the period: Eileen Gray's Transa chair, a model of Le Corbusier's Villa Savoye, etc.

modernism

designing a new world
1914 – 1939

Modernism in design and architecture developed in the aftermath of the First World War and the Russian Revolution – a period when the artistic avant garde dreamed of a new world free of conflict, greed and social inequality.

It was not a style but a looser collection of ideas. Many different styles can be characterised as Modernist, but they share certain underlying principles: a rejection of history and applied ornament; a preference for abstraction; and a belief that design and technology could transform society.

Initially, Modernism was largely experimental, but from about 1926, as economic conditions improved, it moved from the sketchbook to the real world. In the 1930s designers were forced to reassess their work, adapting it to the mass market and sometimes even to the demands of Fascism. But Modernism survived, and it remains a powerful force in the designed world of today.

(Far left)
Alex boutique, Florence (1988) The brief was to provide a clear, simple and uncluttered design with minimal use of colour. Floor, walls and ceiling are in translucent glass, which, together with the monochromatic colour scheme and subtle lighting design, gives an effect of floating structural planes.

(Left)
Joseph shop, Sloane Street, London (1989) A limited palette of finishes was used to create a calm effect: beige limestone floor tiles, grey plaster ceilings, and glass and polished stainless-steel showcases and staircase. The staircase with transparent glazed treads incorporates the balustrade and is suspended from the second-floor slab, braced at each floor.

(Top right)
Joseph Flat 1, London (1982) Low ceilings and windows created an unpleasant, dark atmosphere in the original space. White tiles were used throughout to brighten the environment. A block with space-saving sliding doors moving across a mirrored wall was introduced, containing the bedroom, kitchen and bathroom.

(Below right)
Aspreys jewellery shop competition (1980) This concept is important to Jiricna as, under the influence of Archigram Graphics, the design shows the excitement typical of the time. The interior was conceived entirely in glass: floor, ceiling and display cabinets. It took 20 years for the technology to follow up. Aspreys was the inspiration behind the Marcus jewellery shop, London 1999.

Various projects for Ettegui followed, including many of his clothes shops and the Caprice restaurant in London. Other clients have included Joan & David, Esprit, Vidal Sassoon, Boodle and Dunthorne, Kenzo, The Royal Academy and the British Council. She was in charge of Richard Rogers' interior-design team for the Lloyds Building and has undertaken numerous residential and office refits as well as exhibition designs, most recently the Modernism show at the Victoria and Albert Museum in London. In 1998 Jiricna finally got the chance to work on an architectural project with the construction of the Orangery in the grounds of Prague Castle, which was followed by the Hotel Josef, also in Prague. She is currently working on a concert hall and student library in Zlin, and a private residence outside of Prague.

Jiricna does not like to think she has a distinctive style, instead referring to a uniformity of approach which perhaps gives that perception. She has been thought of as high-tech, a poetic minimalist or, with her concept of unified flowing space, a contemporary modernist. What her interiors do share is a use of similar materials – glass, metal, polished stone – but these are selected not only for their aesthetics but for reasons of transparency, structure and reflection. She employs light not for dramatic effect, but to unify a space and detailing, which she considers fundamental. Without doubt, however, Eva Jiricna's characteristic trademark is the staircase: technical and structural masterpieces which she uses not only as an organizational element but also as a dramatic focal point in her interiors.

(Left)
Hotel Joseph, Prague (2002) The bedrooms have been designed for comfort. Many have glass bathrooms with see-through partitions and sliding mirrored doors which reflect the view and give an added dimension to relatively small spaces.

(Top right)
Boodle & Dunthorne, Liverpool, 2003
The refurbishment included a 'floating' glass DNA staircase, and a cocktail lounge where potential buyers could try out diamond rings and necklaces before they buy. At the time Managing Director Nicholas Wainwright was quoted as saying 'We are creating a very minimalist space which we hope will attract people into the shop.' The interiors are predominantly steel and glass conceived with lightness and immateriality in mind.

(Below right)
Penthouse apartments, London (2002/3)
All four apartments have spectacular views over the River Thames. They are as open-plan as regulations would allow with linear lighting in changing colours to enhance the effect. Not built for a specific clientele, the design is as simple and neutral as possible.

Patrick Jouin

Patrick Jouin was born in 1967 in the small town of Mauves-sur-Loire, France. Of his own admission he comes from a simple background (his father is a wood- and metal- turner and his mother a nurse) and had no idea about design until the age of seven, when he won a drawing competition run by the local bank. The prize was to be flown to Paris to spend a day in the Bourburg Museum. Jouin describes the experience as an epiphany, and from that moment on he decided he wanted to be a designer.

Jouin's early life was influential. From his father he inherited a love of technology and a respect for materials. From his mother he learned the importance of studying the body like a machine, which he believes is essential in his career as an architect as it allows him to perceive space in relation to human needs and demands.

Jouin studied industrial design at Ensci Les Ateliers, graduating in 1992, and was immediately employed by the Compagnie des Wagon Lit, working on the interiors of restaurant cars. A period at Tim Thom, Thomson Multimedia, under the artistic direction of Philippe Starck, was followed by a placement in Starck's studio, where he remained for four years while also producing his own lines for VIA, receiving its Carte Blanche invitation (a grant given to promote young designers) in 1998. He opened his own studio the following year.

(Right)
Chlösterli, Gstaad (2003)
Located in a 300-year-old chalet, the creation of the terrace was the first of Jouin's architectural interventions. In the two-storey-high, disco tongue-in-cheek Swiss references were employed, such as milk churns, buckets and straw-bale tables and chairs. Scottish slate flooring gives way to resin lit from below by LEDs, which suffuse the space with changing colours.

(Left)
Gilt restaurant and bar, New York Palace hotel, New York (2005)
The original building is an eclectic hotchpotch with references to classical civilization, the Renaissance and the baroque. Jouin chose a contradictory rather than complementary intervention. The bar is in Corian and the space is dominated by a structure that appears almost transitory and which brings to mind Buckminster Fuller's geodesic domes while alluding to the faceted nature of the stained-glass windows behind.

Jouin says that having worked for Starck is a mixed blessing. In the light of his own considerable achievements – he was recently described as the designer of the most beautiful restaurants in the world – it is an annoyance that he is still sometimes referred to as one of Starck's *enfants,* but he nonetheless recognizes that he gained a lot from the experience. Not only did he develop connections with leading furniture manufacturers – Cassina, Kartell and Alessi – early on in his career but, more importantly, learned the lesson that an idea is never finished: that a designer should always be struggling to make something better, even at the final stages. For Jouin, designing is an intellectual game with the idea being as important as the finished product.

Jouin's first big break as an independent designer came when, having read an article about his work in *L'Auto Journal,* Rénault invited him to design the interiors of one of their concept cars. This was quite a departure for Rénault, as normally the company used an in-house design team. Their decision paid off, however, with the result gaining tremendous media attention.

It was also at this time that he met Alain Ducasse, the famous French chef and restaurateur, a relationship, which would lead to many of Jouin's best-known restaurant and club designs, bringing him international fame. By employing a modern design aesthetic in his restaurants, Ducasse wanted to change the old-fashioned face of French dining. Initially he approached Jouin as a way of getting to know Starck, but decided against that collaboration, fearing a clash of egos. Ducasse asked Jouin to design the Plaza Athénée restaurant in Paris, which was destroyed by fire shortly after opening. This serendipitous event led to the commission to design the Plaza Athénée Bar, the signature project that launched Jouin on his present trajectory. A wave of projects followed: MIX, New York (now closed); Spoon Byblos, Chlösterli, Gstaad; Alain Ducasse at the Essex House; MIX in Las Vegas; and a new Athénée restaurant; as well as Gilt NY for Paul Liebrant and the BE bakery brand creation in Paris.

Jouin considers himself to be neither a designer nor an architect but a DJ of space. He says his work is connected to fashion, which for him has an ultra-sensitivity and femininity: qualities he finds missing from architecture and which have an important element in his designs. His inspiration comes from the art world: from Leonardo da Vinci's drawings of mechanical devices to the work of the performance artist Vito Acconci and of the lighting designer/artist Herves Descottes. Jouin works to create poetry, mood and ambience in his interiors, creating environments that are luxurious yet functional, traditional yet modern and contemporary yet elegant. He works with light to define a space and experiments with materials and technology to push the boundaries of what is possible.

Jouin considers his largest success to be psychological rather than physical. Creating independently is no fun. He quotes his greatest achievement as being the incredible relationship he enjoys with the 14 people he employs in his studio and his supreme joy at that unique point when everything comes together in a seamless collaboration – the instant he refers to as his 'Moment de Grace'.

(Left)
BE Boulangepicerie, Paris (2002) The concept was to bring the bakery and delicatessen together in one store. The bread is baked freshly in a large stainless-steel oven in the centre of the store. Natural stonework and corroded zinc have been used to add sobriety to the design.

(Top right)
Spoon Byblos, St-Tropez (2002) Inspired by the architecture of the Mediterranean, Jouin designed a restaurant where interior and exterior come together. The restaurant expands outside through large bay windows onto a huge terrace. In the VIP area (illustrated here), a circular bar made of blue molten glass tiles and polished stainless steel takes centre stage.

(Below right)
Plaza Athénée Bar, Hotel Plaza Athénée, Paris (2001) A perfect synergy of contemporary and classical, Jouin divided the area into two main spaces. Here a large glass bar, measuring 8m (26ft) in length is set below mini Murano chandeliers. When touched, the bar glows from within, filling the glass with an other-worldly light.

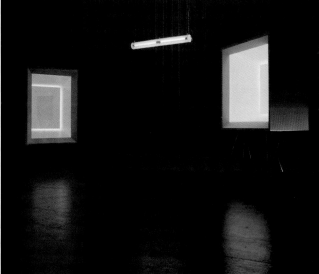

(Left)
MIX, Las Vegas (2004)
Set atop the Mandalay Resort Group's THEhotel, the restaurant has wonderful views over both the strip and the surrounding desert. The space is dominated by a spectacular 8m (26ft) tall chandelier featuring 15,000 hand-blown globes. A VIP lounge seems to float within the ornament. The restaurant has all the razzmatazz one would suspect of Las Vegas but it is tempered by a romantic elegance.

(Above top)
Plaza Athénée restaurant, Hotel Plaza Athénée, Paris (2005)
Five thousand Swarovski crystals glitter around the existing chandeliers, Steel-thread curtains by Sophie Mallebranche act as foils to Herves Descottes' lighting, and reinterpretations of Louis XVI armchairs add colour and an organic touch by being finished in leather and Corian.

(Above below)
The Serial Killer event/ exhibit based on the Bluebeard legend, Exit International Festival in collaboration with Krikov and D. Breemersch, Maison des Arts, Créteil, France (2005)
Jouin interpreted a recorded narrative with an interplay of lights and abstract sounds.

Klein Dytham architecture

Klein Dytham architecture (KDa) is a Tokyo-based multidisciplinary design practice which currently employs ten staff who work very much as a team (the Klein Dytham Allstars). Their portfolio spans the influences of East and West and encompasses architecture, interiors, public spaces and installations. Their Superdeluxe events and parties, hosting informal film screenings, art installations and club nights, feed their appetite for innovation and spawned their now famous PechaKucha Nights (chitchat in English), which originated in Japan, but are now regularly held at ICA and even at Sadler's Wells. During these lively and unorchestrated evenings, designers from all disciplines are invited to take the stage with 20 slides and 20 seconds for each, in a demonstration of creative energy Dytham refers to as a 'fast and furious architectural karaoke'.

Astrid Klein and Mark Dytham met at London's Royal College of Art, where they were both studying for their masters in interior design and architecture. It was an important time for them both and led to a cross-disciplinarian approach to their work which, today, is evident in both their architectural and interior-design projects. 'This school is a fantastic mixing chamber of creativity in art and design – here we got inspiration from the product designers, the chair designers, the glass department, sculpture, even ceramics. It was the energy and stimulation gained from the blurring of boundaries between creative disciplines that we really took away from this experience. The activities that we have initiated in Tokyo, in particular PechaKucha Night, have always kept this idea in mind as a point of reference. By bringing together people and ideas that are normally kept in separate boxes, we cross-fertilize the fields in which we operate, and gain inspiration in the process.'

Astrid Klein was born to German parents, schooled in France, where she studied interior design, and educated in Britain. She is a fervent internationalist with a love of crossing cultural and disciplinary boundaries and has a nose for trends, colours and materials. Mark Dytham was born on the outskirts of Milton Keynes, a postwar British new town which he says engendered in him a 'fascination with the potential of building "the new"'. He is the engineering side of the duo, with a love of technology and gadgets.

Upon graduation, their thirst for the exotic and their desire to experience the architectural buzz which was Japan in the late 1980s led them on what they thought would be a three-month tour of the country, a short vacation from which, as it turns out, they have yet to return.

The Japanese obsession with novelty, their ever-changing urban environments, creative energy, respect of craftsmanship and willingness to experiment resulted in Klein and Dytham deciding to found their practice in Tokyo in 1991, since which time they have slowly built up an international reputation for their imaginative, witty yet unpretentious work. A range which includes flagship retail stores, restaurants, resort facilities, office fit-outs, houses and apartments, as well as temporary constructions,

(Top)
Leaf Chapel, Risonare, Japan (2004) Formed by two leaves, one glass with a delicate lace motif, the other metal with 4,700 perforations, each containing an acrylic lens, light filters through the lenses and projects delicate patterns onto the contrasting interior which is purposely kept dark using black granite on the floor and blackened timber

(Below)
Leaf Chapel At the moment where the bride's veil is lifted, the steel leaf magically opens, revealing the pond beyond.

Gao children's recreational space, Risonare resort, Kobuchizawa, Japan (2005) Various activities (woodcraft, tree-climbing and nature observation) are organized in the space. Inspired by the outdoor programme, KDa presented a 'woodpile' which separates the public space from smaller functionally defined rooms. Hidden treasures – brightly coloured boxes – contain doorways to the playrooms behind.

installations, and events which draw connections to the approaches of the media and advertising worlds.

KDa does not have a distinctive style as such but a love of materials, technology and respect of location all play a big part in its output. Above all, the practice works closely with a client to develop a programme best adapted to his/her needs, finding a unique angle on which to handle their design response. 'We are responsive to the client's requirements. We never attempt to impose some signature design upon the client … It's like cooking. We love to discover the ingredients for the design through our clients. We then put this into our pot, add a dash of KDa spice, and cook up something delicious.'

Their approach is similar whether they are working on a small interior-design project or a large building. Interiors for KDa are small, quick and fun and act as a perfect antidote to bigger, slower and more 'boring' architectural schemes. 'There is nothing worse than having to spend two years on a building – as it all gets too serious and introverted. We always have our staff work on both types of project at the same time.'

Their aim is to 'make spaces that need no explanation, to make spaces that speak for themselves, to make spaces which make people smile and to make spaces that people remember and talk about'. Representative projects include the Leaf Chapel, Bloomberg ICE, Uniqlo, the Billboard building and Pika Pika Pretzel.

(Top right)
Danone Waters, Tokyo (2005) The Volvic area, with carpet and glazing in shades of the logo, contains meeting rooms formed in a zigzag pattern to denote the volcanic mountainous terrain where the water originates from.

(Below right)
Danone Waters The two brands Evian and Volvic are given separate identities, which also act to divide the reception/open-plan areas from closed meeting rooms. The walls in the Evian section are formed by stringing bottles like beads on a string.

(Top)

Museum café, Tokyo (2003) This café in the clouds sits on the 52nd floor of Roppongi Hills overlooking Tokyo. The space is organized by low, zigzaging walls upholstered in pink leather. So that everyone can share in the amazing views, the floors are stepped and convex mirrors have been added.

(Below)

YY Grill, Risonare Resort (2005) The Grill brings the forest indoors. Layered screens in natural wood with a tree motif are positioned against reflective walls to enhance a sense of depth. Dappled shadows are cast through a leaf-patterned ceiling element. The surfaces are branded by hot irons which allude to open-air barbeques.

(Far right)

Bloomberg ICE, Tokyo (2002) Bloomberg harvests data from around the world. Interface design artist Toshio Iwai's iceberg-like screen allows clouds of information to condense. ICE refers to Interactive Communication Experience. When not in use, stock levels are indicated by a line which rises and falls. When approached, sensors activate the screen, which jumps into life, enabling the viewer to play various interactive games with the data.

Lazzarini Pickering Architetti

Coming from vastly different backgrounds (Claudio Lazzarini was born in Rome in 1953 and Carl Pickering in Sydney in 1960), this duo nevertheless have a lot in common. With their shared love of conceptual art, and for the works of twentieth-century architects whom they consider were largely 'misunderstood' in their lifetime (Eileen Grey, Pierre Chareau, Gio Ponti, Carlo Mollino and Luigi Caccia Dominioni), they got together shortly after their architectural training. Lazzarini received his diploma from the Faculty of Rome, La Sapienza, under the tutelage of Ludovico Quaroni, and Pickering, arriving in Italy in 1980, attended the School of Architecture in Venice, where he studied under Gino Valle, Massimo Scolari and Peter Eisenman.

'We are inspired by the architecture of Chareau and Grey – the modernism of spaces and the transformability of functions – in which idiosyncratic and luxurious furniture contrasts with the perfect machine for living. Beloved objects should be part of a modern interior. The key is the total integration of the exterior and the interior; for the dissolution of boundaries between the two. That's the logic of our work. Modernism isn't about forms, it's about approach: understanding spaces, functions and people's lives and trying to make them better.'

Their Rome-based practice was founded in 1985. Although more provincial, they made the conscious decision of locating themselves in the south of Italy. Ancient and magnificent, the Eternal City for them is a constant inspiration: 'Italy is too Milancentric. Here we have the chance to be serene, to not worry about being competitive, to work on our projects and maintain a distance from the stressful world or architecture and design which is Milan.'

Lazzarini and Pickering consider themselves architects who happen to create interiors, and list as their biggest setback commissions for new-build projects which never materialized, reinforcing their reputation as interior designers. They first came to the attention of the international design press with a modular seating system, Acierbo, which won the Compasso d'Oro in 1999. However, their furniture design (mostly conceived specifically for their interiors) talks more of space than product design. Developments from the Acierbo include the Mosaico in 2005, a set of tables, benches, chests of drawers and containers that hang from the walls to create a moveable dining room. 'The relationship between space and furniture is what counts for us. The area around the piece is more interesting than the piece itself. Our furnishings are often comparable to small architectures and serve as a filter from one space to another.'

Nowhere is this more obvious than in the global outlets for Fendi. In these sparse shops of dark wood and metal, the display shelves define the interior, whether they appear to protrude through the windows as in London or are stacked on top of one another in the Paris shop to create a mesmerizing Escher-like tower. Lazzarini and Pickering have used the same components for varying effect. 'While the elements might be the same, the

(Top)
Refurbishment of a Positano villa, Positano (2005) Shot of the living-dining area on the ground floor with 'flying sofa' area cantilevered above.

(Below)
Positano villa. The stairs between the living area and kitchen are designed for sitting on at certain levels.

Wally powerboat The
navigation area is similar
to a flight deck and can
also be used as an office
or dining area, thanks to
sliding tables.

(Right)
**Sai Ram Yacht interior
(2004)** 'Rather than taking
a cruising yacht and
trying to make it faster,
we took a racing yacht
and made it comfortable
and luxurious.' The VIP
cabin contains a king-size
bed, sofas, desk and
glass-walled bathroom.
An unprecedented sense
of space is created by
long visual axes and
spatial fluidity.

configuration/interpretation is specific to
the space. We enlarged the shelves so
much that the display structures became
the architecture.' Correspondingly, the
ground-floor living and dining areas of a
villa in Positano, Italy, are unified by a
brightly coloured ribbon formed from
3,000 Vietri tiles dating from the 1700s to
1890, which winds its way through the
interior, forming a walkway, a table, light
fixture and wall hanging.

The duo do not consider that the practice
has a style, but more an approach or a
language. They call their work 'site-specific
portraits of clients'. 'We listen to our clients
and study the building traditions and
atmosphere of where we are designing,
reinterpreting this for the third millennium.'

Although the pair don't talk about style,
their work does share certain similarities.
The Fendi boutiques, apartments in
Rome, Venice and Monte Carlo, villas in
Tuscany, Positano and Capri, the Iceberg
restaurant in Sydney, the Nil bar in Rome,
the remodelling of an historic building in
Prague, and even the revolutionary
interiors for yachts and powerboats (most
notably the Wally powerboat) all share an
attention to detail, technological know-
how, creative construction systems,
flexibility, transformability and the use of
glamorous materials. Their interiors are a
kind of enriched minimalism: restrained
and rational, yet luxurious and warm.

(Left)
Fendi, Rome (2000)
A futuristic vortex of raw steel and polished surfaces. Vertiginous display shelves pile on top of one another making it almost impossible to tell which way is up and which is down.

(Top right)
Restructuring of a six-storey building in Prague (1999) One of the two 300sq m (3,229sq ft) lofts in the Prague refurbishment. The large skylight is supported lightly by existing beams. The suspended glass volume above the stairs is used by the owner as a bar, and it also acts to bring light down into the entrance area below.

(Below right)
Iceberg Restaurant, Sydney (2003) The space has the atmosphere of a beach house rather than a restaurant. The geometrical heart of the project, defined by four circular chandeliers, contains an entrance, reception, waiting area and the bar of the house. The aquamarine colours bring the seaside location into the interior.

Lewis Tsurumaki Lewis Architects

Paul Lewis, Marc Tsurumaki and David Lewis all studied at Princeton University School of Architecture, a formative experience as they learned to appraise architectural constraints in a positive manner. 'The period we spend at Princeton was critically important to us. The general architectural discourse during the 1990s was very negative, but at Princeton we were taught to be more optimistic, to identify problems in a positive way.' LTL Architects has built its reputation on being able to turn disadvantage to advantage.

Paul and Marc were at Princeton simultaneously while David studied political science at Carleton College, and the history of architecture and urbanism at Cornell. Marc worked for a period at Joel Sanders Architects while Paul was an associate at Diller Scofidio until 1997. Their education, and the experience Paul gained at Diller Scofido (a practice known for its highly conceptual work and architectural research) is strongly theoretical. LTL is dedicated to exploring the inventive possibilities of architecture through what it refers to as the 'close examination of the conventional and the overlooked', and actively pursues a diverse range of work which maintains a creative dialogue between built projects and speculative investigations, analyzing the boundaries between theory and practice.

LTL's early work was mainly exploratory, concerned with competitions, installations and exhibitions in small venues. Its big break came with its own show for Stephen Holl's 'Storefront for Architecture' in New York, followed shortly by the renovation of the Van Alen Institute. However, since founding the architecture and research practice (Paul Lewis and Marc Tsurumaki set up the company in 1993 and David, Paul's twin brother, completed the partnership in 1996), LTL is mostly recognized as the designer of a string of media-grabbing restaurants in New York. These tiny eateries share the common ground of having been designed with low budgets, on tight time-frames and in spaces which were unremarkable, and often derelict.

The spatial restrictions meant that the partners did not have a lot of freedom to work within a floorplan which, for the most part, was predetermined by the site. The alternative was to maximize what they had by working vertically and by working with surfaces. The restaurants examine the parameters and constraints of a commission as a means of catalyzing a design response: 'Architects always have to respond to something – a set of pre-conditions – and we thought why don't we take these limitations and use them as a tool, finding a certain latitude in which to manoeuvre and expand opportunistically.'

DASH Dogs is a good case in point. Paradoxically the 20sq m (220sq ft) hotdog stand is made smaller to produce the effect of a larger space. The ceiling slopes down by 0.6m (2ft) whilst the floor slopes up 15cm (6in) from the storefront entry, creating a forced perspective. The ceiling and floor surfaces are lined with strips of steel, the width of which decreases as the back of the shop is reached, thereby enhancing the illusion of depth.

(Right)
Tides restaurant, New York (2005) The interior of this restaurant explores the different configurations of bamboo. The ceiling is formed by over 110,000 bamboo spikes embedded into a back-lit acoustical ceiling. The effect is an inverted seabed of gently undulating 'grasses'.

(Left)
Fluff bakery, New York (2004) The design is a single surface made from layers of common materials: felt and plywood. The materials and colours adjust to give a darker, softer surface around the seating areas, shifting to lighter and harder on the ceiling. A customized stainless-steel chandelier is comprised of 40 dimmable linear incandescent lights.

(Top left)
Xing restaurant, New York (2005) The restaurant is composed of four distinct but interlocking spaces defined by the use of different materials: the front bar is layered stone, the front dining area is wrapped in bamboo, the toilet corridor is made from coloured acrylic which extends into the dining area and drops down to connect ceiling to bar, and the back restaurant area is red velvet plush.

(Below left)
DASH Dogs, New York (2005) The design for this tiny hotdog stand paradoxically makes the small space smaller in order to produce the effect of a larger space. The strips of steel, which line the interior surfaces, decrease, enhancing the illusion of depth. The customer is visually led from the pavement to the grill, to the cash register, eating counter and back out again. The laminated bamboo plywood counter cantilevers through the glass storefront.

(Top right)
Ini Ani coffee shop, New York (2004)
Originally a fortune-teller's apartment, LTL designed the restaurant as a room within a room containing a take-out area and a small lounge environment. The interior box is constructed from 25,000 strips of corrugated cardboard pressed into a structural steel cage.

(Below right)
Ini Ani coffee shop
Adjacent to the entry doors, 479 cast plaster coffee cup lids form a wall and reference point.

(Top far right)
Lozoo restaurant, New York (2002) The existing space was a combination of six different rooms. Each room has its own floor level and ceiling height, which created a problem regarding space and hence affected its quality. A horizontal level line is used to unify the separate spaces and to highlight the unique volumes of each room. A problem was turned into a design solution.

(Below far right)
Geltner loft, New York (2000) A series of linked elements have been inserted into the loft renovation – a steel and maple stair, a kitchen and a wall of cabinetry for household storage. A tread of the new staircase extends to form the top of the cabinet and to define the outer edge of the kitchen.

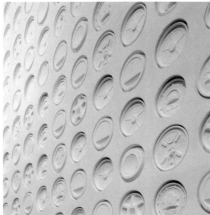

Embedded lights lodged in the gaps between the steel bands form a dotted line which wraps around the space, emphasizing the *trompe l'oeil* effect. A laminated bamboo plywood counter cantilevers 30cm (12in) from the outside through the glass façade and into the interior, acting as a horizontal foil to the sloping ceiling and floor as well as contrasting with the cold smoothness of the steel and the rough industrial aesthetic of the concrete side walls.

'We took the preconditions of the site as a springboard, and then played with materials and perception. We always use inexpensive and prosaic materials in our interiors, whether they be the concrete and steel of DASH, the felt and plywood of Fluff or the acrylic and bamboo of Xing; whatever we use, what is important to us is to build, layer and play with unusual and contrasting combinations.'

Marc, Paul and David do not consider themselves to have a distinctive style but rather a material and programmatic approach. They are now beginning to take on large-scale architectural commissions with exterior content: 'We did a series of restaurants but we now want to move on. We are interested in designing civic or public spaces; projects which will generate an urban condition and have a life beyond the design. We are changing the way we operate, not our methodology. We are just going to have bigger problems to take advantage of.'

Since founding their practice in New York in 1993, Neapolitan architects Ada Tolla and Giuseppe Lignano have received international acclaim for their unique style – an industrial aesthetic achieved by an innovative approach to construction materials and space – as well as their use of reclamation and modern technology. They are involved in residential and commercial projects both in America and abroad, as well as exhibition work and site-specific installations for major cultural institutions, most notably the Guggenheim, the Whitney and the New Museum of Contemporary Art, in New York.

Tolla and Lignano both graduated from the School of Architecture of the Universita di Napoli in 1989 and completed postgraduate studies at Columbia University in New York, a move which has had a huge impact on their work. They perceived New York as a harsh and industrial environment in stark contrast to the ancient beauty of the Italian cities with which they were more familiar. The 'lack of history in America' was a starting point for their artistic articulation: 'A complete freedom of expression, allowing people to build in all kind of ways. To see that was liberating for us,' states Lignano.

As their company name, Lot-ek, would suggest they are concerned primarily with exploring the displacement and transformation of pre-existing low-tech objects which they use in unexpected functional spaces, taking as their starting point an investigation into how the human body interacts with products and byproducts of the industrial age. All their

work shares the same blurring of boundaries between architecture, design, art and performance installation.

Frequently called upon to lecture both nationally and internationally, the duo are known for starting their talks with a slide show of the New York City landscape, while quoting a seemingly miscellaneous alphabetically arranged stream of nouns, adjectives and abstract ideas to describe what is being flashed up on the screen. Gradually, words such as 'abandon', 'cast-off', 'demolished', 'erosion', 'fragment', 'obsolete', 'wasteland' and images of fire hydrants, electrical wires, fire escapes and decaying brick walls come together to form a kind of urban poetry which is the essence of the firm's architectural style – what Tolla refers to as a kind of philosophy-in-aggregate for Lot-ek.

Although employing the latest technological advances, Tolla and Lignano's work is aesthetically anti-computer-age, emphasizing the fact that we do not, in fact, live in a clean and ordered digitally created environment but in one still littered with the detritus of an industrial past. They use heavy-duty objects, petroleum trailer tanks (Morton Loft) and even the fuselage of a jet engine (the student pavilion at the University of Washington, Seattle), as well as raw industrial materials – rubber, distressed concrete, steel, scaffolding and epoxy flooring; objects and substances they find attractive for their sense of history, durability and strength.

Moving from one port to another, it is of no surprise that their trademark is the

Lot-ek

(Right)
Morton Loft, New York (2000) A petroleum trailer tank is cut in two sections that enclose sleeping pods (shown here) and a bathroom, leaving the surrounding space undivided and unobstructed. Hatchback doors cut from either side of the tank are operated by hydraulic pistons and open at the touch of a button.

(Top right)
Boon shoe shop, Seoul (2000) A ribbon made out of translucent fibreglass panels, supported by a steel pipe frame, is placed on both floors of a raw concrete structure. The ribbon glows with fluorescent light produced by tubes attached to the rear of each panel. Different gels can be installed around the tubes to change the colour environment.

(Below right)
Bohen Foundation
The containers are introduced within the rigid square structural grid of the ground floor of a former printing facility, two within each nave of the grid. The containers generate exhibition spaces by sliding along tracks cast in the concrete floor to pre-set locations.

(Far right)
Bohen Foundation, meat packing district, New York (2002)
Interior of one of the eight containers.

shipping container. In the interior of the Bohen Foundation, for example, Lot-ek took eight containers, introducing them into the rigid square structural grid of the ground floor of a former printing facility. Each houses the permanent activities and functioning facilities of the gallery, while exhibition spaces are created by moving the containers along tracks set into the concrete floor to pre-set locations and then releasing movable wall panels attached to the outside of each.

However, it is perhaps the Mobile Dwelling Unit (MDU) that best illustrates the ingenuity of this architectural practice's preoccupation with re-use and transformation: 'a shipping container transformed into a dwelling that nevertheless retains the attributes of a shipping container'. Its interior includes push-out elements used for sleeping, eating, cooking, and so on, which retract into the shell for transportation.

Lot-ek is keen to emphasize that it is not interested in recycling, but rather in matching the needs and characters of clients with found objects. Tolla and Lignano are not ecologically motivated but draw inspiration from their native Naples, '…very much a city where there is an extension between third world and first world, in which people use ingenuity to create new kinds of architecture from existing industrial leftovers … It's the philosophy of the ready-made *bricolage*, of improvising, of using your intuition,' explains Tolla.

(Top right)
MDU, New York (2002)
Cuts in the metal walls of
the container generate
extruded sub-volumes,
each of which contains
a different living function.
When travelling, these
volumes are pushed in,
filling the whole container,
and when in use they are
pushed out, leaving the
interior unobstructed.
The interior is fabricated
entirely out of plastic-
coated plywood.

(Below right)
**Cynthia Broan Gallery,
New York (2005)** The
typical white box of the art
gallery was minimized into
a band of white wall that
wraps around the space
of this former car-repair
garage. Four movable/
flexible elements enable
multiple configurations
of the exhibition spaces
and the formation of
completely different
volumes for each show.

(Top and below far right)
**Guzman penthouse,
New York, NY (1999)**
This comprises the
renovation of a former
mechanical room topped
by a bedroom made from
a container truck. The
interior of the existing
structure is returned to
a simple white shell with
exposed steel pipes and
beams. An external fire-
escape ladder is used
internally and connects the
bedroom to living room.

M41LH2

In case you are wondering, M41LH2 stands for 'Merimiehenkatu 41, Liike-huoneisto 2', the address of the first space rented by the cross-disciplinary architecture and design group after its formation in 2001.

The group was set up by architect and interior architect, Johanna Hyrkäs, architect Tommi Mäkynen, graphic designer and architect Tuomas Siitonen, and architect/journalist Tuomas Toivonen. Before founding M41LH2, the four individuals had built up a network of contacts and collaborators, and had gained experience in Finnish and international architectural and design offices, including OMA, MetaDesign, Heikkinen-Komonen Architects and Tuomo Siitonen Architects.

'Compared to most young architectural offices in Finland we have probably the most multidisciplinary educational background. We think this mixing of influences has been a big advantage for us. The design task is always quite similar: finding formal expression for content and relating these forms to each other; however, different disciplines from architecture to art and graphic design tend to approach these in different fashions. It has been rewarding to learn from other kind of approaches and use them where they are not usually used.'

Not only is the team polytalented within their own practice but in 2002 they got together with Aamu Song, Johan Olin (Com-pa-ny), Nene Tsuboi, Erika Kovanen (Vire), Vesa Oiva, Selina Anttinen, Jussi Kalliopuska, Tuomas

Kivinen, Malin Blomqvist and Mari Talka as part of the Anteeksi collaborative. Although their attitude is not apologetic, *Anteeksi* roughly translates as 'sorry' or 'excuse me'. The Finnish design world is small (*Muoto*, the Finnish design magazine, goes as far as to say, 'A brief chat with a Finnish design name over a cup of coffee will give you a good idea of what's going on'), and this talented young band has probably cornered the market. Responsible for everything from architecture and landscape architecture to graphics, illustration and fashion design, as well as hosting performances and events, the members practice independently most of the time, but when they unite, their reputation has been built on imaginative and quirky work which, in the manner of Droog, inspires fresh ways of thinking about design and architecture. Tommi Mäkynen comments, 'Anteeksi is a sort of continuation in getting close to interesting people working in various disciplines … Collaboration, or even discussion, teaches you to be more flexible. You learn to argue in favour of some ideas and give up on them if something better comes along. Your own truth is not the only one – different angles [equals] richness.'

M41LH2 considers itself to be a firm of architects working on interiors, rather than interior architects or interior designers. Today it has gained a voice within Europe for its youth-friendly interiors: projects which display a zest for the city and urbanism. 'We like the thought that the effect an interior can have can go beyond its physical limits by being

(Top)
Bali nightclub, *Silja Symphony* and *Serenade* cruise ships (2006) The concept was to create a colourful, playful landscape based on various dream locations, from tropical rainforests to islands in exotic locations. Each space provides different moods.

(Below)
Mphis Vaakuna, Helsinki (2002) The location is one of the busiest street corners in the city. To preserve a cosy feel on the inside but maintain a link with the urban environment, M41LH2 used traffic reflector film as one of the main materials.

a space within the space of a city and be read on an urban scale by redefining its context and its surroundings.'

M41LH2's first commission was a concept for a café/bar chain which led to more projects, particularly nightspots (most famously the Helsinki nightclub), but more recently it has managed to procure commissions for a variety of schemes, which include residential and commercial projects

The firm works closely with clients, going so far as to arrange workshops with them to find out what they really want – an exercise that some find an onerous, albeit exciting, experience. This unique approach and the emphasis on conceptual thinking leads to unforeseen results. The style is quirky and fresh yet serious and pragmatic.

The team is inspired by the richness of historic layering, mistakes, imperfections and contrasts. 'I think of small things, new layers on top of old; I think everyday tactics is the new way to go,' states Tuomas Siitonen. 'All the things that come up add to the existing whole. Even if they don't stick around, they will leave a trace.'

Since working in Finland offers limited opportunities with regards to size of market and budgets, future plans include increasing its profile overseas. M41LH2 is also keen to take on more architectural projects and move between different typologies to avoid being type-cast. 'We would love to work on a hotel, or on something for children, a sacred place or a library.'

(Left)
Purple, Helsinki (2006)
The shop sells cheap and trendy accessories to teenagers. To reflect the bric-à-brac nature of the goods and to fit a tight budget, the floor is covered in metallic green plastic grass, smaller merchandise hangs from artificial trees, and a mural of mountains and diamonds adds a space-creating element.

(Right)
Helkama 100, Helsinki (2005) Helkama is a well-known Finnish bicycle and domestic appliance manufacturer which also imports motorbikes and cars. M41LH2 was commissioned to undertake graphics and design for all the exhibitions relating to its 100th anniversary. To maintain the robust attitude to the company, the plywood material usually used in packing cases was used.

(Below left)
Mphis East, Tampere, Finland (2002) Before becoming a restaurant, the space was a bank. In the process of stripping back years of decoration expensive materials were discovered. M41LH2 kept the copper and travertine wall in the street level lounge.

(Below right)
Helsinki nightclub, Helsinki (2003) The island bar is the first area to greet the customer upon arrival and is dominated by a glowing neon cupola which changes colour from green to orange.

(Overleaf)
Helsinki nightclub
The refurbishment of a 30-year-old casino and nightclub was carried out in collaboration with members of Anteeksi. The harmonious spaces are rich in playful and unique details, and wall-to-wall baroque-style carpeting covers walls, ceilings and furniture. The red, orange and white main dance floor can be seen at the rear.

Norisada Maeda

Norisada Maeda was born in Tokyo in 1960, studied architecture at Kyoto University and worked for the Taisei Corporation for five years before founding his own company, N. Maeda Atelier, in 1990. When I asked him what he had gained from his architectural education he replied, 'I studied architecture as phenomenology, which is probably the greatest influence on the way I work today.' This fact is crucial to understanding Maeda's designs. His residences are to be experienced. He draws his inspiration from everything that surrounds him and the results are environments which are alive with reference: 'I do not think that only architecture is architecture. Thoughts of architecture can be found any time and any place. I'm inspired by the natural: in touching the stars in the sky, insects in a park, waves in the sea and in breathing the air. I want to always keep myself the beginner in architecture by challenging various physical fields like surfing and karate. In these areas I am the perfect amateur but a new movement in architecture will never be born from our intelligence alone.'

It is tempting to dismiss Maeda's words as insubstantial and poetic but it is not until you put them side by side with his buildings that you begin to get an idea of their importance. The Borzoi house takes as its inspiration 'tube riding': the surfing technique of entering a wave. The construction is a continuous curved metal structure and the interior walls and ceiling curl around the inhabitant. The Alice house has as its main feature a giant, glass-walled swimming pool which sits in the centre of the interior: 'Rain creates countless patterns on the surface of the water, wind creates waves, a single leaf dropping onto the water changes into a drawing on a blue canvas, snow creates a spectacle of white dots. The pool is a device for extracting nature that is normally invisible in the busy city.'

Maeda quotes The Rose as the project of which he is most proud. Inspiration came to him while eating a square-shaped pudding. He gouged out the sides with a spoon and was charmed by the play on surfaces created by the action. The exterior was no longer the exterior and the interior spaces were defined as gaps or spaces: voids excavated from a solid mass.

For Maeda the distinction between interior and exterior does not preoccupy him. 'Outside is not simply a façade and inside is not simply interior space. The difference is only in the fact that you don't get rained on when you're inside. You will see in my work that gardens exist in the interiors – landscape, architecture, interior and furniture should share the same hierarchy.' When asked which qualities in his work would make a client commission him above the competition, his immediate response was a monosyllabic 'air', qualified by 'not the design of shape'. He continued, 'I always stress that what is of specific importance in architecture is not the visible parts, such as the floor and walls and ceiling, nor the differentiation between exterior and interior, but the "air" encompassed therein, which can be altered by my own spirit or an extraneous

(Right)
Flamingo, Tokyo (2000)
Due to the small floor plan, 20m (66ft) squared, 'passing points' such as the stairwell are also used as the bathroom, lavatory, study and so forth. Instead of conceiving the size of rooms on how they will be used, Maeda broke with precedent and let the client decide which room will be which on the basis 'it just happens to look right'.

(Overleaf left and right)
The Rose, Tokyo (1997)
The design for the house was based on the ideas of scooping out volumes from a potted pudding with a spoon. The interior are defined as gaps or spaces – excavated voids. Glass areas in the floors and staircases provide unexpected views into the inner reaches of the dwelling.

(Top left)
Funes, Funabishi Chiba, Tokyo (1994) Dispelling the normally Western hierarchy of rooms (LDK: living room/dining room/kitchen), the interior is centred around the bathroom. Another feature is the triple-nested glass structure which affords complex reflections and transmissions of light through transparent and translucent glass.

(Below left)
Device#9, Oyumino Chiba, Tokyo (2003) The 'device' is in the flooring of the four internal gardens in mirror-polished stainless steel to reflect the sky, bringing clouds, sunset, moon or gently waving tree boughs to the floor level of this single-storied house. The glass walls of the gardens are angled to allow rain to run off like droplets on a car windshield.

(Right)
Borzoi, Katsuura Chiba, Tokyo (2001) The concept of the house (named after the client's dog) was surfing or, more particularly, tube-riding: the technique of entering a curling wave. Internally the spaces are arranged around several gardens. The walls, floor and ceiling are a continuous curve.

force such as nature. Like Japanese Noh drama, gardening and flower-arranging, rules have to exist in architecture, although within those rules limitless interpretations are possible. Rules are there to stop the creator from creating overblown acts of romanticism, but it is a balance between what I like to refer to as the "removal of self" and the "based upon self" which allows me to mould space, and to harness

the "air" – "the phenomenological" – in a rational, mathematical yet imaginative way.'

Maeda's works are undoubtedly contemporary in both style and use of materials (in most interiors glass plays an integral part in both distributing and modulating light as well as dividing space), yet despite their radical appearance, they reflect ancient Japanese traditions and lifestyles: reducing the distinction between outdoors and indoors, disrupting the symmetrical, building with post and beam rather than walls, modular construction techniques and a symbiotic relationship between water, light and nature. However, to find these kinds of houses amid a culture that places so much emphasis on conformity is surprising. Kathryn Findlay, co-architect of the renowned Soft and Hairy house in 1994, and former associate professor at Tokyo University, could have the explanation: 'The Japanese are so meticulously controlled, maybe when you squeeze people so tight and hard, which is what has happened in the last 50 years, some extreme things pop out at the edges.'

(Far left top and below)
Knock Out The Moonlight, Tokyo (2002) Based on the concept of the Möbius strip – a tape which is black on one side and white on the other but when twisted and linked connects the two colours – the interior of this house imperceptibly becomes the exterior and vice versa.

(Left)
Alice, Tokyo (1997) The spatial configuration is two solid walls on either side bridged by eight chopped floor slabs. Light and breeze enter from above. The glass-walled swimming pool inserted into this frame is the most important element, designed so that the water is visible from any location within the house, even from below.

(Right)
Alice The plot of the house is a long rectangle situated in a busy shopping district. The client required a 'resort' within the city. Maeda both shields and connects the user from his surroundings by isolating the interior in massive concrete walls.

Yasmine Mahmoudieh

Yasmine Mahmoudieh compares herself to an Eastern healer, which may not be as strange as it sounds. She looks on the way she approaches an interior project as being similar to the way in which a shaman approaches his patient: he does not only consider the symptoms but considers all aspects of his client's health and administers in an all-encompassing way. When questioned about her goals as an interior architect, Mahmoudieh told me that her greatest desire was to improve lives through her work and that this could only be done by understanding the background, heritage and psyche of the people for whom she designs.

Born in Germany, Yasmine Mahmoudieh-Kraetz studied art history in Florence, architecture at the Ecole d'Ingenieurs in Geneva, interior design at the College of Notre Dame, Belmond, California (now Notre Dame de Namur University), and architecture (as well as interior design) at the University of California in Los Angeles. Her time in the States was a great influence as she had the opportunity of studying under the illustrious architects Charles Moore, Charles Jencks, Richard Meyer, Frank Gehry and Riccardo Legorreta. Her main tutor, Nathan Shapira, taught her to push herself to the limit – never to fall in love with one of her designs, but to always strive to make it better and look for new interpretations.

She opened her first practice in LA in 1986, followed in 1992 by two German studios, one in Hamburg and the other in Berlin. Six years later, Barcelona followed, and in 1999 an additional office opened in London. She has two brands: Mahmoudiehdesign (for all the typical architecture and design work) and Mahmoudiehconcepts (for conceptual phases, including marketing and corporate identity). Her portfolio includes complete interior-design concepts for hotels, restaurants, shopping centres and office complexes, as well as multi-usage projects. Her best-known schemes to date are the Millennium Center in Budapest; the Fishergate Centre in Preston, UK; the Radisson SAS Hotel in Copenhagen (an Arne Jacobsen hotel, where she had to respect the essence of the 1950s original while bringing the design into the twenty-first century); the Hotel Rheinsberg (the first design hotel conceived for disabled people); and the Resorthotel in Berchtesgaden. Recent work includes the super first class of airbus, the A380, as well as hotel projects in Dubai.

Her designs are distinguished by an individuality mixed with functionality. She likes to come to each project afresh, and for that reason it is difficult to point out a 'style' as such. For Mahmoudieh a good interior is one that does not force itself on you, but creates a feeling of warmth and timelessness rather than being trendy or fashionable. She places great importance on detailing, emphasizing the fact that as the scale of interior architecture is smaller than architecture, the user is physically closer to interior spaces. 'We are linked to walls, floors, materials, furniture, etc. Architecture is viewed from afar as you walk or drive by. We spend most of our time in interior spaces; interior design has a lot to do with psychology and the

(Right)
Resorthotel Berchtesgaden (Intercontinental), Germany (2005)
To emphasize the natural, quiet and relaxing atmosphere of a mountain resort, Mahmuodieh used combinations of stones and woods with varying surface textures.

manipulation of emotion. I always say that entering a building, be it a public environment or a private house, is like reading an open book. You get a sense of the people behind the building.'

The project of which Mahmoudieh is most proud is the Hotel Rheinsberg. She strongly believes in the power of architecture to change perception and to motivate. There can be no more functional a building than an hotel which is designed for the disabled. Not wanting any area of the hotel to remind its customers of their special needs, but instead to leave them feeling comfortable and happy, Mahmoudieh created a luxurious interior with no institutional overtones. She sourced materials from all over the world and from industries not normally associated with interior design – aeronautical, chemical and automotive – to find finishes that were durable but which would not remind the guests of hospital or their wheelchairs. 'I wanted to create a positive environment that would distract people from their handicaps and lead them into a world of enjoyment and happiness.'

Mahmoudieh's aim in life is to design in areas that are not yet considered worthy of a good design – starting with a hospital. 'I am convinced that creative, thoughtful design which is inspirational and innovative will accelerate the healing process of patients. I like to use the best energy to get a positive result in each and every project I tackle.'

Yasmine Mahmoudieh

(Top left)
Radisson SAS Hotel, Copenhagen (2001)
The concept was to create a modern design hotel, to complement the Danish functionalist building which dates from the 1950s. Mahmoudieh used characteristic shapes and design elements such as the lozenge-shaped lights above the bed and horizontal strips of maple wood to maintain the spirit of Arne Jacobsen's original.

(Below left and below right)
Garbe office, Hamburg (1996) A centrally placed reception desk with interchangeable light box panels leads to two corridors servicing the individual offices. To shorten visually the length of the corridors, and to avoid monotony, angular lines and colourful lighting effects have been used.

(Top right)
Five Plus Senshotel, Willisau, Switzerland (2005) The concept was to offer a sensual experience through functional architecture. Five pods are dedicated to each of the senses and prepare the visitor for the actual hotel element, the rooms themselves, which demonstrate new technologies and innovative materials. Translucent Plexiglas dividers are used to define the space.

(Below far right)
Five Plus Senshotel
Glowing wallpapers and carpets with Lurex threads are used in the corridor connecting the room with the suite.

Maurice Mentjens trained initially as a jewellery and product designer at the Academy of Visual Arts in Maastricht. After one year at the Design Academy, Eindhoven he returned to Maastricht to complete an interior design course, graduating in 1990.

Although his interiors are tectonic, he does not look upon himself as an architect, preferring the freedom of calling himself by the broader definition of designer, and being involved more in an artistic interpretation of space than with its structural manipulation. Mentjens' normal approach is to make what he refers to as an installation or theatre set for a specific environment, which may or may not interact with the architecture. 'You may compare what I would do with building a stand at a trade fair or designing a pavilion for a world expo. It would definitely not be a "decorated shed", but rather a "structured décor" or a piece of installation architecture.'

Since founding his own company the year he graduated, he has designed a great variety of different objects – mostly furniture, lighting and watches, as well as exhibition, office, retail and hospitality interiors. However, he is best known as the designer responsible for the branding of Sirius, an outlet for herbal remedies and energy drinks, for which he has developed all the interiors to date. With shops in Maastricht, Roermond and Eindhoven, he worked on a unique look for each successive project. His first creation was an alchemist's laboratory, the second he called a 'smart chapel', then came a holographic cabinet of wall hangings, and the fourth –

Sirius Smart Sounds – is a 'techno temple', the floor of which literally vibrates with bass rhythms emanating from the loudspeakers embedded within it.

More recently, his Grand Café at the Bonnefantenmuseum in Maastricht and the Witloof restaurant, also in Maastricht, have been much publicized and the retail outlet for Stash was awarded the Dutch Design Prize for Interior Design in 2005.

His background in jewellery and product design has had a profound influence on his work as an interior architect. He initially chose his first course as he wanted both to design and handcraft his work. 'The fact that I actually had to produce all my designs taught me an enormous amount in a technical sense, and I consider this to be essential for any designer.' Mentjens was studying at a time when the face of Dutch design was changing and impacting on the design world internationally. Young Dutch designers, many of whom we now associate with Droog Design, were following similar training programmes as Mentjens, producing essentially but unorthodoxly plain, unpretentious, eclectic works, illustrating an original use of materials – products and spaces which were conceptually strong, often interdisciplinary and betraying a unique sense of humour. More importantly, however, this generation of designers recognized the importance of craft in the industrial process.

All of Mentjens' early interior projects were developed in this way. Normally working with only one assistant, he not only designed the spaces but built them as well. He describes his work as a '*couture*

(Top)
Witloof, Maastricht (2005) The Cellar is connected to the Salon by way of a spiral staircase. Having discovered that this space originated from the middle ages, Mentjens chose a medieval, crypt-like appearance. The floor is covered with Portuguese tiles with a gothic-revival motif, and the wall finish repeats the pattern.

(Below)
Witloof, Maastricht Belgian cafés and restaurants are known for their incongruous mix of styles and interior elements. Mentjens didn't want to take this too literally, but the design which resulted kept the aesthetic in mind. The division between the entrance and the tiled section of the restaurant is demarcated by a red neon strip, which symbolizes the division between Flemish and Walloon provinces or between the country and the city.

(Left)
The Tower, Ipanema Grand Café in the Bonnefantenmuseum, Maastricht (2004)
Artist Fons Haagman decorated the walls with huge swathes of heraldic colours. Mentjens' 3m (9.8ft) lamp is an architectonic element forming a tower within a tower. Round tables of varying diameters float through the space.

(Below)
The White Bar, Ipanema Grand Café The wall opposite the bar is covered by *muurbloem* (wallflowers), a patchwork array of cheerful colours and patterns which acts as a foil to the minimal interior.

gown which is conceived and made especially for a particular client'. Because each project is so personal, Mentjens is unaffected by trends which he considers to be superficial and only appropriate for stylists. His work is diverse and site specific, and if pushed to define his style he does so by describing it as 'neo-modern with post-modern influences: aesthetic, well thought out, solidly grounded in details and influenced by technical experiments and the use of new materials and applications'. Function, which he believes to be a 'derived goal rather than a primary one', is not the most important consideration for Mentjens. The conceptual framework based on association, ambiguity and the introduction of sensitive elements is paramount, as this allows an intimate kind of relationship to develop between his clients and their environment.

Maurice Mentjens has no desire to expand. He prefers to work with a small team of collaborators on several small-scale projects a year. He wants to continue to use his interiors as narratives replete with associations and connotations, and for this reason has no intention of working on domestic interiors which he thinks are more suited to the decorator. 'What I need is a story to work with – something to stimulate the imagination and which can be converted into an image.'

(Top left)
Kiki 2, Maastricht (2006)
The Client, Kiki Niesten, requested a chic, luxurious design with a humorous twist. Outlet shops remind Mentjens of storage spaces so he conceived his small boutique as a mini 'warehouse', with walls and ceilings covered with racks and cabinets in grey oak wood to give them a dusty and old appearance. The floor is covered with white clothes scattered randomly and cast in transparent epoxy resin, as if a shopper in a state of high excitement had pulled everything off the shelves in a mad attempt to find just what they wanted.

(Top right)
Sirius shop in Rechtstraat, Maastricht (2000) Copper walls and ceilings, as well as bell jars and chemical apparatus, evoke an alchemy shop. This is a reference to the *genius loci* of Maastricht as an old industrial town and also to the energy drinks and stimulants sold which are extracted from herbs and plants using laboratory techniques.

(Below left)
Bizarre, Maastricht (2001) Walls and ceilings of this DJ-owned fashion shop are covered in different sizes and qualities of paper. The counter is black steel and the DJ tower at the back of the shop is made of white powder-coated steel and neon lights. The tone changes from black at the shaded front of the space to brilliant white under the glass roof at the rear.

(Right)
Kash handbag shop, Maastricht (2004) Handbags don't perch on shelves but hang from shoulders. This was the starting point for Mentjens' design. Magnets attach the bags to steel plates on the wall, maximizing the very small area of the shop. The pedestal along the centre introduces a strong architectural element.

Evelyne Merkx and Patrice Girod have the reputation of being the leading interior architects working in the Netherlands today.

The company was founded in 1995 by Merkx and Girod. Merkx worked as a sales-promotion project manager at the well-known Dutch department store, de Bijenkorf, before undergoing a career change. She studied interior architecture at the Rietveld Academy in Amsterdam and set up her own practice after graduation. Patrice Girod studied architecture at the Technical University in Delft from 1957–63 before replacing Jan Rietveld as architecture lecturer at the Rietveld, while working in partnership with, at first, Abel Cahen and later Reynaud Groeneveld. From 1990, Merkx and Girod worked together on several projects but were not formally connected. Projects included, among others, the early years of the Concertgebouw (concert hall), Hema and Bijenkorf.

The collaboration was formalized in 1996 when the office of Merkx+Girod Architects was officially established. This coincided with the assignment for the interior-design commission for the ABN Amro bank offices in its new headquarters in Amsterdam. In 2003 a second ABN Amro commission – the main entrance lobby – was completed.

The duo's respective expertise has given rise to a body of work which shows a perfect synergy of architectonics and respect for surface finish and styling. 'Space, three-dimensionality and the design of light are crucial within architecture. Skin, materiality and colour are important issues within an interior. Combinations between these two are very common in our designs.'

Their portfolio is impressive, crossing many typologies from new development, expansion, refurbishment, product development, exhibitions, styling and renovation. It ranges from small residential projects, offices and restaurants to strategies for large and complex interiors for retail and public buildings in which the logistic and functional requirements are integrated in an elegant, detailed and coherent spatial vision. They quote as their biggest successes the renovation of the famous Concertgebouw in Amsterdam as well as the concept for the Dutch department store, Hema, which was realized in several sites in Rotterdam, Amsterdam and Antwerp, as well as in 25 smaller shops based on a design manual issued by M+G. Both projects are very different from one another yet are equally representative of the work of Merkx+Girod.

Founded in 1926, Hema is a no-nonsense organization that offers a large range of inexpensive goods but which is patronized by all strata of society. M+G's concept was one of clarity and surveyability (what you see is what you get) easy to follow pictograms and emphatic graphics set against bright colours, and simple but distinctive materials (light wood, aluminium and flooring tiles) with decorative elements kept to a minimum. On the other hand, the renovation of the public spaces, main hall and behind the scene areas of the Concertgebouw is acclaimed for its refined use of colour (over 12 different shades of

Merkx+Girod Architekten

(Top)
Renovation of the Trêves Assembly Hall for the Dutch Council of Ministers, Den Haag (2002) The 3m x 9m (9.8ft x 29.5ft) mahogany table is inlaid with black-leather desk pads and two vases designed by glass artist Bernard Heesen. The chandeliers combine atmospheric lighting with dimmable halogen spots aimed at the desk pads.

(Below).
Textile Museum, Tilburg (2005) The refurbishment of the TextileLab, where craftsmen collaborate with designers, artists and students, illustrates M+G's love of vibrant colours and bold graphics. 'Stitch marks' along the floor organize the space into different clusters. Graphic design by Rene Knip.

white have been combined), elegant spatial arrangements and a combination of modern redesign within a classical context. The comparison of the two projects underlines the fact that in M+G's work, no one style is dominant, but what is common throughout is a clarity of spatial solutions and the use of high-quality materials, colours and details.

Also characteristic of M+G's design is a strong analytical approach. The partners begin each scheme, whether small residential or large public, by defining and redefining the floor plans, considering logistics and technical issues before assessing how natural daylight can best be brought as far into a building as possible. It's only once a space has been sculpted three-dimensionally that they consider materials, treatment of skins and colours.

Full-scale material samples are made. New material and/or new material combinations are developed in their own material-laboratory, and details of surfacing and furniture pieces made and tested.

This pragmatic approach, however, belies the risk-taking nature of some of their work. Asked who or what influences their work, they quote not only key figures in architecture from before the war (Carlo Scarpa, Pierre Chareau and Le Corbusier are particular favourites) but also art, both modern and classic, which they say inspires them to think in unique ways and push boundaries. This attitude is probably most evident in their restoration work, not only in the Amsterdam concert hall but also in the council chamber of the Dutch cabinet in The Hague. Both illustrate an attitude towards the existing that is respectful but which is utterly unafraid to make radical interventions.

Far too often M+G's work is reviewed for its unique 'styling' – use of vibrant colours, graphics, attention to detailing and craftsmanship – and not for the inventive spatial manipulation underneath. 'It's no more than icing on the cake. Remarkable that so many people see only the sauce (colours, finishing touches, materials, a witty element, perhaps) and not the radical interventions that we make in so many spaces. Interior architecture is a three-dimensional occupation.'

(Left)
Hema, Nieuwendijk, Amsterdam (1998)
One of the earlier versions of the Hema concept. M+G opened up the interior to reveal the original glass roof which allows natural light to flood into the building.

(Top)
ArboNed healthcare offices, Utrecht (2000)
The space includes box-like medical examination booths which are adorned on the entrance side with pop-art images of pills, safety gear or graphics based on the kinetic studies of photographer Eadweard Muybridge. Graphic design by Bureau Mijksenaar.

(Below)
La Ruche restaurant in de Bijenkorf, Amstelveen (1998) The centrally placed kitchen is neatly packaged in a big glass box which creates a buffer between restaurant and retail space. M+G photographs are placed between layers of glass on the shop frontage, while the glass is left transparent on the dining side, allowing full view of the kitchens. Graphic design by Rene Knip.

**The Inkwell, Utrecht
(2003)** The head office of
the Dutch railways, this is
a renovation of the largest
brick structure in the
Netherlands. To overcome
problems with the wiring,
M+G inserted an additional
'floor' that acts like a
floating carpet on the
original tiles, which are
kept intact by placing the
carpet free of the walls.

(Top)
**The main hall,
Concertgebouw,
Amsterdam (2006)** The
original hall did not rely on
luxurious materials but
on its ornamental ceilings,
pilasters and columns
which for many years had
been covered by paint.
M+G opted to give the
interior a new and coherent
identity, picking out details
in gold leaf and choosing
an understated palette of
greys and beige offset by
12 variations of white.

(Below)
**City Hall, Alphen aan
den Rijn (2003)** The
central reception area
of the new city hall is
dominated by a bright-red
polyester information desk

Morphosis

The avant-garde Santa Monica based architecture firm Morphosis (derived from the Greek word, 'morphosis' – to form or be in formation), was founded in 1972 by Thom Mayne and Michael Rotondi (who left in 1991 to set up his own practice RoTo Architects, leaving Mayne as sole principal). Mayne studied architecture at the University of Southern California School of Architecture, graduating in 1968. He received his masters ten years later from Harvard University's Graduate School of Design and worked for the planner Victor Gruen (the inventor of the American-style shopping mall) before going into independent practice.

Over the past 35 years Morphosis has progressed from restaurant interiors and modest residential additions to major commissions from the US Government and the California Transportation Authority, school boards and international developers. The company is interdisciplinary, concerned with architecture, graphics, city design, and industrial and interior design. It employs over 40 people who work collectively and are directly orchestrated by Mayne. He looks on his job as a film director: 'I think of myself more as a thought-leader than as a designer. My role is to produce continuity and direction and stimulate a large group of people. It's like Ingmar Bergman or Woody Allen. You need to put a group of people together who can operate collectively given the many implicit issues and shifting variables.'

Although for Mayne architectural interiors carry their own knowledge base and set of requirements, he sees no significant division between interiors and the architecture itself. Even though the scale of Morphosis' work has grown, interiors remain an important element. 'We approach each project not only from the outside (its site and urban context), but also from the inside (its programmatic and user requirements), affording each set of parameters equal weight. To provide a fully integrated design, our architectural interiors often incorporate built-in elements, such as custom millwork, built-in seating, light objects and supergraphics.'

Today Morphosis is considered one of the most influential practices of the past twenty years. Its work is site-specific, and these days work is being carried out everywhere, both nationally and internationally. The company is known for a portfolio which reflects the dynamic vibrancy and alienated society of Los Angeles and the unique, somewhat rootless culture of southern California. The firm has won countless accolades, culminating in 2005 with the Pritzker Prize for Architecture being awarded to Thom Mayne. The jury characterized Mayne as 'a product of the turbulent 1960s, who has carried that rebellious attitude and fervent desire for change into his practice.' Lord Palumbo, the Jury's chair, added, 'Every now and then an architect appears on the international scene who teaches us to look at the art of architecture with fresh eyes, and whose work marks him out as a man apart in the originality and exuberance of its vocabulary, the richness and diversity of its palette, the risks undertaken with confidence and brio, the seamless fusion of art and technology.'

(Top)
New academic building for The Cooper Union, New York (2008) The space is conceived as a stacked vertical piazza, contained within a semitransparent envelope that articulates classroom and laboratory spaces. A central atrium rises through the space. The mesh is made from glass fibre reinforced gypsum, a material which is extremely plastic and sculptural.

(Below)
Building, California (2006) A redefinition of circulation and vertical movement provides opportunities for chance encounters. Open work areas lie at the building's perimeter and private offices and conference spaces in the core, which allows natural light to fall on 90% of the workstations. Exposed concrete is complemented by maple doors and colour-accented doors. The project features a series of public art pieces.

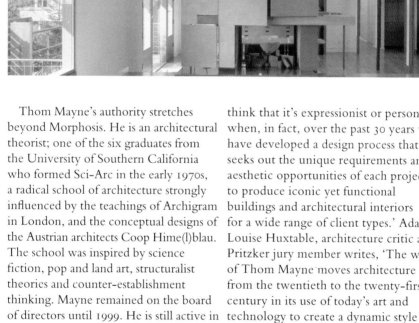

Thom Mayne's authority stretches beyond Morphosis. He is an architectural theorist; one of the six graduates from the University of Southern California who formed Sci-Arc in the early 1970s, a radical school of architecture strongly influenced by the teachings of Archigram in London, and the conceptual designs of the Austrian architects Coop Hime(l)blau. The school was inspired by science fiction, pop and land art, structuralist theories and counter-establishment thinking. Mayne remained on the board of directors until 1999. He is still active in the academic world, inspiring his students with his thought-provoking and open-minded theories, and is a tenured professor at UCLA.

Mayne maintains that teaching has helped him to communicate better with his clients. In formulating his methodology for his students he has built up an expressive yet clear language to help his clients – often conservative bureaucrats – to better understand the logic behind his work. 'Because the work of Morphosis is strong, they somehow think that it's expressionist or personal when, in fact, over the past 30 years we have developed a design process that seeks out the unique requirements and aesthetic opportunities of each project to produce iconic yet functional buildings and architectural interiors for a wide range of client types.' Ada Louise Huxtable, architecture critic and Pritzker jury member writes, 'The work of Thom Mayne moves architecture from the twentieth to the twenty-first century in its use of today's art and technology to create a dynamic style that expresses and serves the client's aims and today's needs.'

Mayne concludes: 'Architecture is a way of seeing, thinking and questioning our world and our place in it. It requires a natural inquisitiveness, an openness in our observations, and a will to act in affirmation. I'm chasing an architecture that engages and demands inquiry. Architecture is not passive, not decorative; it is essential … it affects us directly and profoundly. It has the potential to impact behaviour and the quality of everyday life.'

(Below left)
Tsunami Asian Grill, Las Vegas (2000) The geometrically manipulated planes allude to the 'idea' of the style of architecture in Las Vegas. Rebeca Méndez' graphic elements refer to Asian culture through colour, density and imagery, and are emphasized by the black ceiling and floors.

(Below right).
Kate Mantilini Steakhouse, Beverly Hills (1986) The double-height dining hall features custom-designed barstools, build-ins and sculptural elements. The murals and imagery are based on the cult of personality surrounding the boxing world (Kate Mantilini, the client's aunt, was a legendary promoter). A conceptual orrery acts as a sculptural element and descends from a large oculus at the far end of the hall, expressing the intepretative intentions of the project.

(Right)
University of Cincinnati Campus Recreation Center, Ohio (2006) In the food court, hand-painted murals by Rebeca Méndez animate the large scale tilted cones that envelop each food-service island. The materials used consist of honed concrete, rubber flooring, cement and metal fibre panels, and a metal mesh ceiling.

Torsten Neeland

Although Torsten Neeland's work is concerned with the manipulation of space rather than superficial styling, he insists that the fact he studied industrial design means that he cannot call himself an interior architect. He trained at the College of Fine Art in Hamburg under Professor Lambert Rosenbusch, himself an architect, who believed strongly that architecture and design shouldn't be disconnected from one another – a lesson that had a lasting effect on Neeland's work. 'I wouldn't relate my work to interior decoration because I find the tectonic and spatial elements in an interior more important. I always try to modify or reveal the presence of space. However, the balance between space and objects is important to me.'

Neeland was born in Hamburg in 1963. After his studies he worked for a while in Germany before moving to London in 1997, where he now lives and practices. His portfolio ranges from private interior design and retail outlets to product design and large-scale exhibition spaces. The project which made his name was the Rusing furniture shop in Düsseldorf (2000); however he maintains that the Go shoe shop built in 1993 had a big impact on his future success, as he started to explore new ways of illuminating space. More recently he has been concentrating on domestic interiors as well as working as art director for the German upholstery and furniture manufacturer Cor/Interlübke to formulate a new image and identity for the company, designing fair stands and shows throughout Europe. Similarly, he has been asked by the advertising agency ZOO Werbeagentur to come up with a visual appearance for the new Audi brand 'Audi GW Plus'.

His work has been described as 'sensual minimalism' and he would agree that simplicity is the philosophy of his life, 'It is like a natural desire.' What he achieves throughout his work is an elegance, consistency and timelessness, which he manages by honing a space to its essential. 'If simplicity would be a fashion, it should become a permanent one. I strongly believe that good design is timeless. I like to think that my designs don't look dated or old-fashioned after ten years.'

Above all, Neeland is recognized for his unique, ethereal use of light and lighting effects to transform space and create different moods. In this respect he is an artist, yet one who is grounded with a solid understanding of how he is harnessing lighting design to create or distinguish architectural volumes and infuse his interiors with emotion. It is not surprising, therefore, that he quotes as one of his greatest influences the work of the artist James Turrell, and also Dan Flavin. 'My discovery of light artist James Turrell in the early 1990s had an impact on my work as it helped me to explore a new way of perceiving light.' He uses space as a testing ground for lighting, pushing the boundaries of what is possible, and enjoys the element of uncertainty this research can cause. 'I find creating space with light always has an irrational impact, because you can control light only to a certain extent when your work is an experiment.'

(Right)
Go shoe shop, Hamburg (1993) This was one of Neeland's earliest experiments with the use of light to control space. He also worked with Corian, a material that was little known in the 90's.

Top left)
Rusing shop, Düsseldorf (2000) Subtly changing light emphasizes walls and ceilings as separate forms. Gaps of light separate wall from ceiling, and ceiling from floor. The display cabinets similarly 'hover', which allows the interior to remain open, uncluttered by the furniture and lighting on show.

Below left)
Flat in Germany, location withheld (2004) For Neeland, creating an interior for a private client is like designing a bespoke tailored suit. The space has to reflect the needs, desires and lifestyle aspirations of the person who occupies it. Private interior architecture is often a platform to try out new lighting ideas.

Right)
Duravit showrooms for Philippe Starck Series 3 (2004) The wall was painted with an invisible paint which responds to UV light (black light), giving the illusion that the room was partly illuminated by a massive screen, and adding a theatricality to the set.

Asked what qualities he thought made clients commission him above the competition, Neeland quotes his signature style which he is able to mould to the identity of a brand (creating spaces that are unusual while remaining commercial), or the lifestyle of a private client. He collaborates very closely with the people who employ him, choosing only those who share his vision and are able to understand both the expectations and limitations of his concepts. The relationship is pivotal and dialogue is two-way and ongoing. 'Every project includes alterations, things that need to be adapted to the client's needs. However, the client often finds out more about his needs once he sees the designs.'

Future ambitions include Neeland's desire to become associated with inclusive design. He is impressed by the work of Roger Coleman, the head of the Helen Hamlyn Foundation, who has been a pioneer since the early 1980s. 'I would love to be more involved in inclusive design in ensuring that environments, products, services and interfaces work for people of all ages and abilities. It has the potential to improve the quality of life for everyone, but it needs to be made available via mainstream solutions in order to create a more integrated society. I like to think about a holistic vision of an inclusive world.'

(Top)

Flat in Holland Park, London (2000) The clients of the 111.5 sq m (1,200 sq ft), third floor duplex felt that it was important to create a dialogue between old and new. Custom-made furniture such as *chaise longue* seating, cupboards, lighting and a bed were especially designed for this project.

(Centre)

Frankfurt Fair Exhibition of Tools and Everyday Objects (1997) Tools and everyday objects being sold at the fair were selected to create an exhibition where the objects, display and space are in perfect balance. The products are only visible from within the stand and were exhibited according to the time of day they are used.

(Below)

Audi showroom, Berlin (2005) The idea for this project was developed in partnership with ZOO advertising agency. The brief was to create a new visual interior for the showrooms that would effectively separate second-hand Audi cars from new ones.

(Far right)

Cor/Interlübke Fair stand, Milan (2006) The company is targeting a younger and more cosmopolitan clientele. Neeland has worked with the company since 2004 and is responsible not only for its exhibition stands but also with helping to choose colours, fabrics and accessories for re-branding.

Fabio Novembre

If you ask Fabio Novembre to supply a biography, you get the following:

'Since 1966, I've responded to those who call me Fabio Novembre.

Since 1992, I've responded to those who also call me "architect".

I cut out spaces in the vacuum by blowing air bubbles, and I make gifts of sharpened pins so as to ensure I never put on airs.

My lungs are imbued with the scent of places that I've breathed, and when I hyperventilate it's only so I can remain in apnea for a while.

As though I were pollen, I let myself go with the wind, convinced I'm able to seduce everything that surrounds me.

I want to breathe till I choke.

I want to love till I die.'

If you visit Fabio Novembre's website there are nearly as many pictures of him in various disguises, or states of undress, as there are of his interiors or furniture pieces. If you ask for a studio portrait you are as likely to get an aggressive finger-pointing stance as a fibre-optic haloed Jesus demanding you should be your own messiah. The man is unique. He lives by no-one's rules; in fact he considers that the world we live in today is lawless – nothing is recognizable and there are no prevalent political theories or ideologies. The only *modus vivendi* is to *Vivere* with a capital V and to *Amore* with a capital A. He is anti-establishment or maybe just a law unto himself. His eccentric view on life was learned in the University of the Street and his motto comes from Lou Reed: 'Take a walk on the wild side'.

When I asked what defined his design style, Novembre replied, 'It's an unavoidable consequence of my being an individual different from the remaining six billion individuals living on this planet. I am what I am and I do what I do. I just tell my own stories and I believe that the more they are personal, the more they have the possibility of becoming universal.'

Yet he does have a style. He is the master of narcissistic baroque and his interiors – mainly hotels, retail spaces, nightclubs and bars – are thrilling and surreal experiences which stir the imagination and delight the senses. They are a bizarre, colourful, original, luxurious and sensuous cornucopia of mosaics, leathers, lamé, poetry and imagery. His inspiration comes from the naked female body and he uses organic, soft, round and comfortable shapes. 'Architecture is like a beautiful

(Right)
Spazio Novembre, Milan (2004) For Novembre his own studio is relatively restrained. The living quarters on the first floor, however, are dominated by a mosaic of green foliage, across which the giant serpent of Eden twists and coils, proffering the apple of temptation to the diners below.

(Left)
UNA Hotel Vittoria, Florence (2003) Novembre wanted the hotel to be different from the average boutique hotel by bearing distinctive reference to its Tuscan location. His starting point was the city under the Medici with its connotations of Machiavellian conspiracies and seduction. The swirling mosaic which forms the entrance and twists into the reception desk is a reference to the baroque adornments in the regal villas surrounding Florence.

(Top left)
Tardini Showroom, New York (2000) Like the skin of a python, the sensuous mosaic dominates the luxury handbag and accessory store, forming floor, ceiling and display stand. The minimal white Corian walls act as a backdrop.

(Top right)
Bar Lodi, Milan (1998) The entrance to the bar is framed by a monochromatic tiled entrance of concentric squares. The small bar seems much bigger by Novembre's use of a large mirror down one side, and subtle lighting effects on the ceiling and beneath the bar to draw the eye in and emphasize the linearity of the space.

(Below)
Bisazza Showroom, Berlin (2003) The Bisazza flagship showroom takes the art of mosaic to the extreme. The result is a dramatic series of spaces dominated by colour, form and stunning visual effects. The theme is Beckett's *Waiting for Godot* (Novembre considers Berlin to be the city of eternal waiting). Beckett's words can be seen at the rear of the picture.

(Right)
Shu bar and restaurant, Milan (1999) In contrast to the glowing green bar, the restaurant's interior is almost entirely black, with a black mosaic tiled floor and padded walls. The giant arms which sprout from the halo of floor-mounted spotlights are a reference to the Egyptian god Shu, who held the heavens aloft.

(Left)
Stuart Weitzman shop, Rome (2006) 'Ultimately all a shoe shop needs is shelving. I wanted an infinite shelf that would wrap the inside of the whole shop as if it were the outside of a preciously packaged gift'. A Corian ribbon, with discreetly integrated lighting, winds and spirals across every surface. Such is the craftsmanship that not one seam remains visible.

(Right)
Blumarine Shop, London (1994) This early project shows the beginnings of Novembre's fascination with baroque adornment and sensuous lines. The store looks more like a bar than a retail outlet, the customer entering between a pair of nubile legs encased in Bisazza Oro tiles.

woman: you want her nude, sculptural in her most intimate and structural forms, perfectly true, like a picture by Helmut Newton, with a fierce, self-declared sexuality.'

Novembre was born in Lucce in southern Italy, the country's baroque capital. 'I don't believe in architectonic DNA but for sure I breathed that atmosphere for 17 years.' He decided to study architecture, although he had thought photography or fine art would be less limiting; but once at Politecnico di Milano, his eyes were opened to the possibility of architecture. 'I completely reassessed architecture, because it is the ultimate challenge of three-dimensionality.'

As you would imagine, Novembre does not like definitions, yet more than architect or designer he considers himself a storyteller. 'After my architectural training I moved to New York and studied movie direction for a while. I'm fascinated by film; it's about giving way to dreams. In a way my interiors are like short films and my architecture like a feature movie.' Of his own admission

he cannot draw, but he says he excels at writing, making up narratives that turn into sets and then projects. 'When I think of a place I see it already made in all its detail. The main effort is not in imagining but in conveying. It's important to be able to put across to a client, consultant or craftsman the spirit or the mood that I'm trying to achieve.'

So far Novembre has worked mainly on interiors, although in 2007 his first built project, a new headquarters for fashion house Meltin' Pot in Apulia, is due for completion. 'For many years architecture has been considered a subject for big guys and interiors for little girls. In a way it is very much thanks to the Italian tradition that interiors have merged into architecture and vice versa. What I've always wondered is: how can you build boxes without imagining the content? Shouldn't it be called sculpture instead of architecture? We should talk about space – that's the only thing that matters. True architecture is like a body where everything is related – where the heart and brain depend on each other in order to coexist.'

John Pawson

John Pawson is today's leading proponent of minimalism. His austere yet luxurious interiors are known worldwide and have played an important role in opening our eyes to the spiritual, ethereal beauty of reductionist architecture. He carves space with light, subtracting all that is superfluous, honing and paring down until all that is left is the essential. Yet he is not dictatorial. 'The life my sort of architecture follows is not one which feels right for everybody. I am passionate about my work, but I am not out to make converts. The only universal measure is whether space feels comfortable and right to the people who use it.'

John Pawson came late to architecture. The son of Methodist parents, he was schooled at Eton in the UK before returning home to Halifax to work in his family's textile mill. He travelled to Japan, where he spent time in the studio of Shiro Kuramata. 'For the first time in my life I found myself looking at work which I could recognize, which set something resonating inside me.' He was never Kuramata's apprentice, but the relationship was both inspirational and influential: inspirational as Pawson inherited a belief that space is more interesting than form, and influential as it was Kuramata who persuaded Pawson to become an architect and encouraged him to begin his training at the Architectural Association in London.

Pawson founded his own company in 1981 and started his lifelong research into the fundamental problems of space, proportion, light and materials. His architectural career to date has spanned a wide variety of projects, ranging in scale from a compact apartment for writer Bruce Chatwin to Calvin Klein's flagship store in Manhattan and airport lounges for Cathay Pacific in Hong Kong. He was responsible for the design of the 2002 Venice Architecture Biennale and returned two years later as one of the ten architects showcasing their work in the British Pavilion. More recent projects include a number of private houses around the world, a condominium in Manhattan's Gramercy Park for Ian Schrager, a residential tower in San Francisco and the Sackler crossing for Kew's Royal Botanic Gardens, London.

It was the Calvin Klein limestone and glass store in New York which was to become of seminal importance for Pawson. The story that a band of Cistercian monks wandered in off the street and were so taken by its elegant simplicity that they made it their mission to find the architect and hire him to work on the design of their monastery in the Czech Republic is apocryphal; what is true is the fact that the order's abbot came into contact with Phaidon's book on Pawson's work, *Minimum*, and found in it a philosophy compatible to the rebuilding of their monastery in Novy Dvur. The simple and exquisite exteriors apart, the resultant interiors serve to emphasize the connection between minimalism and spirituality: from the soft shadows of the cloister ceilings onto which rays of reflected light are cast by aquaducts edging the windows, to the deep cuts in the

(Right)
Jigsaw, London (1996)
Two adjoining town houses have been stripped and knocked together to form a shop on two levels with offices above. The double-height entry was formed by cutting back the first floor, allowing for dramatic light effects and display areas.

**Lobby, Hotel Puerta
América, Madrid
(2005)** Each floor of
Puerta América has been
designed by a different,
world-famous architect.
The lobby, reception
and meeting rooms are
Pawson's contribution
and offer a sense of
tranquillity in the heart
of the hotel. The effect is
achieved by using natural
wood and the design of a
semicircular reception area
that shelters guests from
the busy lobby.

church's walls which allow light to fall
directly onto the altar at certain times of
the day. The project was very close to
Pawson's heart, so much so that he offered
his services for 50 per cent of the fee
proposed by local Czech architects.

However, it is Pawson's house in
Notting Hill Gate, London, which stands
as a testament to his minimalist beliefs.
Renovated in 1999, he lives there with his
wife and two children, all of whom gave
their personal briefs for the project. His
wife wanted a comfy sofa; one son wanted
Chelsea FC wallpaper on his bedroom
walls, while the other wanted a room that
locked – and all of this to be contained
in a series of spaces devoid of clutter.
Stone is the predominant material, its
elemental quality appealing to Pawson's

austere sensibilities. Light is added to the
simplicity of the house, filtering through
windows veiled in white mesh and
through the glass wall of the rear eleva-
tion. Falling on the stone surfaces and
the white plaster walls, it produces a soft
and sensuous luminance.

'Minimalism is not an architecture of self-
denial, deprivation or absence; it is defined
not by what is not there, but by the rightness
of what *is* and the richness with which this is
experienced. What could be more sensuous
or tactile than an expanse of honey-coloured
limestone? This is not about creating the
architectural equivalent of the hair shirt, but
about making the best-possible contexts for
the things which matter in life – on paring
back the accretions of surface and behaviour
to what is essential.'

(Top)
Cathay Pacific lounges, Hong Kong (1998) Pawson's sphere of influence extends to Sir Norman Foster's Hong Kong International Airport where he designed the first- and business- class lounges for Cathay Pacific. The key was to preserve the view of Foster's architecture as well as the spectacular arrival and departure of planes outside. Pared-down monumental walls with vistas to the exterior promote an air of tranquillity.

(Below)
House, Notting Hill Gate, London (1999) Pawson's personal monument to minimalism. The exterior of the house was renovated while the interior was gutted and rebuilt, challenging the traditional London terraced-house standard plan by placing an emphasis on horizontality rather than verticality. Natural light is supplemented by the clever use of indirect lighting, which makes the monochromatic walls glow.

(Left and below right)
Novy Dvur Monastery, near Pizen, Czech Republic (2004) The design emphasizes simplicity and serenity. The materials used throughout are simple and durable, from wood for the furniture, polished concrete for the floors and plaster for the walls.

(Top right)
De Carnet House, London (2005) The brief was for a relaxed family home, suited to the display of the client's art collection. The interiors are a series of spacious, well-proportioned and light-filled volumes with open, long views through the depth of the house.

Pentagram

With the battle cry 'all for one and one for all', Pentagram is a utopian company run by designers for designers. Colin Forbes, one of the five (along with Alan Fletcher, Mervyn Kurlansky, Keneth Grange and Theo Crosby) who founded the company in 1972, wrote in the Pentagram publication *Transition*, 1992: 'The idea of equality goes back to our first company, Fletcher/Forbes/Gill, where the three partners decided on equal equity and equal incomes. However, each partner's profitability was openly declared, which contributed to a competitive element.'

Pentagram is run along much the same lines today. There are now 17 partners scattered among the various offices: Angus Hyland, John Rushworth, David Hillman, William Russell and Daniel Weil in London; Justus Oehler in Berlin, Michael Gericke, James Biber, Lisa Strausfeld, Michael Bierut, Paula Scher and Abbott Miller in New York; Lowell Williams and DJ Stout in Austin, Texas and Kit Hinrichs, Robert Brunner and Lorenzo Apicella in San Francisco.

The company is egalitarian and without a hierarchy of leaders and management. Owned by individuals, the pyramid grows horizontally rather than vertically. Each partner is given equal shares and takes an equal division of the profit, the understanding being that some will be having lean periods while others have success at any one time. All the offices work this way, although, for currency and economic reasons, they act independently on an international basis.

William Russell, who in 2005 was the last of the partners to join Pentagram, told me, 'I was made an offer to join Pentagram which I couldn't refuse. Initially I was worried about losing my independence, but working here is the best of both worlds as I'm in charge of my own projects, yet have the security, technical and administrative support as well as the financial back-up to concentrate on the job in hand.' Russell's sentiments are not unusual. Most of the partners would concur. Nearly all came from a background where they had run their own companies for several years, gained national and even international recognition for their work, expanded as much as they could but were looking towards the future and an opportunity to progress unhampered by having to increase in size to compete with global companies and risk becoming managers instead of designers. Pentagram's *modus vivendi* offers the solution.

The company is multidisciplinary. When it was founded, the division was three graphic designers, one architect and one interior designer. The percentage balance is roughly the same today, the interior architects being William Russell, Daniel Weil, James Biber and Lorenzo Apicella.

Although the London office is large employing 50 staff, the atmosphere is relaxed and friendly. The first-floor offices, designed by Pentagram's Theo Crosby in the mid-80s are open-plan with the partners sharing a 'cloister' along one of its edges. Rather like a train carriage,

Daniel Weil came to Pentagram in 1992. He takes a 'Darwinian' approach to architecture, interior and product design; projects have a beginning but their ending is determined by the process allowing consequential ideas to inform the outcome. This approach liberates creativity, meaning that nothing is 'out of bounds' but is based on a consistent purpose and a rigorous editing of methodology. It informs not only spaces, forms, materials and identities of buildings, but also the detail, function, tactility and aesthetics of products.

(Top)
Israel Museum's Bronfman Archaeology Wing, Jerusalem, 2009 The project involves working with the curators to display some 8,000 objects through the wing, spanning prehistorical times to the sixteenth century and to develop a cohesive interpretive concept.

(Below)
The Autogrill/A Café, brand identity for European coffee-bar chain (2000) The interior-design concept was prompted by a desire to reclaim Italian coffee culture from multinational competitors, and covered all aspects of branding from graphics to the soft furnishings.

James Biber joined Pentagram in 1991. He sees architecture as an extension of the clients' search for meaning in form. He is strongly influenced by graphic design and has developed a keen sense of how buildings and interiors can be an articulate expression of 'legible design'. Whether working on domestic commissions, for corporate clients and their brands or institutions, he believes that architecture speaks at least as loudly as any other aspect of public or private personas.

(Right)
The JEHT (Justice, Equality, Humanity and Tolerance) Foundation, New York (2004) The offices were expanded to include a large new meeting area for conferences and events. The space was a former renowned photography gallery.

(Top far right)
Loft Space for a film producer and writer wife, Greenwich Village, New York (2002) As well as living areas, the brief included the design of a screening, and a multi-use room. The solution was to create very distinct spaces united by a single view through a set of soundproof doors.

they are lined up one behind another in individual compartments with shoulder-height divisions creating a space amenable to dialogue, collaboration and constructive criticism. Downstairs is devoted to the reception, meeting rooms and most importantly, the canteen. Each lunchtime the staff breaks at the same time and gather to socialize and talk through ideas.

William Russell told me, 'I think this is part of the reason people come to Pentagram. Our clients are confident because they are working with a long-established company with a good track record for an intelligent, witty and elegant portfolio but, significantly, we are known as cross-disciplinarian, as we specialize in so many fields, from graphics and branding to product design, interiors and large-scale architectural schemes. For me, it was inspirational to get a glimpse into other disciplines. We offer a unique package because we can take charge of all aspects within an individual project, yet with each partner finding and being in charge of their own commissions we can also offer individual characteristics and ways of working.'

A company comprising so many partners has the unparalleled opportunity of being able to continually re-invent itself, as longstanding members depart and young blood is brought in.

Lorenzo Apicella began his career working on skyscrapers in Houston, Texas, followed by urban design in London as well as interiors, exhibitions and theatrical environments throughout Europe. His work combines a fascination for hybrid creativity with articulate communication and technical precision, and is respectful of the physical, cultural and historical context of each project.

(Below left)
Natural History Museum – Investigate, London (2000) An interactive science facility for children in the Natural History Museum's listed Waterhouse building was conceived as a hands-on centre for investigation and interaction with natural objects.

(Below right)
Bene showroom, London (1997) The bright, airy atmosphere of the showroom's neutral white and silver envelope has been complemented and animated by bright furnishings and elegant glass partitions.

The latest partner, **William Russell** (joined Pentagram in 2005), found international recognition with his string of outlets for Alexander McQueen and Margaret Howell and most notably for his much-publicized residence in Bacon Street, east London. He does not consider that he has a particular style, preferring to be led by an empathetic consideration of client, site stipulations and context. Russell draws on the accidents of vernacular architecture as well as the random collisions and juxtapositions of materials and forms which he reinterpretates reusing materials and techniques in new ways while referring to the principles of modernism as the design work progresses.

(left)
Alexander McQueen concept, outlets in London, Milan and New York (2002–04) Elegant, sensual and ethereal interiors using limited materials and colour palette reflect the luxurious qualities and craftsmanship of McQueen's work.

(top right)
Cass Arts flagship store, London, 2006 This is the largest art material emporium in London, totalling 7,500 sq ft over three floors. In keeping with the 1930s commercial property, materials used included galvanised steel and Douglas fir whilst the building's original concrete floors were retained. The store has a simple, customer friendly layout showcasing world-renowned manufacturers.

(below right)
Margaret Howell, Fulham Road, London (2006) Designed to express Howell's timeless, relaxed style and commitment to traditional and pure fabrics.

plajer & franz studio

Primarily associated with their work for BMW, plajer & franz studio are known internationally for their sensational exhibition designs, showrooms and display halls. They have far reaching experience in retail design, working for such large brands names as Timberland, Samsung and s.Oliver. Based in Berlin, their studio was founded in 1996 since when they have also successfully created platforms for local clients Brille 54 and Caras Gourmet Coffee.

The duo studied architecture in Germany before moving to the States. Werner Franz was employed by New York-based Tsao & McKown, working on large-scale developments as well as fashion interiors, gaining experience in major architectural developments as well as the necessary attention to materials, fixtures and fittings required in the detailing of fashion boutiques. During this period he received a tough drafting education as he was schooled in the I. M. Pei tradition (Calvin Tsao worked for the Japanese architect before going into partnership). The doctrine at Tsao & McKown is 'a structured hand drawing requires structured thinking'.

Alexander Plajer inherited an interest in craftsmanship from his father (the manager of a large aluminium importing company who was always bringing home wooden packaging for his sons to construct swings, slides and so on), who showed him how to work with wood and metal. As a child Plajer and his brothers played in their huge adventure garden, constructing houses and machines out of pieces of scrap. These childhood experiences instilled in him a love of architecture and design. His experience with interiors began while still at university, designing retail spaces for Swatch watches. Once in America he worked for Richard Meier, where he became involved with high-end detailing on such projects as the Stadthaus in Ulm and Siemens headquarters in Munich. He returned to Germany in 1993 and founded his own company before going into partnership with Franz three years later.

Both partners consider themselves interior architects rather than designers. 'To create a big trade show booth like the one for BMW requires coordination as well as knowledge of the latest technologies and how to use them in construction. Even with retail spaces, technical issues such as mechanical and structural engineering have to be solved in order to shape the space perfectly. If you cannot handle these things, you will not be able to do a good project.'

Their work does not have a uniform style, although there is a consistency in all they do. They take as their base a minimalist interior and then enrich it with the use of contrasting materials, tactile experiences and luxurious materials. Nikas Maak, writing for the *BMW* magazine in January 2005, describes their interiors as a perfect interplay 'of Dionysian and Apollonian, the smooth with the rough, the ice-cold with the hot'.

They base their work on the dynamic and futuristic designs of the 1950s and 1960s, on the sensuous work of Le Corbusier and the South American form

(Right)
Most stand, Cologne international chocolate exhibition (2006) The concept was 'delightful seduction'. plajer & franz studio emphasized the values of the brand: luxury, modern design and sensual delight using a clear choice of colours and lines in a hybrid of the contemporary and art deco styles.

(Left)

BMW iaa 2005, 61st International Motor Show, Frankfurt BMW demanded that the design of the temporary building and the material expectations should reflect the high-quality aesthetic features of the group. Four new models, four revolving platforms and four LED screens with reverse rotating systems performed a car 'ballet'.

(Top right)

Relaunch trade show concept for s.Oliver Shoes/Comma Shoes, Düsseldorf (2005) Two brands – one creative and young, the other stylish and cosmopolitan – had to be linked cohesively. White and grey were used as the uniting colours for both brands, which were further joined by an encompassing band. The translucent material made the walls appear animated

(Below right)

The newly built access staircase for Tendance Astrale jeans outlet, Galeries Lafayette, Berlin (2005) Jean Nouvel's architectural concept for the shop was based on the cone. plajer & franz studio took this as well as circular movement as their motif.

(Right)

Anastasia concept for s.Oliver Munich stand (concept completed 2005) plajer & franz studio have been responsible for 11 'shop in shop' concepts for s.Oliver. The brief for Anastasia was to design a space which would reflect the lively and charismatic nature of the pop icon. At the centre stands a swirling display, which loops around alternating lighting schemes, and a textile column which stretches from floor to ceiling, allowing the possibility of showing products from both sides. The large visual on the back wall – videos showing Anastasia, as well as the 'tattoo' graphic custom-designed by plajer & franz studio – sustain the design concept.

(Below left)

SIS concept for s.Oliver (concept completed 2005) The SIS concept shows plajer & franz studio's commitment to function, consistent detailing and their signature affinity to the intelligent, considered use of materials and graphics.

(Below right)

75th Geneva Motor Show (2005) The design of the stand revolved around the important premier of the new BMW 3 Series, which was presented on a dais in the middle of the space. Striped walls gave the feeling of speed while the slogan, 'The Driving Force', was translated into dynamic film sequences.

of modernism found in the energetic works of Oscar Niemeyer. Their reinterpretations translate a functionalist design language using a human and contemporary idiom by employing an unusual combination of materials from the traditional to the modern.

Whether designing an exhibition stand for BMW, a retail concept for s.Oliver or a trendy nightspot such as the Universum lounge in Berlin, the spaces they create are dynamic and restless, engaging the user on an emotional level.

Nowhere is this more evident than in their work for BMW. They have designed stands in Paris, Frankfurt and Geneva, showrooms in Berlin, and lifestyles concepts throughout Europe and in China. A good example is the stand for the Geneva Motor Show 2005 which presented the M-series for the first time. Concentrating on the concept of velocity, plajer & franz studio made 'speed' the key word for their design. The area is road-burning red, dressed with grey lamellas placed at irregular and, what appears at first to be, randomly placed intervals. In fact, the patterning is based on the gear sequence of a Formula 1 car driving on a curvy coastal road, which they then transformed into a diagram and ultimately into the finished design. To emphasize the point, plajer & franz studio hung a real-life Formula 1 model on the wall, which appears to race around the space.

'We want to turn space into something more interesting – something you relate to instead of a bare box. We want to create sensation and make people a bit more sensitive to the environment in which they spend their lives.'

(Above)
Tendance Astrale jeans outlet. The central area is dominated by an inverted glass cone. The area has a DJ and animated LEDs which react to the music. Circular dressing rooms have out-of-focus images behind a double-layered Plexi skin, giving the impression of girls undressing.

Francesc Pons

Francesc Pons works across all fields, from offices, showrooms and retail spaces to restaurants and expensive penthouses. The hallmarks of his interiors are an obsessive eye for detail, the use of sumptuous, contrasting materials and a theatrical glamour and sophistication which evoke a romantic bygone era of luxury and opulence.

Born in 1967, he trained as an industrial designer at the Elisava College of Arts in Barcelona, but moved into interior architecture over a decade ago when a friend asked him to design her flat. Disillusioned by the vernacular, outdated forms and bland interiors he saw around him in his native Catalonia, he has systematically set himself the task of breaking down the status quo since the founding of his studio in 1995.

Although Pons refers to himself as an interior architect, he considers that a successful interior can only be achieved through looking at all aspects of its design. He feels that the barriers created by defining architecture and design are artificial, and his own work is concerned not only with the physical manipulation of space but also with how that space should be detailed, finished and decorated. Not content to stop there, he also takes into consideration how an interior will be used: who will visit it, how it will be run, in the case of a restaurant, what food will be eaten, what the waiters will wear and what music will be played. He considers himself a global creator.

A good example of this was his first significant project, Sandwich & Friends, a modern eatery in the trendy Bom area of Barcelona, which he conceived as a whole new social experience: an interim venue to drop into and party over a coffee and a *bacadillo* before moving on to the next nightclub or bar. Situated in a restricted site, Pons opened up the interior to the street by way of a glazed façade through which can be seen his signature use of what he refers to as 'modern classic materials' – Formica, mirrored glass, chrome and pvc chosen for their durability and reflective qualities. The space is given a strong identity by adopting bold graphics and bright canary-yellow planes. Pons goes for instant effect and would rather his work be disliked than ignored. Sandwich & Friends was a departure for Barcelona at that time (1999) and launched Pons on his career as a designer willing to take risks in a conservative climate – to, as he says, 'do different things with different ideas at a moment when everybody seemed to be working in the same way'.

Subsequent projects – the Amaya Arzuaga flagship store, the 501ª hairdressing salon, the Noti restaurant, the Outumuro studio and BSB showroom – have continued to surprise, questioning preconceived notions of what is expected from certain types of interior.

The design of the Amaya Arzuaga shop is based on the timeless qualities of a vintage Jaguar. Using lavish materials – black lacquer, pearly metallic veneers, leather and brass finishes – Pons has recreated the romantic, super-glam days of 1950s Balenciaga, Chanel and Dior. A luxurious space which stands in direct

(Right)
BSB showroom, Barcelona (2004) Visitors to the showroom enter the main display area via a corridor from the reception. Lined with mirrors which give a rather disconcerting labyrinthine feel. This small space contains a bar and is used to entertain clients.

(Left)
5º1ª hairdressing salon, Barcelona (2001)
Walls and centrally placed styling table are made from zebrano wood. Pons asked the question why a salon had to look like a salon and has created a 1970s boardroom instead.

(Top right)
The Ottimo restaurant, Barcelona (2004) Chrome runners, mirrored ceilings, green wallpaper and wood panelling create a more restrained aesthetic than Pons' earlier work.

(Below right)
Sandwich & Friends fast food restaurant, Barcelona (1999)
A yellow-and-black-glazed box with a striking mural of Barcelona youth painted by Pons' friend, controversial artist Jordi de La Banda.

contrast to the neighbouring minimalist interiors more frequently associated with *haute–couture* boutiques, 5º1ª re-examines the function of a salon. It looks more like a boardroom, with its marble and zebrano clad walls acting as a sobering backdrop to the centrally placed styling table (also in zebrano wood), where clients sit together on either side as if at a conference.

Noti, a restaurant known for its unusual cuisine, now has a theatrical interior to match. With a difficult circulation, deliveries and guests both have to arrive through the same door. Pons has created a design statement from a problem by making the service area into a stunning feature. He has inserted a wall of highly polished brass panels set against shocking pink Formica to mask the working areas from the dining room.

Instead of being content with a mere stylish refurbishment of the seventeenth-century Renaissance palace, which houses Outumuro, Pons has divided the photography studio into three radically different yet complementary zones, while the BSB carpet showroom demonstrates a more restrained, sculptural quality that successfully contrasts the softness and richness of these famous rugs with the reflective, metallic finishes of the entrance corridor above.

When asked what distinguishes his style he replied, 'The look, *le charme*, elegance, comfort, modernity, the wonder to be different and original as well as an attention to detail which was so important in my career as a product designer and which I've carried on in my work with interiors.'

Francesc Pons

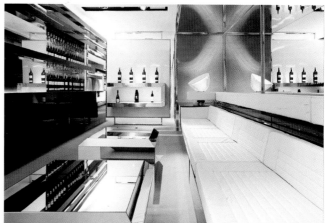

(Left)
Noti restaurant, Barcelona (2002) This restaurant is housed in the offices of the former newspaper *El Noticiero Universal*. The interior layers materials and finishes to create a rich jewel-box of velvets, linoleum, black glass, brass and shocking cerise Formica.

(Above top)
Outumuro studio, Barcelona (2003) The photography studio is housed in a Renaissance palace. The two-tiered library reception area has a reflective back wall and is finished in rich tones of brown and ochre. The floor mosaic dates from the nineteenth century, and the table is in rosewood and ebony-coloured laminate.

(Above below)
Amaya Arzuga flagship store, Madrid (2000) Pons has quickly become known as the designer's designer. The collaboration with Arzuga, the *enfant terrible* of the Spanish fashion world, resulted in a two-floor outlet with womenswear on the ground floor and menswear and a small bar in the basement. Display modules made from polished black lacquer and metal reflect their surroundings and magnify the space.

Pugh + Scarpa Architecture

Pugh + Scarpa have redefined the role of the architect to produce some of the most remarkable and exploratory work in America today. They do this not by escaping the restrictions of practice, but by looking, questioning and reworking the very process of design and building, to produce entirely inventive work that defies categorization.

Lisa Iwamoto, Department of Architecture, UC Berkeley, 2004.

Pugh + Scarpa was founded in 1991 by Gwynne Pugh, who holds a degree in science from the University of Leeds and a masters in architecture from the University of California in Los Angeles, and Lawrence (Larry) Scarpa who studied architecture at the University of Florida. In 1998, architect and expert in sustainability Angela Brooks joined the partnership to serve as project manager at their Santa Monica office. Scarpa has been their lead designer since 1993, and I spoke to him for the purpose of this feature.

Pugh + Scarpa is known for new-build, engineering and interior-architecture projects, with the percentage balance today falling into full-scale architectural projects. 'It was a different story five years ago, when a major proportion of our portfolio consisted of interior interventions. Schemes such as the offices for Creative Domain, Jigsaw, Reactor Films and XAP, and the residences Orange Grove, Redelco and my own house, the Solar Umbrella, were publicized so widely and acclaimed by our peers by way of design awards that they have led to bigger projects. They have allowed us to get into

markets which were closed to us when we established ourselves in the early 1990s: multi-family housing, educational projects and civic and institutional work.'

Pugh + Scarpa first got into interior architecture fortuitously. They were working on an engineering project for Stoney Road Productions, which needed an apartment interior completed in ten weeks and on a limited budget. Pugh + Scarpa was the only architectural practice foolhardy enough to take it on. They teamed up with building contractors and finished it on time. The excellence of the space gained them recognition for being able to complete quickly without sacrificing quality, and a flood of commissions soon followed.

Interiors are still very important to Pugh + Scarpa, who look upon them as a laboratory to experiment with materials, innovative construction techniques and flexibility. Scarpa comments: 'I'm very influenced by artists and their working methodology. Architecture is so tied up with technicalities and constraints that I think a lot of architects have lost a sense of freedom and creativity in their work. I'm a sculptor and I consider that my approach lies somewhere between art and architecture. Our interiors tend to put 80 per cent of the budget into 20 per cent of the space, by that I mean most of our projects contain free-standing forms, or sculptural details as inherent architectural elements.'

Although they may not have a distinctive style, familiar concerns creep up over and over again in Pugh + Scarpa's work: *transparency* – openness and flow are

(Right)
Orange Grove, West Hollywood, California (2004) Located in an area of traditional-style bungalows, Orange Grove stands out due to its modernist aesthetic. The residence is similar to the nearby iconic Schindler House, with elements such as windows and porches forming an abstract sculptural pattern. The interior volumes are large and simple and are based on space, light and the kind of industrial materials normally found in a loft.

(Above)

Creative Domain headquarters, Los Angeles (2004) Central to the overall design was Scarpa's decision that the space should be viewed as one giant sculpture. The eclectic result included the use of materials to define space, a wall of light-filled Dixie cups, and a 4m (12ft) -long spiral steel sculpture which punctuates the raw industrial ceiling into the sixth-floor lobby.

important elements in all their projects; *emphasis on public spaces* – kitchens and cafeterias are usually placed at the entrance of an office and used as an area for staff and visitors alike; *displacement of the reception* – this is frequently placed as far into an interior as the client will allow, to encourage visitors to enter a space under their own terms and explore; *use of prosaic materials innovatively*.

Scarpa often quotes from Venturi's *Complexity and Contradiction in Architecture*: 'A familiar thing seen in an unfamiliar context can become perceptually new as well as old'. Pugh + Scarpa reveals the extraordinary from within the ordinary by using natural and composite materials in a non-traditional sense, and familiar objects in unfamiliar contexts: pingpong balls create a wall in Jigsaw, industrial

broom heads form a screen to the second-floor balcony of Scarpa's home, Dixie cups are filled with light and stud the entrance to Creative Domain, and a shipping container forms the conference room at Reactor.

Goals for the future are to continue to diversify and be challenged, to be involved in public architecture which impacts on the community and the city, but above all to stop being considered as 'green' architects. 'Of course it is important to us, it's fundamental, but our architecture comes first. We make places people *enjoy*. All our architecture is sustainable to a lesser, or usually greater, extent and that is how it should be. If it were made legal, like disabled access, then the media could stop using it as a tag-line. Sustainability is not a concept for design; it's just a layer.'

(Left)
Solar Umbrella, Venice, California (2005)
Inspired by Paul Rudolph's Umbrella House, 1953, Scarpa's own house provides a contemporary reworking of the solar canopy. The transparency of the interiors allows light to penetrate from front to back. The living room layers colourful domestic materials over concrete. Copper is used in the fireplace nook and cherry wood for fittings, both of which lend warmth to the open space.

(Top right)
Jigsaw, Los Angeles (2004) The offices of a film-editing company need dark, hermetic spaces. The brief was for an inviting, stimulating environment that allows for social interaction. The result is a series of free-standing sculptural elements which house the office's library and editing rooms, the latter suspended over a shallow pool of water. The social areas are in the negative space volumes carved out of the former warehouse.

(Below right)
AP, Culver City, California (2001)
Restrictions imposed by the building's architect and owner meant that none of Pugh + Scarpa's interventions should impede on the original structure. The board and conference rooms of this Internet information management systems company are housed in organically shaped forms ('sculptural follies' (raw on the outside, finished on the interior) – and are a physical manifestation of Pugh + Scarpa's ongoing experimentation with form and materials, and with making and construction.

Pugh + Scarpa Architecture

(Left)

Reactor Films, Santa Monica, California (1996) Housed in an art deco building, this TV commercial office focuses on the centrally located conference room which is located in an ocean shipping container. The circulation of the space is based on a street-scape. To emphasize old and new, the surrounding interior pushes and pulls against the walls, revealing and concealing the original building.

(Top right)

COOP Editorial, Santa Monica, California (2003) The remodel of a 1963 Frank Gehry commercial structure, the design for this post-production company office reflects Pugh + Scarpa's ongoing inquiry into ways of approaching interior architecture in an innovative way. Without redefining the architecture they responded to the material qualities of the location intuitively. A second skin, a back-lit wood and plastic wall, moves in and out, alternately concealing and revealing the building's fabric, and adding a new layer to a previous usage.

(Below right).

Redelco residence, Studio City, California (2004) Originally started in 1994, work stopped during the early construction phase (due to unforeseen circumstances), to be restarted a decade later. The problem was how to rebuild innovatively on an outdated footprint. Pugh + Scarpa achieved this by opening up the interior by removing all the planned room dividers and, by way of 7m (22ft) -high sliding glass doors, allowing the interior and exterior to become one.

Andrée Putman

Andrée Putman is the *grande doyenne* of interior design but, although she might recognize her status, she would hate the classification. She is without doubt one of the most accomplished manipulators and decorators of space, creating masterpieces from emptiness; however, she approaches each project not as an architect but more like a musician, writer, film director or artist. Functionality and technical expertise are a given; what she brings to her work is her character, her memories, associations, perceptiveness and humour: 'My goal is to bring a touch of humanity to my work in what is a very sombre moment.'

Born in 1925 into a wealthy, ancient (her grandfather's family were descendents of the Montgolfiers) and powerful French family, her parents were artists and eccentrics. Her mother, who played the piano, visited the Louvre every day until she was 90, and insisted on taking her daughters to daily concerts and on frequent trips to monasteries and *châteaux*. She cocooned them in a world of passion and beauty, making clothes for them out of antique lace and satin ribbons, creating costumes which made them look more like characters from Virginia Woolf novels than schoolchildren. 'This is how I lived, like an Egyptian mummy wrapped in bandages which prevented all movement or speech. I lived in this abstract, incommunicable world of music until that decisive point in my life when I won this prize.' The prize to which she refers is the highest award at the Paris Conservatoire where she studied harmony.

(Right)
Gildo Pastor Offices, Monaco (1966)
'I promised a staircase like a necklace of light.' Space is sculpted and then enhanced by a delicate and playful luminescence.

(Left)
Private residence, Shanghai (2004)
Putman's design for the penthouse apartment of the tycoon daughter of design patron Pearl Lam is lavish yet minimal. Shown here is the entertainment area, with a blue glass-walled staircase leading to the master suite.

(Left)
Guerlain boutique and spa, Paris (2005)
In collaboration with interior architect Maxime D'Angeac. The original building was listed and the marble could not be touched. M. d'Angeac linked the boutique to the spa with a golden ribbon on the mezzanine. Once the architectural modifications were in place, Putman added her signature style with glass-bead curtains representing perfume droplets, a 3.06m (10ft) tall chandelier in the shape of an atomizer, a wall dispenser to refill customers' perfume bottles and a Felliniesque atmosphere in the spa.

She did not stay at the Conservatoire for long. She knew that she would never be a virtuoso, but her ability to play complicated pieces faultlessly and the rigorous discipline of her musical studies instilled in her a love of harmony and composition which is evident in the severe, mathematical yet sensual lines of her design work.

On leaving the Conservatoire she rebelled against her cloistered upbringing, living the life of an artistic bohemian in 1950/60s Paris. She wrote on design and style for L'Oeil and became heavily immersed in contemporary painting, working for Prisunic, persuading them to sell lithographs of the artists she admired at accessible prices. Her collaboration with Denise Foyelle, whom she had met at Prisunic while designing a range of home accessories, led to the formation of a style consultancy, Mafia, which promoted the Utopian ideal of beauty for all through various events and communications. In 1971 she founded Créateurs et Industriels with Didier Grumbach, which attempted to align the arts with industry but had limited success and then only in the realms of luxury and fashion.

However, the experience she gained from having founded the two agencies made her realize that her strengths lay in uniting people, spaces and objects. The result was the formation of Ecart in 1979, a studio which she perceived as a vehicle to re-edit objects and prototypes she found in the flea markets of Paris but which later went on to re-issue the giants of the 1930s – Robert Mallet-Stevens, Eileen Grey or Mariano Fortuny – and

Andrée Putman

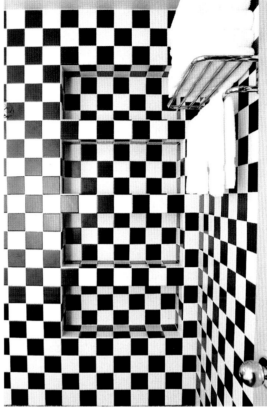

(Opposite, top)
Bayerischer Hof Spa, Munich (2005) The spa won the 2006 Gala Spa Award. Covering three floors, it is topped by a swimming pool under a glass roof which can be retracted during good weather.

(Opposite, below left)
CAPC, Bordeaux (1984) The CAPC is the largest avant-garde museum in France. Putman transformed a beautiful and gigantic warehouse into a sophisticated exhibition space, succeeding in combining a modern classic aesthetic with historic industrial architecture.

(Opposite, below right)
Orchard House, Kobe, Japan (1992) A vast, 400m (1,308ft) rectangle of space has been transformed into a club comprising lounge, restaurant and bar. The concept explores half-light.

(Above left)
Concorde, Air France (1993) Height and space were gained by subtly enlarging the capacity of the luggage compartments. Elegant details in the cabin add sensuous comfort to what is normally a very utilitarian environment.

(Above right)
Morgan Hotel, New York (1984) The first ever boutique hotel. Intended for the traveller in search of rest and privacy, the Morgan Hotel eschewed an outdated, uniform luxury aesthetic in favour of an elegant and, at that time, unique home-from-home atmosphere. The black-and-white tiles in the bathrooms have become legendary.

eventually to design original pieces and also to work on interiors. Commissions such as the Morgan Hotel in New York, the conversion of a water tower into the Wasserturm Hotel in Cologne, the interiors for Air France's Concorde, the renovation of a warehouse into the CAPC Museum in Bordeaux, the Gildo Pastor offices in Paris, the Bayerischer Hof Spa in Munich, the Pershing Hotel in Paris as well as various residential and retail interiors (notably her long-standing collaboration with Karl Lagerfeld) and the sets for the stylized Greenaway film *The Pillow Book* have sealed her success. Today, working under her own name, Andrée Putman's human brand of minimalism has made her an icon.

Putman's designs are primarily concerned with space and light, with special care taken over details and the use of luxurious materials. Together with her team of architects and designers she produces timeless, simple, elegant, familiar, non-trendy interiors which are innovative, courageous and often subtly humorous. Like the woman herself, her work is enigmatic, which makes it timeless. 'I believe my designs have a mystery which protects them from possessing only momentary stylishness. They don't seem to age over time. It's almost a guarantee that comes with my creations – like buying a sweater with a tag that says "won't shrink when washed".' Above all, Putman does not believe in being too 'clever'. 'The most successful interiors are not those that one notices because of their originality but those in which one simply has the feeling of being at ease.'

Muti Randolph

Muti Randolph's route to interior design was not the usual one. He studied industrial design at the Pontifícia Universidade Católica do Rio de Janeiro, graduating with a degree in visual communication, and then worked as a graphic designer and illustrator, creating advertisement campaigns for Coca-Cola, packaging and branding for British Tobacco, and album covers for major recording companies (as well as flyers and sleeves for smaller indie labels). The three-dimensionality of his illustration and graphics projects (some look more like architecture than two-dimensional design) resulted in commissions for set and event designs from major clients such as Globo TV and *Vogue*, as well as for underground house parties. 'I began to design elements of sets, and soon whole sets for TV and theatre. Now people could go inside my illustrations, and that is exactly what fascinated (and still fascinates me) about designing spaces.'

His first interior-design project was for the U-Turn Club in São Paulo. The client wanted to employ a set designer rather than an architect and the initial intention was to change the interiors every six months. Such was the success of Muti's design that the club remained exactly as conceived until a brawl in 2001 put it out of business. 'Because of U-Turn, people started hiring me to design other clubs and now my main activity is interior design.'

Although in many instances (D-Edge Campo Grande, Galerie Melissa and the more recent D-Edge in São Paulo) Muti is responsible for both the architecture and the interiors of his built projects, he prefers to describe himself as a designer to reflect the multidisciplinary nature of his studio; he still, on occasion, works in graphic design, set design, furniture design, animation and software design. For Muti, interior design is the link between industrial design and architecture as it contains aspects of both. 'An interior-design project is where the most intense human interaction takes place: a total immersion at an intimate distance. When you walk into an architecture project, it is the interior-design part of it that you mostly interact with.'

All Muti's interiors have a sense of unity and he designs everything from the graphics to the furniture and fittings. So unique is his style that anyone else's work inside of one of his spaces would immediately look out of place. 'I'm always aiming for a distinct, coherent, almost natural feel. I see my interior and set projects as illustrations – as paintings that invite visitors to come inside. Each element must clearly belong to the whole.'

Muti says that he is a geek as far as computers are concerned, having been obsessed with them since childhood. He constantly researches new technologies: 'Two years ago I was surprised to find out that no VJ software would sync live audio to video in a direct way. I started then to develop a software that does it and I now use it in several of my projects. It is good to be able to contribute to the development of technology and not be limited by it.'

Both D-Edge, São Paulo and Diesel Brazil's second-anniversary party in the

(Top)
Diesel Brazil's second-anniversary event, Prestes Maia Gallery, São Paulo Museum of Art, Brazil (2004)
The white-painted MDF sheet 'cubes' covered tables, chairs, bars, the DJ booth and the hostess stand. Some, arranged in stacks, are wrapped around the marble columns in the space and rotated randomly. These unify the space, conceal the projectors and break down the projected visuals.

(Below)
Diesel Brazil's second-anniversary event
Projections cover most of the visible surfaces. Diesel's marketing campaign was titled 'Work Hard'. Muti has used tilted black-and-white stripes to recall 'Caution: Men at Work' road signs.

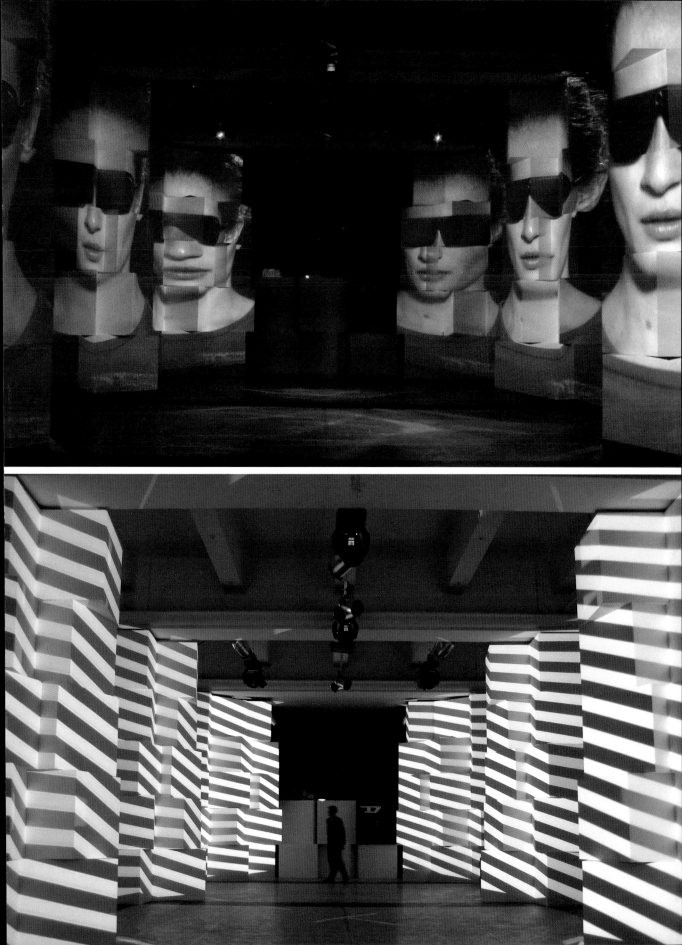

Prestes Maia Gallery of the São Paulo Museum of Art were shaped by synchronized music and light: physical manifestations of Muti's exploration of the relationship between sound and vision. The former – a black box with resin floors and faux wooden walls – has a Cartesian grid of white Plexiglass lights embedded in all its surfaces. A light jockey (LJ) works with the DJ to produce a sophisticated lighting effect which moves with the music. On different nights different colours are used to suit the atmosphere of varying music styles. One sequence features lights flickering, seemingly randomly, superimposing disorder on the rational. For the Diesel event, the client's concept was to create 'maximum visual impact' and the space was defined and distorted by light. The company's logo is red – the dominant colour in the light show. Muti conceived a cornucopia of film and animations using images of models, people using Diesel products and advertisements which, run by software, moved perfectly with the music played by the DJ and were projected onto white intersecting MDF sheets laid onto one another to resemble cubes.

Muti's interiors, especially those for nightclubs and parties, not only find a beautiful solution to a client's needs, but also create sensorial experiences for the user, proposing as they do new relationships between people and their environment.

(Left)
Galerie Melissa, São Paulo (2005) Melissa produces fashion accessories in plastic, especially footwear designed by famous designers. Muti has created a hymn to plastic. The products are displayed in transparent plastic bubbles which emerge from organically shaped, shiny white plastic 'horns' set against a psychedelic background of off-axis stripes.

(Top and below right)
D-Edge, São Paulo, Brazil (2003) The vibrant nightlife of São Paulo, a city of sight and sound, is manifest in the design for the second D-Edge venue. The grid of light on a dark background is analogous to the computer screen which depends on light to bring it alive.

(Top left)
Colcci Fashion Show, Rio de Janeiro (2006)
A huge sculpture of a sea with breaking waves was mounted in one of the seating areas of the main tent at Fashion Rio. It was made of 120, 10cm- (4in-) wide slices of painted Styrofoam, and eight trucks were needed to transport the waves.

(Below left)
MTV Brasil set, São Paulo (1999–2002)
The set was used for journalistic programmes, each one of which happened in a different area (subset), as well as live shows. The futuristic retro aesthetic, with Pantonesque curves and bright, primary colours, is typical of Muti's love of the 60s. 'What excites me about the 60s is its sensuously stimulating nature, its humour and its freedom. Its all about fun.'

(Right)
São Paulo Fashion Week, Niemeyer's Art Biennale Building (2005)
SPFW was the biggest project undertaken by Muti in terms of both space and data: two terabytes of animations as well as live interventions were projected from 12 computers on irregular angulated panels. The projections formed images up to 50m (164ft) wide and 5m (16ft) tall. The project consisted of two giant video installations that embraced most of the building interior, as well as video booths and a seating area.

Karim Rashid

Karim Rashid is best known as an industrial designer. He is ubiquitous and prolific and has been credited for bringing exceptional, affordable design to the masses via iconic products such as his Garbo rubbish bin which, to date, has sold over three million worldwide.

He was born in Cairo in 1960, is half-English and was raised mainly in Canada. He received a Bachelor of Industrial Design in 1982 from Carleton University, Ottawa, and pursued postgraduate studies in Italy, working with Ettore Sottsass and Rodolfo Bonetto. He founded his own practice in New York in 1993, since when his rise to fame has been meteoric.

Although we associate him primarily with his product designs, Rashid regards his office as multidisciplinary. It is his aim to create a Warholian factory that produces buildings, interiors, fashion, objects, products, furniture, art, installations, music and film. Recent work includes two hotels, six restaurants, various shops, furniture, lighting, jewellery, houseware and fashion accessories, and his approach remains the same whether he is working on a perfume bottle or an interior. He describes himself as an intellectual and as a cultural editor, and sees the ideas behind his work – or rather the importance he places on design as an instigator of social change – as in some ways more important than the physical object itself.

For Rashid the move into the twenty-first century is a landmark. New cultures demand new forms, material and styles, and his latest designs, interiors and graphics are conceived to reflect the digital age, which he considers the third Industrial Revolution. He proposes objects and spaces for new behaviours and produces work that suits the cosmopolitan, casual, trendy, laid-back consumer of the computer age. Design does not just serve or reflect changes in the way we live; for this pluralist it is instrumental, as he believes it is capable of altering human behaviour and creating new social conditions.

Rashid has coined the expression 'Sensual Minimalism' to describe his style, which has an emotional appeal while staying minimal. He uses soft and tactile forms as they are more human and signify comfort and pleasure. The 'blob' is Rashid's trademark. For him it is a visual reaction to mechanization and an expression of the biological nature of all existence.

Rashid's interiors reflect his philosophy that we are living in a disposable age. 'I think that in the future we will own nothing; we lease cars, we lease houses, and soon we will learn to lease everything, experience it for a short while, and go on to the next.' His spaces relate to the senses, are organic, soft, physical, brightly coloured and fun but are designed to evolve and are ultimately transitory. 'I believe that the design of an interior is a metaphor for how technology, housing, furnishing and space can work together to evocate an increased sense of experience, affect our psyche and bring us a better contemporary life.'

Although at first glance his built environments may appear merely

(Right)
Nooch Express, New York (2005)
This contemporary noodle restaurant interacts with the city through its openness. A large plate-glass window acts as a 'section' dividing street from dining area. The pan-Asian mode reflects the nature of the food served.

decorative, they are in fact holistic, with a sound understanding of space. For the Semiramis Hotel in Athens, Rashid has designed everything from the building itself (a conversion of a 1921 hotel) to the soaps in the bathrooms. His apartment in New York was initially a stable and a 100 year-old pumping supply company which he turned into a Cartesian white 'blank gallery' which serves as a living gallery for his latest prototypes. The fast-food restaurant Nooch uses bright techno colours and strong curvilinear forms to emphasize speed, and the entire restaurant is open through the full-length, wrap-around glass façade. The city is welcomed in and the diners have the energy of the streets as their backdrop. And, in his first restaurant design, Morimoto in Philadelphia, he took as his base a strict geometric grid of glass booths containing LEDs which subtly change

colour throughout the evening to reflect the different moods associated with dining: relaxation=lilac; love=pink; conversation=orange; and taste=green. Surrounding this he imposed a gently undulating biomorphic space of white stucco which is continually washed by the morphing hues. 'Light is the best architectural element because it is immaterial and therefore can transform a space completely.'

In Karim Rashid's book *I Want to Change the World*, the musician David Byrne writes that since the mid-1990s there has been a growing design current that emphasizes joy, exuberance and optimism, all of which he recognizes in the work of Karim Rashid. Design does not stand on its own but is part of our sociological, psychological and political world. 'Design is the whole experience of living,' says Rashid.

(Left)
Four Food Studio, Long Island (2005) Rashid has used colours and digital images to associate each area of this contemporary American restaurant to one of the four seasons. Seen here is the bar (Spring), the dining area (Summer) and in the background, a lounge (Winter) complete with igloo fireplace.

(Above left and right)
Semiramis Hotel, Athens (2004) Karim conceived the hotel as a sensory experience and uses pinks and techno colours to add the vibrancy and energy he associates with the digital world.

(Below right)
Askew restaurant, New York (2005) Karim plays with the notion of 'askew', creating a dynamic perspective through angled surfaces that interact with one another, allowing the eye to wander across the room in several directions.

(Top left))
Morimoto, Philadelphia (2001) A symbiosis of geometric and biomorphic forms washed with ever-changing hues of digital light.

(Below left)
Kit house (2006) Constructed from sandwiched panels of various customized surface finishes – outdoor-quality polycarbonate for the exterior and plastics for the interiors – it is held together by a simple aluminium frame. The decorative language speaks to the new computer-age generation.

(Right)
Karim Rashid's New York apartment (1999) This was designed as a blank Cartesian space to serve as a backdrop for Rashid's latest products and prototypes.

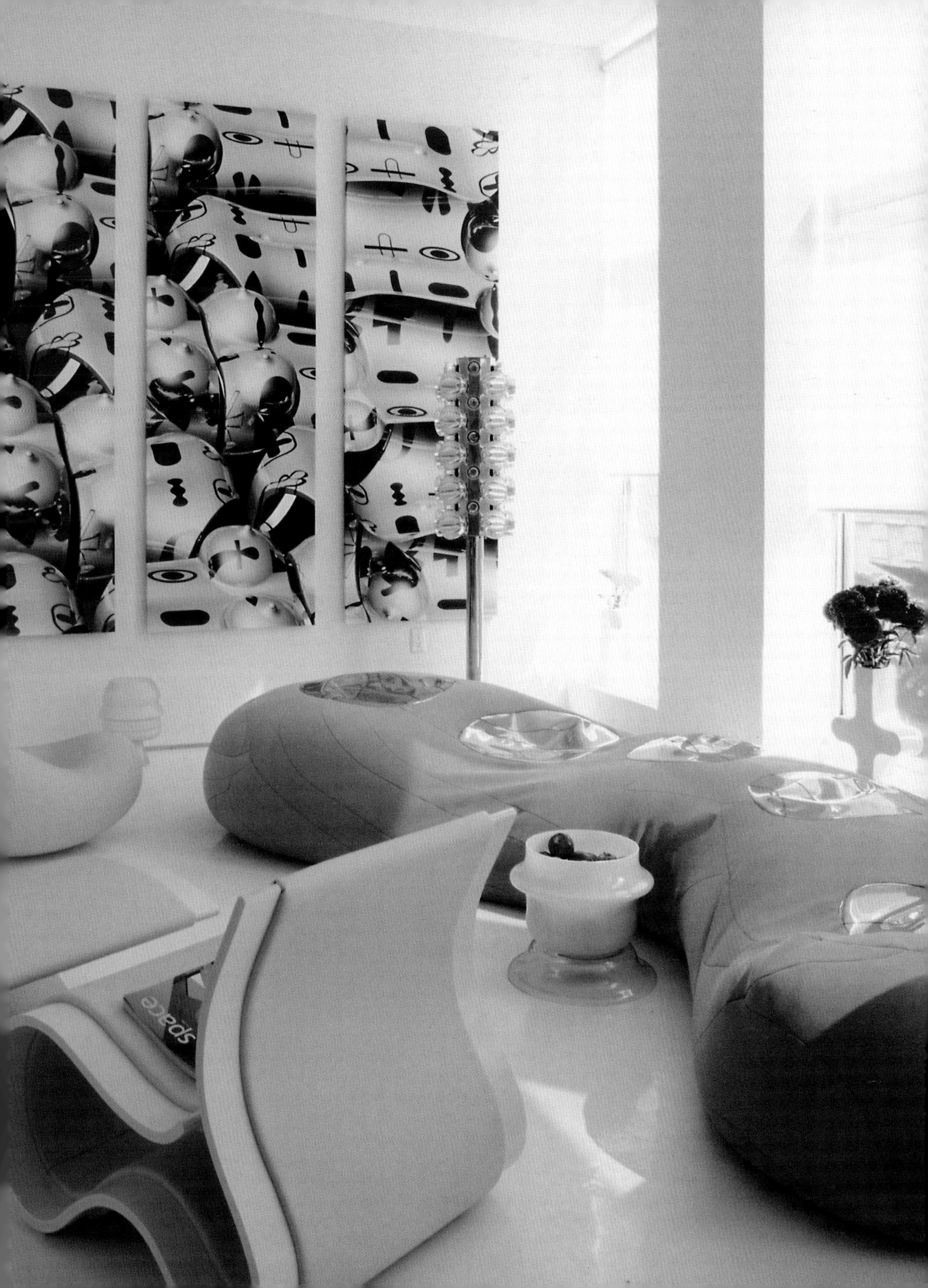
space

Francesc Rifé

Francesc Rifé, the Spanish interior and industrial designer, was born in Sant Sadurní d'Anoia in 1969. His career started as an undergraduate. Rifé studied interior design at the Escuela, DIAC-Eiade/La Llotja, industrial design at Escuela La Llotja and architecture at Universidad Politécnica de Cataluña, Barcelona. While studying architecture he simultaneously undertook independent commissions for various design and architecture studios, as well as working on his own projects. He founded his architecture studio in Barcelona in 1994 and has since built up a national reputation as a designer concerned with spatial order, geometric balance and solemn rational form. 'True luxury' for him is 'to marry the function of an interior with sober consideration of space'. His work is without frills; it is considered, serene and elegant, showing a committed eye for detail and a mastery of proportion.

He works mainly in the commercial and private sectors and is probably best known for The Can Fabes restaurant, which has been widely publicized. Other notable projects include the Duplex Josefina Martí, Barcelona; the Duravit offices, Parets del Valles; Professional Bookkeeping Services (PBS) office/showroom, Barcelona; and the Nuba restaurant in Manresa, the popular university area of the city.

The fact that Rifé refers to the people who work in his studio as 'interior-volume sculptors' is not surprising. Viewing the work the practice produces is like looking at the graphic paintings of Mondrian: harmonious and ordered with slabs of colour broken up by strong lines into cubic forms. For Rifé, decoration is very much secondary; in fact, at first glance it would almost appear that to add furniture and fittings to his interiors is at worst sacrilegious and at best unnecessary. 'I always look for the purity of space; for me luxury lies in that … it is only by balancing form and space that the neutral cleanliness which defines our style is created.' Any auxiliary objects are added to the interiors with a careful deliberation, creating a refined still-life. There is nothing out of place, nothing which isn't in keeping. 'Fashion' or 'trend' are words with which Rifé is not familiar.

Rifé selects clients who share a similar vision to his own, a process that is becoming progressively easier as he has become better-known. Because his work is seemingly straightforward, he is trusted. Each commission he undertakes he approaches differently after considering the personality of the client involved, yet each has to be solidly founded in his own philosophy.

The Can Fabes restaurant refurbishment is a case in point. Not just a place to eat, this accolade to culinary delights includes a meeting place, a new kitchen, extended cellar, a lecture hall and hotel rooms above. The qualities which define the chef/client's success are the same that Rifé took as the starting point for his design. Just as the selection of the raw materials and their unsurpassable quality are the secrets of Santi Santamaria's dishes (natural and pure ingredients which he transforms

(Right)
Duplex Josefina Martí, Barcelona (2002) To compensate for a shortage of natural light, a palette of various shades of white and careful illumination have been used. The walls are in limestone and the custom-made furniture is shiny white MDF. The effect is one of elegance and serenity.

into innovative recipes), Rifé similarly distilled and interpreted the original stone and wood of the restaurant, adding a new cubic volume of limestone and steel. Inside and out had to be related not only to the old construction but also to the new one. The wood of natural oak is dyed to a darker tone, and the original wood and copper have been substituted by sheets of black iron protected with resins to transmit the idea of time advancing. The interior of the dining area is dominated by a laminated smoked box of reddish glass which denotes fire. All is pared down, the flavours intensified into a perfect reduction of style and elegance.

Francesc Rifé's character is as modest as his designs are understated. 'I have no particular goals and I will continue not to. I never thought I would be where I am and I prefer to continue working to try to continue being here.'

(Top left)
PBS offices, Barcelona (2004) The space has an open façade which allows natural light to flood in. Rifé has used a neutral palate of black and white to enhance the effect. The workbenches have an almost monastic feel and serve to draw the outer profile towards the interior.

(Below left)
Nuba restaurant, Barcelona (2004) The space has been opened up by the introduction of randomly placed lattice windows, and is divided into three areas by means of slatted wooden 'curtains'. This allows for extra privacy and helps with acoustics.

(Top right)
San Fabes restaurant, cellar, lecture hall and boutique hotel, Sant Celoni, Spain (2003) Rifé's design is inspired by the cooking skills of the owner/chef Santi Santamaria. He has mixed materials – masonry, stone and wood – to create a space dedicated to the art of good food. ...re is represented by using laminated, smoked red glass.

(Below right)
San Fabes The principal element in the restaurant is the staircase which leads to the basement cellar. Illumination is embedded into the ground. A large stone table with hidden black oak chairs is used by the sommelier for wine tasting.

(Left)
Duravit offices, Parets del Valles, Spain (2004)
The 7.2m-high (23.4ft) spiral staircase joins the ground floor, which house logistics and storage, to the attic which contains 1,000sq m (10,764sq) of offices. The overall effect of the design, both in spatial terms and the use of materials, is one of sobriety, balance and order.

(Right)
Duravit offices The conference room contrasts with the neutral black and oak surfaces of the office spaces. Green was used to connect the project with an earlier scheme for Duravit in Hamburg. Fluorescent lights snake across the plaster ceiling.

(Right)
**Parkhouse studio,
Barcelona (2005)** This
wooden flooring company
is housed in a long and
narrow space. Rifé has
created a tunnel with
hundreds of samples
forming an unique
collage of textures.

Ever since he made his name with the Planet Hollywood restaurants, David Rockwell has been known as the king of theatrical dining, yet it may be surprising to learn that these high-class eateries form just 20 per cent of his overall output. Founded in 1984, the New York-based practice employs around 160 staff and specializes in hospitality, cultural, healthcare, educational, theatre and film design. Crafting a unique and individual narrative concept for each project is fundamental to the Rockwell Group's successful design approach, whether it be for Nobu Fifty Seven, Terminal 5 at John F. Kennedy International Airport, the W Union Square Hotel, stage sets for the popular Broadway hits *Hairspray* and *Dirty Rotten Scoundrels* or the Children's Hospital at Montefiore in The Bronx.

'Our interior design leads to a strong conceptual design, which is defining a space with a narrative, be it a story of a culture or of an era, a festival, a geographic place, a temporary location or an emotion. We use craftsmanship, new and surprising materials and technology to further the idea. We combine the traditional architectural notions of procession, direction, function and style with non-traditional aspects of perceptual design.'

Rockwell's upbringing has had a major influence on his work. His childhood was one of transitions and impermanence. His father died when he was two and he was raised by his mother who was a touring vaudeville actress and later a choreographer at a community theatre in New Jersey, where David and his brothers also performed and worked on the sets. When he was nine his stepfather moved the family to Guadalajara in Mexico, where David was to remain for most of his teenage years. He returned to the States to study architecture at Syracuse University followed by postgraduate training at the Architectural Association in London and an internship with lighting designer and theatrical consultant Roger Morgan. 'The spectacle of colour, energy and surprise is something I try to create in my designs. My experiences on stage and my mother's theatrical background, as well as my time living in Guadalajara, being constantly surrounded by vibrant colours, people, markets, festivals and bullrings are particular memories that I kept with me throughout my studies, as well as in my current practice.'

The theatre, from Broadway and stage lighting to the work of Fritz Lang, Anton Furst and Boris Aronson, continues to inspire his designs, and his involvement with restaurant interiors (more like stage sets in their own right) allow him ample scope to be as innovative and experimental as he dares. 'Restaurants have been an incredible laboratory for us to try out ideas.' If you commission David Rockwell the result will certainly not be low-key.

Take, for example, the Rosa Mexicano's floor-to-ceiling translucent, blue-resin water-wall illuminated with strings of LEDs, or the vast glowing onyx mountain cut in facets the size of doors for Nobu Downtown, or the ceiling of the private upstairs room at Nobu Fifty Seven which is constructed from 107,000 sea urchin

(Right)
Nobu Fifty Seven, New York (2005) The inspiration is Japanese fishing villages with the ocean providing the pervasive theme. The terrazzo floor of the bar is patterned with ripples. The walnut bar top floats on onyx-like driftwood and the walls and columns are sheathed in timberstrand shingles as a reference to Japanese vernacular houses. The chandelier is made from abalone shells.

(Right)
W Union Square Hotel, New York (2000) The hotel is located in the early twentieth-century Guardian Life building. Rockwell recreated the glamour of the *beaux arts* period with a monumental staircase made from mahogany and steel which rises from the reception to the second-floor ballroom.

(Top far right)
Pod restaurant, Philadelphia (2000) Coloured lighting, organic curves and cutting-edge materials – moulded rubber, sculpted plastic and resin – give this Asian-fusion restaurant a futuristic aesthetic. The white epoxy walls and creamy concrete floor reflect the rainbow of light. The bar features a red polyurethane sculpture for lounging and ottomans that glow when sat on.

(Below far right)
The Children's Hospital at Montefiore (2001) Taking as inspiration his belief that sick children are 'explorers on a journey to healing', Rockwell has created an unintimidating interior that encourages curiosity, wonder and learning. Each floor has installations by individual artists which relate either to the treatment on that floor or the developmental level of the child.

shells, or the futuristic Kubrick-inspired interior of Pod, with its lozenge-shaped bar of transparent amber resin embedded with white neon lights. 'We attempt to create memorable spaces which people want to come back to again and again. To achieve this, we pursue an ambitious programme for each project. We create multiple styles relevant to many functions, not just one: hybrid design as opposed to purity, making the familiar unfamiliar.'

Since he first created Nobu Downtown in 1994, Rockwell's design approach has had a significant impact on the cultural and economic phenomenon which has come to be known as destination dining. However, his interiors are not without

their detractors. Loved by the populace but derided for what architectural purists call 'stagecraft', he is often criticized for his overblown theatrical experiments and his eschewal of modernist clean lines. But to do so is to miss the point. What Rockwell offers is not only a dining experience but also a form of escapism: 'I want to design spaces where people have the opportunity to lose themselves and enjoy the moment.'

The human factor is given a high priority. He works closely with his clients to understand their points of view and needs, but his prime concern is for the eventual user and the ritualistic social functions that these spaces allow them to perform.

(Top right)
JetBlue Terminal 5 at JFK, New York (2009)
The project includes way-finding graphics and a signage system to ensure efficiency. Circular information screens float overhead, while terraced seating areas allude to New York's brownstone stoops. The floor is kept clear by linking signage, platform seating and viewing areas on upward swirls of steel cables.

(Below right)
Chambers Hotel, New York (2001) Located on upper Fifth Avenue, known for fine art, fashion, literature and film, the lobby at Chambers has all the elegance and refinement of a private collector's home. Original works of art by young artists are displayed. The furniture and fittings are of an Ottoman inspiration and the fabrics, luxurious silks and velvets come from the neighbouring couture houses.

(Top right)
**Set of John Waters'
Hairspray, New York
and Seattle (2002)**
Rockwell has re-created
the humour of the original
1988 movie which follows
Tracy Turnblad's quest to
feature in a dance show
at her local TV station.
Television informs the
aesthetic with graphic
patterns and abstracted
forms, including a
suspended latticework of
microphone booms and
an LED wall of 610 circular
pegs, resembling a giant
piece of Lego.

(Below right)
**Kodak Theatre,
Hollywood and Highland
(2001)** Inspired by the
glamour and panache
of a Busby Berkeley
production, the home
of the Oscars features
balconies with surfaces
of cast glass, swirling
silver-leaf latticework, an
auditorium which can seat
a maximum of 3,300 and
a hydraulic-driven media
cockpit in the centre of
the orchestra.

Fernando Salas

Fernando Salas was born in 1950 in Santa Cruz de Mudela, Ciudad Real, Spain. His father worked on the railways and the family moved to Andalucía and Barcelona as his career progressed. Salas' childhood was a mixture of influences from the wild countryside of the south of Spain to the Barrio of Barcelona. He had a natural talent for draughtsmanship and the luck to be noticed by an observant high school teacher who recognized his potential and guided him in the right direction.

Salas had no formal architectural training, serving an apprenticeship from the age of 14 with MBM Architects under Oriol Bohigas, José María Martorell and David Mackay. He opened his own company, Salas Studio, in 1975, since when he has built up an international reputation for his atmospheric, simple and down-to-earth designs, making him the leading interior architect working in Spain today.

He has completed a number of commercial, retail, hospitality and restaurant designs, including fashion boutiques (Ekseption, Torremolinos; Zastwo, Barcelona and Zas, Barcelona), franchises (Robert Verino, Love Store and Custo), offices (Silver Sanz, Barcelona; Barcelona Empren and Twenti showroom and office, Barcelona), bars, restaurants and hotels in collaboration with Javier Mariscal (Calle 54, Madrid; Ikea restaurant, Vitoria; Domina Hotel, Bilbao, and a floor in the Hotel Puerta América, Madrid). The occasional collaboration between Mariscal and Salas combines their experience: Mariscal's creative, fresh art and Salas' interior-design experience. The result is a creative boiling pot, which combines the passions of both of them and produces some very special results

Salas' influences are varied: his love of Bauhaus which he considers the 'father' of modern architecture; his respect for the Mediterranean vernacular which creates spaces specific to the geographic and climatic needs of the user; the functionalism of the 1950s – architecture which liberated Spain from the 'grey, boring and formal architecture of Franco's rule, but above all his love and respect for nature which he says is fundamental to his work, instructing as it does his choice of colours, textures, atmosphere and aesthetics.

Salas believes that architecture should be intuitive and not be too concerned with stylistic artifice. 'A plastic result can be achieved without being opportunistic. An interior can be beautiful without having a signature style. An intrinsic sublime value can be created by harnessing, for example, natural light, using it to add brilliance and texture. We have a wealth of "materials" in sensation and experiences which we should employ to come up with a solution which will work well for the end user.

Natural comfort is important. Often these days architecture has become too modified and has lost touch with the human element. For example, the climatic elements of a building are often missing; the consideration of air currents and the aroma that a gardenia from the back porch might give to the interior of your house. The Romans and the Arabs had this sensibility and knew how to live. I think it is important to re-learn some of these basic qualities. Sometimes I feel that

(Right)
Hotel Domina (in collaboration with Javier Mariscal), Bilbao (2002) The interior of the hotel is a gathering of different styles. The main atrium is dominated by a giant sculpture of stones.

(Right)

Hotel Puerta América (in collaboration with Javier Mariscal) Madrid (2005) Eighteen architects and designers were invited to create inspirational spaces. Salas' floor takes its theme from the functionalism of the 1950s. The rooms are designed to look long, the view over the city reinforcing the deception.

(Below left)

Silver Sanz offices, Barcelona (1993) The construction of the stairway is made from one single piece of metal covered in the same marble as the floor. The concept for the interior was to be as simple as possible without showing excessive design intervention.

architects have the wrong sense of progress and have lost the knowledge of what "proper" architecture is all about.'

Salas' design is understated. He does not intervene unnecessarily and has lost projects because for some his work is over-simple. 'Clients have told me this is very poor in the sense that it is lacking or missing something that appears to make it plain. I don't feel my approach has changed much from the start of my career. I keep fresh by exploring the properties of new materials, but the way of understanding things is still the same – sincere and first-hand. I don't put cherries on top. If you make a great cake, why decorate it?'

Proof of his success, however, has come in countless citations and awards, including many FAD prizes, the latest given in 2005 for the interior of the Formica restaurant in Barcelona. Peer recognition is important to Salas. 'It means so much to me as I work and have created a style, an attitude which has remained coherent for the last 35 years. It is important to be given the reassurance that I haven't been wrong and that I haven't been making stabs in the dark.'

As well as architecture, Salas is active in exhibition and graphic design. He paints, and recently held an exhibition of his own photographs. His current projects include a series of warehouses for wine merchants Ribera del Duero, and hotels in southern Spain and in Canada.

(Top)
Calle 54, Madrid (in collaboration with Javier Mariscal) (2002) A thematic restaurant inspired by the world of Latin music. The idea was to create a dark, authentic space with references from the streets of Havana. The floor and bar is in black granite. The space is dominated by a graphic mural showcasing the names of famous jazz artistes.

(Below)
Custo, Barcelona (2001) Located in an historic building, the interior is lined with light and transparent materials (aluminium, transparent glass and methacrylate) to emphasize the products.

(Opposite page)
Restaurant Ikea, Vitoria (2005) Not to be confused with the Swedish brand, *ikea* in Spanish means small hill. The restaurant was conceived as a small country house surrounded by oak and beech trees. Salas brought the forest inside, using natural woods for the floor and a branch-like wooden construction on the ceiling which allows artificial light to filter through.

Office design has changed dramatically over the past ten years. A technological revolution which has seen the rise of the Internet, and wireless communication has resulted in a mobile workforce no longer tied to the bland office interiors of the past: those globalized spaces where everything was the same from the colour of the carpet to the design of the furniture and the standardized size of an office for a particular grade of worker. Today's workforce is team-based, knowledge-driven, community-orientated, mobile and self-deterministic, and the spaces in which it works are changing to reflect this trend.

Sevil Peach Gence Associates was founded in 1994 by the Turkish-born interior designer Sevil Peach and the architect Gary Turnbull who met during their time at YRM Architects, where they worked as design director of interiors and associate/project director respectively. Their practice is multidisciplinary and has completed a variety of projects both in the United Kingdom and abroad. Although they have gained a wide range of experience in retail, healthcare, exhibition and residential design, they are best associated with their cutting-edge workplace design and have built up an impressive list of clients: Barclays, Sony, Mexx, Novartis and, most significantly, Vitra, for whom they completed the refurbishment of the existing offices within one of the factory buildings designed by Nicolas Grimshaw in Weil am Rhein in 1997. This groundbreaking project launched SPGA on the path to being recognized as one of the leading architectural companies exploring the new ways we work today. Their office interiors go beyond the expected, creating new questions and different ways of looking at new working patterns and relationships.

Being multidisciplinary means that they draw together architecture and interior design in a seamless fashion. 'Our buildings provide exciting and usable interior spaces. Our interiors are informed by and respect the buildings they inhabit.' For Peach, Turnbull and their team there are three key approaches that will result in an innovative yet timeless design: the rational (does it make sense?), the emotional (does it feel right?) and the strategic (will it function and result in better business?). They believe in conceiving what they refer to as a holistic environment that will be comfortable, inspirational and motivational for the people working there.

Their interiors manipulate form, volume, colour and light with close attention to detail and materials, and are informed by a thorough understanding of technological innovation. They employ devices to create spaces which reduce the stress of the workplace which are increasingly governed by the speed of new technologies and also the demands of 24/7 working methods. 'Work is a matrix of friendships and social interactions; to work efficiently, we need interaction, communication and collaboration.' SPGA recognizes that there is no longer one way of working and that an interior should recognize and reflect that people work in different ways during different parts of the

Sevil Peach Gence Associates

(Left)
Vitra, Weil am Rhein, Germany (1997)
SPGA was asked to design an open-plan office which would encourage interaction and teamwork, changing methods of work as well as reflect Vitra's brand, showing its furniture in a real working installation.

(Below)
Vitra Throughout the floor, users can enjoy both views to the outside across the internal 'terrace' (seen on the right), as well as a variety of interior vistas. The open plan is broken down into human scale and intimate work areas by the use of movable canvas-wrapped panels.

(Top right)
Novartis Pharma pilot office, Basel (2003) The commission was to create a 'campus of knowledge' which challenged cellular office culture. The area is compartmentalized into intimate work areas centred around a range of shared support facilities. To the rear is the communal workbench and in the foreground a break-out area for informal gatherings.

(Below right).
Novartis Pharma office, Basel (2005) Commissioned after the success of the pilot scheme, SPGA worked on the interiors of the Diener+Diener new building. The ground floor is designed as a fluid space and houses the lounge, restaurant, enclosed meeting and presentation rooms as well as concentration rooms.

(Far right)
MEXX International Design Centre, Amsterdam (2004) SPGA softened the interiors of the former 1990s Nissan European headquarters to be more suitable for a creative fashion business. Office areas are connected to an indoor 'garden', running the length of the atrium which has visitor seating, product-display, coffee-point, Internet and relaxation areas.

day: singular work, concentrated work, relaxed work, formal interaction and communicative group work.

SPGA includes architects, interior designers, historians, artists, and theatre and product designers but they consider themselves 'Designers' with a capital D. 'I think we are quite clear in our definition: we see design as a problem-solving discipline. We "design" together to create environments, buildings, interiors, exhibitions, ways of working. We respond creatively to challenges, human and environmental.'

The company considers its key success and greatest limitation to be one and the same – the conscious decision to keep the practice small. Although this means they are frequently turning down work, it also means that they have a more intense and

personal relationship with their clients. An important word for Sevil Peach is 'dialogue' – connectivity with their clients, colleagues, consultants and contractors is the starting point for any project. It's only through listening to what the client needs, how the office is run, and what the workforce demands from its office environment that the partners can begin to get an idea of the concept for the design. 'The work and the clients inspire us to do what we do. We always seek to establish a close personal working relationship with our clients as well as with all members of the design and construction team. At the heart of our working process is dialogue. Throughout each project we are open to discussion and explore all possibilities to achieve the best and most appropriate solutions.'

(left)
Hilarion House, Girne, Northern Cyprus (2002)
Shielded and screened openings give a variety of framed and open views, and provide diffused daylight throughout.

(top right)
Workplace, London (2001) A concept office exhibition stand which explores the issue and nature of 'a working day', drawing on our experience of the changing nature of work culture and life at work. Lifestyle components are introduced to make the user feel comfortable about blurring the boundaries between work, rest and play.

(below right)
Euroshop, exhibition stand for Vitrashop Group, Düsseldorf (2002)
Zona, the design branch of Vitrashop, show a range of retail design concepts. The 'visions' (transparent, organized, glowing, floating, horizontal, playful, curved, mobile, etc) took on their unique identities using fluctuating shapes, various materials and different colours.

Shubin + Donaldson

Robin Donaldson received a bachelor of arts degree in art and art history with an architectural history emphasis from the University of California at Santa Barbara, and his masters in architecture from the Southern California Institute of Architecture (SCI-Arc). He studied with Thom Mayne and Michael Rotondi but, more importantly, worked for Morphosis (see page 198) during his period at SCI-Arc, which absolutely informs the work of the practice. From them he learned never to accept the status quo with regards to design. His partner Russell Shubin graduated from California Polytechnic in San Luis Obispo, where he was taught a process-driven design approach with an emphasis on learning through experience, and studied at L'Ecole de'Art et d'Architecture at Fontainbleau, France. They founded their architecture firm in 1990 and now have offices in Culver City and Santa Barbara.

Shubin + Donaldson work across the board, specializing in residential and commercial architecture, stores and community buildings but they have built up a worldwide reputation as the leading interior designer of offices for creative production companies. They count

(Right)
Ogilvy & Mather Advertising, Los Angeles (2000) 'The Tube' dominates the entrance to the offices, at the end of which is a gigantic portrait of the company's founder.

(Left)
Brand New School, Santa Monica, USA (2005) The space had to reflect the company's informal style and personality. The result is a building within a building. A tightly planned interior construction containing open and closed spaces sits inside the high aluminium ceilings and concrete flooring of the original shell.

amongst their clients The Firm (a talent-management company so hot that its phone number is unlisted); the highly successful production company Brand New School; Ground Zero, a young band of high-profile advertisers; and Ogilvy & Mather, the Culver City-based, internationally known heavyweight advertising company. Eager to impress and stamp their corporate culture in the competitive worlds of media and advertising, clients such as these give the duo the opportunity to work on wonderfully cool and experimental concepts, often, but not always with spectacular budgets.

These 'youth-led' firms often work in a very flexible, anti-hierarchical way. Blurring the boundaries between home and the office they want amenities such as kitchen, recreation areas, break-out spaces, and even rooms for showering and sleeping, to be designed with what Shubin + Donaldson refer to as a 'hipness quotient'.

The results are dynamic interiors which seem to owe more to science fiction or *film noir* stage sets than they do to the wood-panelled boardrooms we associate with the world of American corporations. With a directness and honesty in the choice of simple materials which are employed in innovative ways (bamboo flooring hung vertically, off-the-shelf structural pieces selected to pattern and direct space, or insulation materials adapted for aesthetic usage), these avant-garde, bold, sharp, angular, masculine and dramatically lit spaces take design to the edge but never slip into parody. Many of the projects share a similar aesthetic: skeletal frames, translucent skins and raw materials which reflect the less permanent, fashionable, technology-led culture of the companies which employ the duo.

Such a specialized field demands a different design approach. Instead of working in the traditional way of programming, schematic design and design development, Shubin + Donaldson add what they call a 'portrait', or 'concept visualization' of the company concerned.

Shubin + Donaldson

Once Shubin + Donaldson have established the character of the client, they create a digital, as-built 3-D context model of the space, generating imagery to explore spatial organizations, ordering or disordering constructions and graphics which are consistent with the company's vision. It is only after this process that the architects concentrate on functional concerns. Although it is obviously important to keep in sight the fact that no matter how 'trendy' the concept the interiors must work efficiently and effectively for the client, the primary concern in the early stages is to create an image that will successfully reflect and promote the client's business.

The project of which Shubin + Donaldson are most proud (and it's certainly the most publicized), is Ogilvy & Mather's Los Angeles headquarters. They were chosen as the architects over impressive competition such as Gensler, precisely because the long-established

'blue-suit' advertising company knew S+D could provide the new identity it desired. The office areas are separated from the glazed exterior by a large, perforated aluminium entrance tube which resembles the stranded fuselage of a jet engine. With its LCD display screens programmed to greet guests with images of the company's work, it leads the visitor into the heart of the building, bypassing a 4.9m-high (16ft) dividing wall made of 1.23m x 1.23m (4ft x 4ft) acrylic plates that sport Scotchprint super-graphics of quotes by the company's founder ('We sell or else' … 'We sell or get fired') whose large face takes up half the glass wall.

For Shubin + Donaldson, interior architecture is not just a functional means to an end but is used as a communication tool to promote not only clients' business but their very identity. From the first glimpse you know that you are going to get exactly what's on the packet.

Philippe Starck

What could I possibly write about Philippe Starck that has not been written a hundred times before? To the person in the street, the world of architecture and design barely exists, in so much as he or she would be hard-pressed to name more than a handful of architects – and even fewer designers. The exception is Philippe Starck. The *enfant terrible* of design, whose personality as well as his much-publicized prolific output has guaranteed him rock-star status, he is the most celebrated and commercially successful designer in the world.

Written by the journalist Ed Mae Copper, the biography posted on Starck's website is eulogistic. Describing Starck's childhood as one spent making his own objects and dismantling others under his father's drawing boards (his father was an aircraft designer), it continues: 'Several years and several prototypes later, the Italians have made him responsible for our furniture, President Mitterand asked him to change life at the Elysées Palace, the Café Costes has become Le Café, he has turned the Royalton and Paramount in New York into the new classics of the hotel world, and has scattered Japan with architectural *tours de force* that have made him the leading exponent of expressionist architecture.'

Philippe Starck was born in Paris in 1949. He studied there at the École Nissim de Camondo and set up his first company producing inflatable objects in 1968. A year later he became the artistic director of Pierre Cardin. Having spent a period in America, he returned to Paris in 1978,

founded Starck Product in 1979 and designed his first nightclub, Le Main Bleu. From that point his rise to fame was expediential. His portfolio encompasses major architectural projects (from commercial buildings in France, Japan and the USA, to private residences – including a whole street block, La Rue Starck – to an air-traffic control tower in Bordeaux), interiors of unparalleled louche luxury (from the string of hotels he has created for Ian Schrager to boutiques for Jean Paul Gaultier, shops for Taschen, the Maison Baccarat in Paris and the Yoo apartments throughout the world), as well as mass-produced, playful, sometimes just absurd consumer goods (toothbrushes, chairs, the emotionally charged electronics for Thomson Multimedia, kit-houses and, more recently, the gold-plated Kalachnikov lamps manufactured by Flos).

Yet one senses today that maybe the tide is turning for Starck.

Writing for *Metropolis* in March 2006, Philip Nobel refers to a 'Y2K crisis *chez* Starck, marking a moment of high ambition and higher insanity from a designer well known for both'. Quoting the Yoo condominiums, the design-for-everyone range of products for Target, and the plans for a spaceport in New Mexico for Richard Branson, Nobel sees a watering down in Starck's recent work and a concurrent attempt by the designer to claw back some of the 'bad-boy street cred that his success – and that of the designers he inspired – had helped to sap from his image'.

There is an element of truth in what Nobel writes, but it is not the whole story.

(Right)
Bon restaurant, Moscow (2006)
The concept behind the Moscow example of the Bon chain was to create a world of luxurious chaos. There are no regular shapes, with tables of different sizes placed in the main hall alongside missmatching chairs; carpets and finishes have negative images; gilded armchairs are half-burned and stools and side-tables are in the form of car-tyre casings. The Limoges ware, cut-glass tableware and silver service were all custom-made for the venue and are placed on the table in total disarray.

(Top right)
Kong restaurant, Paris (2003) Located on top of the Kenzo headquarters, the brief was to link East and West: chic with traditional. Holograms on the back of the chairs in the penthouse restaurant mix the geisha with modern-day trendy Japanese women and European models.

(Below right)
Maison Baccarat, Paris (2003) The custom-made crystal table in the transparent room is 128m (420ft) long and is used to display glassware. Starck's design for the flagship store gives the 240-year old company a new image while respecting the interiors of the eighteenth-century mansion.

(Top right)
Purple bar, Sanderson Hotel (2000) A private sanctuary in the heart of the hotel (owned by Ian Schrager), the bar is a baroque candle-lit cave-like space contrasting highly decorative Venetian etched glass with the rough rock surface of the front of the bar. The area is soundproofed and subdued, and can only be used by residents and VIPs. Light is directed away from the users towards the glittering array of bottles reflected in the glass.

(Below right)
Theatron, Mexico City (1995) This theatrical nightclub is situated in the basement of Mexico City's National Auditorium. The giant staircase gets narrower and steeper as it leads up to an illuminated bar. A distorted and hugely enlarged Richard Avedon photograph – 9m x 12m (30ft x 39ft) – entitled *Killing Joe Piro* dominates the space and adds to the rather disturbing surreal atmosphere.

Philippe Starck

(Above left)

Jean-Paul Gaultier Store Boutique, Paris (2002)
The *enfant terrible* of fashion meets the *enfant terrible* of design. The boutique offers an architectural portrait of Philippe Starck with irony, elegance and surprise; a dreamlike, sophisticated setting for the latest Gaultier collections.

In a lecture given by Starck at the Lisbon Experimenta Design Festival in 2005, it seems that the answer lies in a more deep-rooted sense of self-doubt, in the role of design and the designer in today's society: 'Design is useless. I'm ashamed of being a designer. Three or four years ago I gave my company to the people who work for me. I want to be less involved. I am no longer interested in architects or designers and I no longer want to talk about design … I never stop producing but you might say I produce out of sheer idleness. I design in seconds, in spare moments. I'm a Faust-like character, selling my soul to the devil: a hotel takes one and a half days, a boat an afternoon, and a product five minutes. The only solid thing in life is relationships between people and the vibration caused by a look. Quantum physics expounds that nothing really exists – atoms, time and images. In that case, do we actually *need* anything? I continue to work for my ego, for money and fun, but there is no real reason.'

Of course this could be one of the outbursts to which Nobel refers, but I think it would be more generous to interpret it as genuine questioning by a man used to being treated as a demigod in the small universe that is the fashion-led design world of today.

The future for Starck lies in the democratization of design. 'Design was about elitism; my duty now is to duplicate it and give as many people as possible a share in the idea.'

(Above right)

Taschen Bookshop, Paris (2000)
Benedikt Taschen has been quoted as saying that Starck does with design what Taschen does with books. 'I love Taschen. He invented completely democratic publishing' says Philippe Starck. 'For me, Taschen is political'. Starck has used bronze surfaces, theatrical lighting, as well as exotic woods and customized furniture, to create a spacious and luminous theatrical stage setting against which to display Taschen's stunning coffee table art, design and photography books.

(Above)
Clift hotel, San Francisco (2003) Starck plays with scale and the surreal in the reception of the Ian Schrager hotel, which is furnished with an array of eclectic and strange objects, including the outsized Italianesque bronze and gilt chair which alludes to the hotel's past, a once glamorous hotel in the Italian Renaissance style.

Seth Stein

Seth Stein was born in New York in 1959. He graduated from the Architectural Association in London and worked for both Richard Rogers and Norman Foster before founding his eponymous small design-led practice in Notting Hill in 1989.

He is greatly influenced by the works of the architect Luis Barragán who re-invented the International Style with his sensuous use of colour and his mastery of space and light. By adopting vivid colourful highlights, textural contrasts, the artful employment of light and water, and accentuating his buildings' surroundings, Barragán brought some of the warmth and vibrancy of his native Mexico into his work. Often referred to in the same breath as John Pawson or Claudio Silvestrin as one of the UK's leading modernists, Stein prefers to look on his work as purist rather than minimalist. 'I'm constantly develop-ing my own philosophy, playing with textures and materials and contrasting modern, very technical features with natural elements. For example, glass installations/staircases placed next to sand-blasted oak, and pared-back walls enlivened with sheets of colour.'

The majority of Stein's work is domestic, including new-build and reconstructed houses in the UK, South Africa, Canada, the Caribbean, a recent refurbishment of an Italian town villa in Vincenza, and a house off the coast of Finland. Although personally Stein would prefer to live in a white box, he recognizes that he has to work with families and, therefore, has to take a more practical and holistic approach.

'With my residential projects I am more than just an architect; I'm somehow a kind of architectural therapist. I work with my clients on a very personal level, taking into consideration not only the physical aspects but also the psychological: examining and reflecting on how they live their life, how they would like to live their life and what got them to the stage where they were able to commission such a project.'

Stein's domestic interiors, although incredibly refined and elegant, do not come with a set of rules for their inhabit-ants, as Philip Nobel, writing about the Toronto house, succinctly sums up: 'They are not temples to an idealized lifestyle … [but] part of that other modern tradition: homes that embrace contemporary forms, materials and effects but do not impose impossible codes of conduct. The house encompasses robust space that suits every hue on the domestic spectrum, from contemplation to rowdy play.'

(Right)
Summer house, Helsinki Archipelago, Finland (2000) The layout is basic: the kitchen and fireplace in the centre, the living room with full-height glass wall facing south, and the bedroom facing east to catch the morning sun. Twelve photo-voltaic panels provide the energy for the house. The materials were sourced locally, prefabricated in neighbouring workshops during the winter months, transported and erected during the summer.

(Left)
Car-lift house, London (1996) The brief required flexible accommodation to be provided for either living or car parking. The lower deck of the lift is clad in acrylic panels that bring natural daylight into the depth of the house, activating the lift base as living accommodation. A continuous flight of glass stairs connects the three floor levels.

(Far left)
House in Toronto (2000)
From the street the setting
is suburban while the
rear opens up to face a
forest ravine. The plan is
conceived as a cluster of
individual houses linked
by a double-height, top-
glazed communal space.
Adjustable aluminium
louvres modulate daylight
within the living areas,
washing the interior
spaces with zebra
stripes of light.

(Top left)
**House in Vincenza, Italy
(2004)** The restoration
and reconstruction of an
early nineteenth-century
palazzetto, the site is
narrow and deep and
the space is moulded
by light.

(Below left)
**Baltic Restaurant,
London (2001)** Located
within an early nineteenth-
century building consisting
of a large shed dominated
by substantial exposed
timber trusses, the main
dining area is flooded
with light from above and
retains remnants of the
original building which
add colour and texture.
The amber fibre-optic light
installation is a reference
to the materials found in
the northern seas.

(Right)
S J Berwin solicitors' offices, City of London (2006) One of London's most enviable workplaces, according to the capital's top listings magazine *Time Out*, the Berwin office is located in a 1980s speculative building overlooking the River Thames at Southwark Bridge. Working in association with HOK International and John Robertson Architects, Stein designed the office environment housing 1,500 staff as a series of cellular offices, meeting rooms, accessible libraries and break out spaces. The strategic use of coloured glass insertions transform the quality and the flexibility of the space.

(Far right)
Kensington home, London (1995) Seth Stein's London home is located in a former Victorian stable which later became a builders' yard before falling into disrepair. The site consisted of a series of buildings and outbuildings which Stein transformed into a light and airy house based on a courtyard plan, by the addition of a new entry structure and glass gallery.

The two projects which brought Stein fame were his own much publicized house in Kensington and the car-lift house in Knightsbridge, both completed in the mid-1990s and both highlighting some of the main themes which run through his work. They took inspiration from their sites: the former spreading itself over the foot-print of a Victorian stable yard, the latter extracted from the smallest-possible parcel of land – a 6m (20ft) wide and 8m (26ft) deep plot at the end of a mews. They both continue exterior into interior, are studied exercises in volumetric juggling, and manipulate light by playing with reflection and transparency. But there the comparison stops.

Stein's house is essentially modernist in spirit but interwoven with a respect and retention of original architectural features which anchor it strongly with its original usage. A series of interlocking spaces, it is centred around a number of courtyards with water features (owing a debt to Barragán). Light falls into the building from numerous strategically placed apertures.

Having worked in the offices of both Rogers and Foster, the technical innovation of the car-lift house comes as no surprise. A small pied-à-terre for a car collector,

Stein has taken the technology used for parking cars in a city garage – the car lift – to turn parking space into living space and vice versa, creating an interior which changes as living patterns evolve. When empty and raised, the two-storied hydraulic lift provides a ground-floor room, with a translucent floor, next to the entrance, and a basement-level living room with a translucent ceiling. When occupied and lowered, the owner's classic cars 'occupy' the interior space but become part of the decoration. Transparent stairs, floors and walls allow light throughout the building, giving a greater illusion of space.

Currently Stein is moving away from the domestic arena, concentrating on more new-build and large-scale challenging projects as he does not wish to be branded a fashionable architect. Completed projects include new offices for the London law firm S J Berwin, as well as the restoration of the courtyard stables at Harewood House, Yorkshire. He is currently working on a government-funded drop-in centre for homeless women in East London for the charity U-Turn, and a London showroom for furniture manufacturer Wilkhahn.

Tarruella and López

Sandra Tarruella and Isabel López studied interior design in Barcelona at the Escuela Diac and Escuela Elisava, respectively. They met when they were both working with the Spanish architect Pepe Cortés, leaving to found their own interior-design company in 1992. Prior to joining Cortés, Tarruella had collaborated with various practices and gained experience working on the designs of retail and restaurant interiors while López had worked in design administration, first with the ARQ-INFAD board and later as organizer and member of the jury for Habitàcola in 1988.

They both look on their time with Cortés as fundamental to their present careers. From him they learned much of their technical know-how and also managed to build up powerful connections, most notably with the Grupo Traguluz for which they have subsequently completed numerous restaurant designs, including El Japonés, which secured their position as one of Spain's most exciting young interior-design outfits. Most importantly, however, from the moment they started to work together they knew that it was a relationship which would endure. Their personalities complement each other perfectly. Tarruella is holistic in her approach, while López is a perfectionist, and they look on their partnership as a 'third person' who combines their best attributes.

Although the duo has worked on retail, hotel and domestic interiors, the majority of the work they undertake is in the design of restaurants, a fact Tarruella and López attribute to the economic slowdown experienced by Barcelona after the Olympics, during which a lot of building work was put on hold except, apparently, places to eat. The Spanish are well-known for dining out regularly. Tarruella and López's experience and success was built up on the back of this trend and continues to play a part in the commissions they undertake today.

They quote four rules for the successful design of a restaurant. First and foremost is that the food should remain the star of the show; neither the interior design nor anything else should overshadow it. Secondly, the acoustics are as important as the aesthetics. Thirdly, the local vernacular should be respected. And lastly, as the space is devoted to enjoyment, all the senses should be engaged: hearing, touch, smell, sight and taste. Their designs are therefore adapted to suit the menu, clientele and location of each restaurant and are rich in reference, with a strong emphasis given to details and surface finish. Acoustics can direct the types of materials they use, and they never hang pictures in their interiors as they believe that the space itself should act as an artistic centrepiece.

Tarruella and López's style is elegant, colourful and sensuous yet essentially modest and restrained. Although they are happy to go along with the fact that they have been described as minimal, they do not believe that purity of aesthetics should get in the way of functionality or comfort. Their interiors are warm and appeal to the senses largely through their use of a fine balance of different materials, never over-

(Top)
Cuines Santa Caterina, Barcelona (2005)
The idea was to create a space where different cuisines meet different cultures. Using simple and natural materials – stoneware, marble, wood and non-treated metal – the aesthetic is one of the marketplace with all the products on view. The plants represent a vegetable patch, giving the idea of natural, fresh produce.

(Below)
Restaurant Bestial, Barcelona (2002)
The main access to the restaurant is via a big glass window by artist Frédéric Amat. The dining area and bar are two separate volumes connected to the entrance hall. The ceiling is made of wood and acoustic material which comfortably soundproofs the space.

(Top)
Restaurant Negro Rojo, Barcelona (2005) The restaurant, located in the basement of the two-floor 672m (2,184ft) space, serves oriental food. The use of red metal mesh iron plates and iroke wood creates a feeling of the east.

(Below)
Vialis shoe shop, Madrid (2005) Because of its small size, 22sq m (237sq ft), the idea was to create a showcase shop. Four main contrasting materials have been used: Cor-ten steel, back lighting, tightened PVC and solid oak continuous flooring. White is the predominant colour, and the rest of the materials show their natural colours and textures.

using one above another. They are no strangers to decoration and they frown at those who look on it pejoratively or underestimate its importance. To be able to integrate finishes and decorative elements successfully requires intuition, vision and the ability to imagine an interior as it will be perceived by the user.

'It is a point of view, shared by many, that decoration is only an addition or surface intervention. This way of thinking can be repressive and limits the intention to go further than what is simply correct. A house is lived in and a deep relationship is established with it, but a commercial space – a restaurant or a hotel – is visited with a certain, clear intention. It is important to transmit sensations and give importance to the superficial without dropping into the superfluous.'

(Top)
Mercats de la Mediterrània exhibition, Barcelona (2003)
Mirror, glass and virtual images create an idea of movement and lively activity. Music and smells complete the order and chaos of a Mediterranean market.

(Below)
Restaurant El Japonés, Barcelona (1999) The key to the project was to provide an oriental aesthetic reinterpreted through an occidental one. Straight lines and basic volume create a zen-like atmosphere. The materials are all sourced in the West but chosen for their Japanese connotations.

(Above)
Santa Margarita house, Mallorca (2001) The use of a minimum range of elemental materials (concrete, glass and wood) emphasizes the basic geometric volumes of the space, creating an austere atmosphere. Only what is absolutely necessary is added. The furniture is monumental, linking the interior to the scale of the exterior.

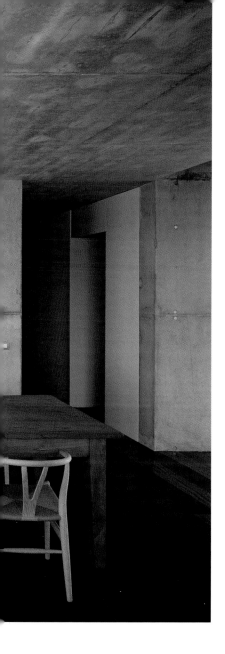

(Above)
**Hotel Omm, Barcelona
(2003)** The project is
based on simplicity of
line, colour balance,
volume, texture and the
use of materials with no
adornment or artifices.
The entire ground floor
is a restaurant which
also acts as the hotel
reception, alleviating the
normal boredom of hotel
vestibules, and creating
a meeting space for the
people of Barcelona.

Adam D. Tihany

Adam D. Tihany distinguishes his design approach as 'singular and original thinking with attention to every little detail and quality of execution'. Architecture for Tihany is a little-understood profession which profoundly affects the way we live. His interiors take as a starting point the building itself: 'How does the space work? How can I shape movement in the space? How do the architectural proportions feel?' Once he has settled on an appropriate space plan, it is only then that the interior design begins.

He graduated from the Politecnico di Milano in the late 1960s at a time when the student movement and revolt had more or less made the academic part of his curriculum obsolete, and maintains that, like the apprentices of the sixteenth and seventeenth centuries, he learned his profession by working in various architec-

tural and design studios assisting trained and experienced architects.

Tihany was born in Transylvania in 1948, raised in Israel, educated in Italy, trained throughout Europe and then moved to New York in 1976. Two years later he founded his own multidisciplinary studio which today encompasses all aspects of design, from commercial and residential interior architecture to furniture, products, exhibitions and graphics. He is considered the pre-eminent hospitality designer, with a string of famous restaurants and hotels to his name including the Bice and Spago restaurants worldwide; Le Cirque in New York; the Aleph Hotel in Rome; the Mandarin Bar at the Mandarin Oriental Hyde Park, London; hotels in Rome and Prague for the Boscolo chain; The Dan Eilat Hotel and Resort in Israel; The Per Se at the Time Warner Center in New York; and the Bouchon at the Venetian hotel in Las Vegas, as well as the futuristic Bar Teatro at Las Vegas' MGM. As a bit of a departure (no pun intended) he has recently completed Hanger One, the $29m private aviation club in Scottsdale, Arizona.

Tihany would argue that he does not have a signature style, yet all his projects share a sense of theatricality, spontaneity, exuberance and surprise, using luxurious materials, fittings and furnishings in a sensual, contemporary way. He does not have a fixed formula, preferring instead to explore new forms, new materials and innovative technology. His prime concern is that his interiors should be multidimensional, 'never two-dimensional or surface-deep'. His work is timeless,

(Right)
The Library Lounge, Blue Heaven Radisson SAS Hotel, Frankfurt (2005) A sense of fluidity is created by using architectural features and furnishings instead of dividing walls to define different areas within the hotel. Narrow-beamed stainless-steel chandeliers enclose the library lounge, which contains platform seating and laptop plug-in facilities.

(Left)
The Members' Lobby at Hanger One, Scottsdale, Arizona (2003) The architectural language Tihany employed was chosen to reflect the exhilaration and 'techno-focused accoutrements' of flying.

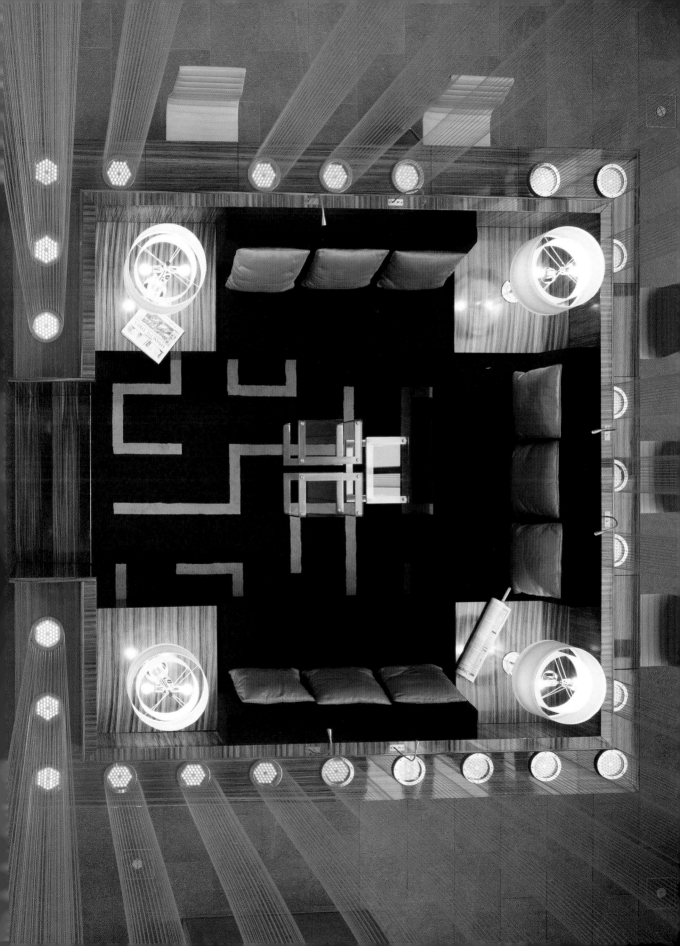

which he hopes will add to the longevity of his hotels and restaurants: interiors for an industry acknowledged to be one of the most fickle.

Well known for the holistic approach he brings to his interiors, Tihany is in charge of every aspect of the design, from the architecture and interiors to the graphics, furniture and tableware. It seems that the only thing he is not in charge of is the cooking (although he has written a cookbook, *Venetian Taste*, with chef and co-owner of his New York restaurant, Remi).

A key word for Tihany is 'connectivity'. He only takes on projects he knows he will enjoy and he has to feel strongly connected to a project, whether it is in the understanding of the concept, a rapport for the space and how it will affect the future design, or a thorough understanding of the demographics involved. He is a great advocator of site-specific design. For him, a successful restaurant designer should have a sound knowledge of, and a desire to integrate, 'social norms, local mores and ethnic or regional traditions into the overall design scheme … the customer should be able to feel the rhythm of the city.'

His starting point is always the hotelier, restaurateur or chef who commissions the work. 'I design portraits of my clients, and the portraits are as diverse as the personalities.' Tihany's strength is that he has the ability to extract from his clients exactly what they want. He collaborates rather then dictates. He has even been known to ask a chef to cook for him as, from the way a dish is put together and presented, he feels he can deduce how the restaurant should look. Thomas Keller, the owner of Per Se, writes in the Tihany monograph, *Tihany Style*, 'He helps lead you to those right choices, without losing sight of your overall vision. I think one of Adam's great abilities is to realize the image you have in your mind in reality.'

Adam D. Tihany's goal is to design the best hotel or restaurant (or both) in every great city in the world. As he says, 'You can imagine I still have a lot to do…'.

(Top right)
The dining room at the Per Se restaurant and bar, Time Warner Center, New York (2004) The design concept is built around the personality of the owner/chef Thomas Keller. It is a study of contrasts, featuring a wealth of natural materials enriched by customized fabrics and finishes in a soothing palette. Floor to ceiling torchères are an unusual lighting feature.

(Below right)
The Wine Tower at the Aureole Hotel and casino in Las Vegas (1999) Tihany is known for his sense of fun. The Wine Tower was inspired by the image of Tom Cruise suspended mid-air on cables in *Mission Impossible* (the wine-angels fly up and down the tower to retrieve the wine), New York skyscrapers and the huge towering bulk of the Aureole's chef, Charlie Palmer.

(Top left)
The Jade restaurant at the Pudong Shangri-la Hotel, Shanghai 2005.
References to the regal past of the Ming dynasties litter the restaurant. Here giant back-lit interpretations of miniature glass perfume bottles set in the ebony wood wall panels act as stunning lighting accents.

(Below left)
The Line ultra-modern all-day-dining area at the Shangri-la Hotel, Singapore (2005)
Ten different dining experiences from dim sum to Italian are unified by a series of glowing orange boxes travelling throughout the whole space. The four forces of nature are represented by varying finishes and colours: white=air, orange/red=fire, carpeting=earth, and blue=water.

Marcel Wanders

Marcel Wanders grew up in Boxtel, the Netherlands, and graduated from the School of Arts, Arnhem, in 1988. He is best known for his product designs, the project which brought him to international fame being the iconic Knotted Chair, which he produced for Droog Design in 1996 and which was later taken up by Cappellini. Today he is pretty much ubiquitous, designing quirky and decorative yet technologically ingenious products for the biggest European contemporary design manufacturers, while at the same time working on architectural and interior-design schemes, and most recently turning his hand to consumer home appliances.

In 2000 he created Moooi and today, although B&B Italia own 50% of the company, he is still its artistic director. Because of generous state subsidies given to designers in Holland, and the creative freedom taught in its design schools, Dutch design is still largely conceptual. It may have influenced the way the rest of the world looks at design but it has yet to develop a way of translating this commercially. Moooi tries to redress this imbalance. In control of both the design and the manufacturing process, it provides the opportunity to reconsider artistic aesthetics and produce products in realistic and industrial ways.

Wanders does not consider himself a Dutch designer. In fact, he refuses to categorize his work. What he is adamant about is his desire to contribute something to make the world a better place, to make objects or interiors that mean something in everyday life. Although often using innovative materials and techniques, his products tap into human emotions and have universal Proustian connotations.

Marcel Wanders is probably one of the most flamboyant characters on the design circuit today. Tall, handsome, loquacious, mischievous, confrontational, mercurial, opinionated, he is above all passionate about his work. 'I want what I do to increase in complexity.' Talking about the difference between product design and interior design he resorts to body language. Cupping his hands together as if he is holding on to something precious and delicate, he told me, 'Designing a chair is like this, whilst an interior is more like this,' gesticulating wildly he stretches out his arms to draw towards him an imaginary harvest of plenty. 'It's a narrative, rich in meaning and connotation; it's a layering, one thing on top of another, a kind of ordered chaos.' He goes on to say, 'I want to take the imagination of people and make it soar to new places. My work has to be in constant motion.'

Wanders is fairly new to interiors. Today his work in this field consists of 'Wander-Duck', the Mandarina Duck store in London; the 'Stone House' organic meeting rooms in the Interpolis offices in Tilburg, the Netherlands; the VIP room in the Dutch Pavilion at the Hannover Worldexpo; the Lute Suites apartment/hotel suites in Amstel in the Amsterdam suburbs; the public spaces of the Hotel on Rivington in New York; the interior of the Dutch Embassy in Berlin; and a small restaurant, Blits, in Rotterdam. He is currently working on the Villa Moda store in Bahrain.

(Top)
Mandarina Duck 'destination' store, London (2002) The central space is dominated by a 7m (21ft) tall mannequin inspired by *Gulliver's Travels* which contains an audio system. Forty additional normal-scaled dummies appear to breathe. The space has no internal walls. A huge spiralling silver staircase rises through the double height, behind which a chromed wall 'inhales' and 'exhales' by changing rhythmically from convex to concave.

(Below)
Thor restaurant, Hotel on the Rivington, New York (2004) The design makes reference to its location and also the notion of the past and the future. Wanders created a city plan with four distinct areas: entrance, lounge, bar and the restaurant itself. A pink plaster corridor leads from the foyer into these areas.

(Top right)
Blits restaurant, Rotterdam (2005) The building was designed by Dutch architect Francine Houben. Wanders redesigned the interiors as a theatre-like restaurant where the diners are both actors and audience. Everything is dramatic, from the curtain which swoops down over the bar to the red love-suite, with heart-shaped detailing.

(Below right)
Royal Wing Room, World Expo 2000, Hanover To maximize the small space, Wanders covered the domed roof with silvery twigs which reflect the light, as does the shiny white floor space which is surrounded by VIP chairs.

(Far right)
The Lute Suites, Amstel, near Amsterdam (2005) An innovative and unparalleled concept in hospitality, the suites are half-hotel/half-apartment and are conceived as a home-from-home for long-stay guests. Everything, from the space (all have their own front door, living room, bathroom, bedroom and kitchenette) to furniture and fittings was designed by Wanders in collaboration with Boffi, Moooi and Bisazza mosaics.

Whether working on an installation, a retail project or a hotel, Wanders' approach to any interior design project is always the same. His first consideration is scale, which he perceives in an architectural way. 'An interior has to be understandable. It has to have a story with a beginning and an end. Order is all-important and each interior has to be readable.'

The Lute Suites, however, were an epiphany for Wanders as, during the development of the project, his approach to interior design changed. Although still with an underlying order and a sound understanding of tectonics, he considers this set of apartments/hotel suites to be a design without a concept in which space is organizing itself. Unlike, for example, the Mandarina Duck outlet which was conceived in a linear way, working towards a clear goal, the Suites are less rational and more emotional. 'It has the complexity of a music score; I started from a familiar refrain and then added layers of meaning and history.'

His latest scheme in Bahrain is conceived in a similar way. 'I refer to the Villa Moda store as an international souk. It's a city plan without a plan – one idea piled up on top of another.'

Is this development something Wanders would like to take further? 'Space needs to equate to time. Maybe an interior shouldn't be understood at first sight but to be experienced as a journey of discovery. A project should perhaps develop itself. There should be no rules. It's fun to do different things, to cut through the red tape, to even look for the barriers in order to broach them.'

(Left)
Soap Stars, Exhibition Fuori Saloni, Milan (2005) In collaboration with Bisazza, Wanders' exhibition mixed his latest range of baths, sinks and toilets, 'Soap Series', with the most opulent of Bisazza mosaics. The result is a rich installation that combines the minimalism of Wanders' products with the baroque opulence of Bisazza's highly ornate mosaics.

(Top right)
Stone House, Interpolis' Headquarters, Tilburg, the Netherlands (2003) The concept was to create a series of office spaces within a network of 'cities, squares and neighbourhoods'. The 'clubhouse', break-out and meeting areas were all designed by different architects, providing inspirational collaborative environments. Wanders' brightly coloured boardroom sits in a cave-like space surrounded by work desks and shines like a beacon in the gloom.

(Below right)
Thor restaurant. The ceilings and floors are lined by wallpaper specially created by Wanders. Like a magic-eye puzzle, black and white layered patterns – foliage, circles, hexagons – blur and blend, becoming, as Wanders says, 'a wonderful pattern-less organization of atoms and neutrons, energy and purity'. The outhouse leads to the toilets. The chandelier is from Maarten Baas' Smoke range for Moooi.

Wells Mackereth

We like to create beautiful buildings and inspirational spaces designed to thrill and empower; spaces that people truly enjoy being in – to work, interact, live and relax.

Since founding their company in 1995, Sally Mackereth and James Wells have built up a reputation for creating buildings and interiors which, taking the client's brief as a starting point, reinterpret its essence from the master plan down to the smallest detail.

One of their latest projects is a case in point. Leviev is the flagship store for a Russian/Israeli diamond-mining company. New to retailing, they approached Wells Mackereth to work on an interior for their Bond Street shop, which would challenge the usual anodyne design conventions of competing diamond retailers.

For Wells Makereth, retail spaces are all about seduction; the product should never be upstaged but the interior should reflect the mood, spirit and life of the brand. On a day-to-day basis, Leviev has £150 million worth of diamonds on the premises, yet the clients wanted a welcoming atmosphere. This dichotomy resulted in the concept for the store. To visit Leviev is to visit a Mayfair home: there is no apparent security (with specialist consultants on board, security is present but kept as unobtrusive as possible); the spaces are furnished with luxurious upholstered furniture; the floors are of stone; the walls are lined and spaces are divided by layered silk chiffon and brass between sheets of glass. The colour scheme is neutral – a perfect backdrop for the sparkling and coloured diamonds on show – and the varied display boxes, ornament-like, are integrated into the furnishings. It is a departure from the traditional and is indicative of the approach of Wells Mackereth.

James Wells and Sally Mackereth met while working together for architect Stanton and Williams. Wells studied architecture at University College London and the Bartlett before working for the postmodernist Quinlan Terry. Mackereth was at Oxford Brookes University and the Architectural Association (AA) prior to employment at various architectural practices, including CZWG and the 'charismatic, inspirational' Piers Gough.

Their time at Stanton Williams instilled in them an obsession with detailing as well as the desire to break away from a modernist approach to architecture. They wanted to incorporate a range of materials, colours and warmth into their work. Their big break came with one of their first projects in partnership, the refurbishment of a loft space in New York. The client owned a castle in Scotland and wanted the Soho apartment to be the complete antithesis – a decadent, urban pad. The modern, yet luxurious interior was much publicized, including a three-page feature in the UK's *Sunday Times* 'Style' section, which greatly helped to launch Wells Mackereth's new practice.

Today their portfolio of work incorporates a broad range of typologies, from new-build to interiors, including residential, retail, high-end bar and restaurant design, and art gallery and exhibition

(Right)
Smiths of Smithfield, London (2001)
Conversion of a former meat-market warehouse into four floors of bars and restaurants, including a new steel and glass roof extension. Open all day, the spaces change to suit the mood of diners, from the breakfast crowd to late-night clubbers. The design is 'inclusive', appealing to young and old, city-slicker and trendy fashion addicts alike.

design. 'It's a conscious decision of ours to mix projects from installations to major developments. If you start to specialize, there is a danger of getting bored and boring – to become formulaic is stifling. We have an approach, a handwriting, which we carry throughout our work – tried and tested ways of handling detailing, the seductive use of contrasting materials, etc. – but our aim is to push the boundaries and create spaces which do not intimidate or patronize but enhance the quality of life and, above all, are enjoyable. We like to touch people with a subtle form of wit, and each of our projects has its own quirk.'

The duo draws influence from the city and the street: from the world around them. They admire people who work outside the industry – the Rolling Stones' set designer, Mark Fisher, and Thomas Heatherwick, whose work refuses to be defined or boxed. In Mackereth's case, her time at the AA (whose motto, incidentally, is 'Design in Beauty, Build in Truth'), in particular her association with David Green of Archigram fame, instilled in her the importance of experiencing places and situations to the full as well as the belief that architecture is for people, not for architects.

Their goal as architects is to work more in the public sector on buildings that will affect many rather than a few, and as interior architects to eventually have one of their spaces listed. Mackereth comments: 'If you go into this profession saying you only want to design something that will outlive you, then you are in for a bit of a shock; but wouldn't it be wonderful to leave behind you something like the UN interiors or the Soane Museum?'

(Left)
Leviev, London (2006)
The style of the store is clean and modern, yet fused with rare antiques. A muted colour palette of ivory and mink is accented with bronze showcases, creating a strikingly seductive environment.

(Top right)
Stone Island/CP Company, London (2000) The challenge was to reinforce a cult clothing brand by providing a suitably 'techie' environment. Working with German product designers, the design includes a double-height magnetic wall and an 'intelligent' floor of sockets with interchangeable 'light sabres' and video links from which the clothes are displayed.

(Below right).
Goya and Brassai exhibitions, Hayward Gallery, London (2001) Two major art retrospectives. The design for this show set out to create a dramatic journey through large-scaled gallery spaces where the main subject matter consisted of small-scale works on paper with tightly controlled lighting levels.

(Top)
Beach house, Sussex, UK (2005) A new-build steel-frame house. A large quantity of sliding and folding glazing allows the views of the beach to become a part of the interior.

(Centre)
Triyoga, London (2000) In this conversion of pre-war factory into a yoga centre, the architects employed a simple use of colour, modest materials and filtered natural light to create an atmosphere of peace and calm. Coloured gels on the windows create subtle light effects on the white rubber floors.

(Below)
Pringle of Scotland, London (2002) Commissioned to facilitate a major repositioning of this long-established fashion brand, the Bond Street flagship store reinforces a subliminal message of Pringle's historical Scottish roots through scale, colour, materials and witty references. 'Our skill as designers is to be able to re-invent a little bit of history – to celebrate what's there with subtle interventions.'

(Right)
Bumble and Bumble, New York (2006) B & B is a major hair salon and retailer housed in eight-storied building in the downtown meat-packing district. The design introduced a series of movable layers and elements to the vast top-floor space to break it down into pockets of activity, blurring boundaries between retail, gallery, café and photo-shoot areas. The main device is a series of Perspex tube screens on casters, reminiscent of giant shampoo foam bubbles.

Clive Wilkinson was born in South Africa and was educated at the University of Cape Town and the Architectural Association in London, where he studied under Peter Cook and Ron Herron of Archigram fame, as well as Rem Koolhaas and Zaha Hadid. 'My architectural education was very influential and my thinking was largely established at that time.' He worked for Terry Farrell and Partners before being attracted by the greater creative possibilities offered by a move to LA, and the promise of a client base eager to push the limits of creativity.

He founded his own practice in Los Angeles in 1991, having been hired and fired by Frank Gehry, whom he nevertheless refers to as his 'literal mentor'. The project which made his name also indirectly resulted from this collaboration. 'My involvement with interior architecture was accidental. I was working on large building structures for Gehry, and had a side job designing the interiors for Chiat/Day advertising. When I started my firm they were the first people to give me work. TBWA/Chiat/Day put our firm on the map. We are probably still most proud of it as it also set a new paradigm for workspace design for large creative companies.' This 'city' of stacked canary-yellow, customized container offices heralded the start of what is now known as the break-out office environment, and from its completion in 1998 and the media coverage it attracted, big-name ad agency commissions began rolling in.

Since that time, the firm has completed over 90,000 sq m (a million sq ft) of creative workplace and educational projects. Its portfolio includes urban design, creative workplace design, and educational, residential and retail projects. Notable schemes include the HQ offices for Foote Cone & Belding; an urban regeneration project for Max Maier, in Ludwigsburg, Germany; the LA headquarters of Pallotta TeamWorks; the New York headquarters of ad agency J. Walter Thompson; several projects for the Fashion Institute of Design and Merchandising (FIDM); and the interior of Mother's London offices with its now-famous 76.2-m (250-ft) -long concrete table. One of their biggest successes resulted from winning the competition design for the master plan of Google's 'campus' in Silicon Valley.

CWA (the practice prides itself on promoting collaboration and teamwork as the most effective way of delivering a creative end-product) does not consider having a definitive style, stating that what might be perceived as such comes from their method of putting things together. They often quote the film director Jean-Luc Godard's adage that 'style is the outside of content', yet their interiors layer raw, often industrial, environments with bright colours, creating spaces with the wow factor which break down the barriers between work and play, and between solitary and group effort.

Wilkinson strongly believes that there is no boundary between architecture and interior architecture and does not mind how people label him, as long as 'it is not reduced to interior decorator'. Talking to

Clive Wilkinson Architects

(Top)
Pallotta TeamWorks, Los Angeles (2002)
The concept for the office derives from the mobile 'tent cities' that the client (a charity fundraising company) uses to stage events. Circulation areas are treated as external streets. The 'tents' are anchored to prefabricated shipping containers, which accommodate private offices and meeting rooms. To cut down on MEP, CWA have allowed the tented structures to breathe while the communal communication areas are left without air conditioning.

(Below)
FIDM's Annex, Studio East and Studio West, Los Angeles (2004)
The client's brief emphasized individual and collaborative work as well as a space which would reflect regional LA culture. Primary elements use the height of the old banking hall, and the design abstractly alludes to natural elements indigenous to southern California.

Frame magazine for its celebratory fiftieth issue, he commented, 'It's always depressing having this profession confused with interior decoration. Real creativity is like writing a book. Decoration is like copying lines from a newspaper and trying to make your handwriting look pretty.'

Wilkinson draws his inspiration from the faces of people engaged in the struggle of life. 'I am constantly aware that what we do is a flash of history which will take others to decide its relevance.' His greatest influences come from the literary world: T. S. Eliot, Ezra Pound, John Donne and Henry James as well as the later revolutionary writer/critics Walter Benjamin and Marshal McLuhan. Architecturally, his heroes are Le Corbusier, Louis Kahn, Alvar Aalto and Frank Lloyd Wright. Again, in conversation with *Frame*: 'Today there is a wonderful opening up of opportunities and a loss of dogma, which is liberating. Architects have mostly accepted the world itself as the largest contributor to the culture of architecture rather than irrelevant academic obsessions.'

CWA is known for working closely with its clients: 'Clients choose us when they want a creative and distinct brand expression, and because they think we will listen to them well (which we do).' The company's members spend a major part of their time helping their clients understand what they want and the results, interiors very much of the moment, are a blend of pragmatism coupled with creative invention.

'We want to do work that affects people and makes their lives richer. It needs to function on many levels … we have little interest in work that is part of a culture of luxury and personal gratification for the elite.'

(Top)
TBWA/Chiat/Day, Playa Vista, LA (1998)
The brief called for an 'advertising city' to be constructed inside a large warehouse. A small urban environment was developed with multiple levels, green park space and an irregular 'skyline'. Traditional planning concepts: Downtown, Main Street, neighbourhoods, parks, alleys, civic functions, building façades and street furniture all became elements necessary to humanize the raw industrial space.

(Below)
Google headquarters, Mountain View, California (2005) The master plan follows a simple distribution of work neighbourhoods and a main street. All shared resources, from meeting room to micro-kitchens and library lounges, are located here.

(Far right)
Mother, London (2004)
The main activity takes place on the third floor of a large warehouse space in Shoreditch. To unite this with the two floors below, CWA constructed a new concrete staircase which cuts through the building and turns into the agency's cast-in-place worktable which circuits the room like a racetrack. The design is based on Fiat Lingotto in Turin, Italy.

Yabu Pushelberg

George Yabu and Glenn Pushelberg met while still at school and studied interior design together at Ryerson Polytechnic University, Toronto, in the mid-1970s. They worked independently before founding their partnership in 1980. 'Many design companies are started by people who worked for another company, but, we're kind of self-invented – there's no history of any other practice in our association.'

Today Yabu Pushelberg is one of the leading interior-design companies in North America with offices in Toronto and New York employing over 70 staff. Its portfolio crosses all typologies, from retail to hotels and from restaurants to showrooms. It works internationally and has built up an impressive blue-chip client list. Notable projects include the W Hotel with its famous Blue Fin restaurant, Times Square, New York; Four Seasons Hotel, Tokyo (a further two are on site in Dubai and Hawaii); the Amore Pacific skincare shop, New York; two Lane Crawford outlets in Hong Kong; the Graves 601 Hotel in Minneapolis; and St Regis hotels in San Francisco and Mexico City, with a further due for completion shortly in Hawaii.

The architect/client relationship is an important one for Yabu and Pushelberg. The individuals and companies with whom they work are famously high-maintenance, and it is noteworthy that the duo does not settle for the simple route of producing a unique design to fit a client programme. 'You've really got to form the client. You've got to say, "you've given me a brief and the brief is missing key parts", or "the brief is missing the essence of what it should be, and this is what we think it should be and this is why".'

The results are sophisticated and tranquil interiors which avoid trendiness but are not lacking in both the innovative use of luxurious materials or signature details which include specially commissioned finishes, such as the 'Wave Wall' at Blue Fin, and installations. Particularly impressive is Hirotoshi Sawada's backdrop of recycled pieces of paper behind the reception desk at the Graves 601 Hotel in Minneapolis. Yabu Pushelberg is often quoted as saying that its work goes beyond an aesthetic to the idea: 'We seek to evoke feeling and visual emotion without an excess of design. We're kind of like design sociologists looking for an angle which is not gimmicky but which will engage a user on a human level and draw them back again and again.'

The chairman and CEO of Four Seasons Hotels & Resorts, one of the world's largest operators of luxury hotels looks on the practice as one of a kind: 'The team at Yabu Pushelberg has an unusual talent and a unique style that is both contemporary and timeless. They truly create interiors that will endure the test of time'.

What Yabu Pushelberg aims to achieve in its work is the creation of interiors which are 'different' and push artistic limits but do not pander to today's trend for fashionable designer spaces. 'It's important to keep on doing new things,

(Right)
Blue Fin restaurant, W Hotel, New York (2001) The area adjoining the lobby is dominated by a textured wall, in front of which hangs a sculpture b Japanese artist Hirotoshi Sawada. Together they represent a school of fish swimming upstream. The interior is cool and refined with a touch of the exotic.

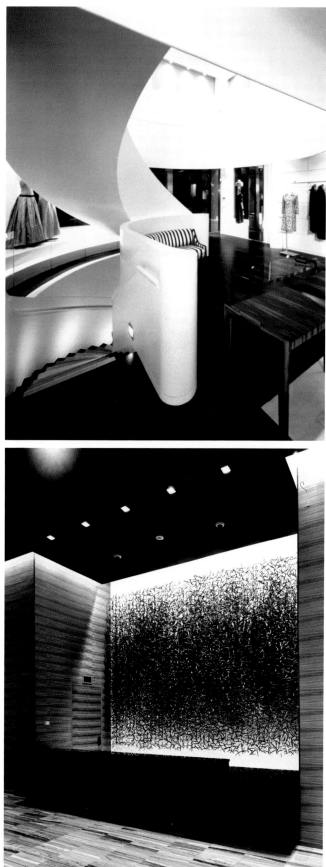

but in a more restrained way: reducing
design to a clean and simple level.'

Early work focused mainly on retail
and residential, via their big break coming
with a series of commissions in Taiwan,
Japan, Hong Kong and South Korea,
where the firm made an impression in the
late 1980s and early 1990s by developing
different solutions for individual clients
rather than adopting a blanket formula as
was more common with other American
practices working in Asia at that time.
This approach got them noticed, and in
1998, Neiman Marcus, which owns
Bergdorf Goodman, commissioned them
to design the jewellery and perfumery
departments in the basement of its Fifth
Avenue department store: 'We took this
grand dowager and made it fresh but still
respected what it is.' The pair's understanding of the emotional history of the
store resulted in Tiffany contacting them
to work on the revamp of its famous New
York premises. Because of its special place
in the city's culture, this was a sensitive
renovation which the duo carried out
floor by floor. 'We had to work like good
plastic surgeons to ensure it looked better
than ever after the operation. The idea
was that no one should recall what it once
looked like.'

Masters of both renovation and the
contemporary avant-garde, Yabu
Pushelberg create environments which
are distinctive, diverse, thought-provoking and original but which, at the same
time, are in tune with the commercial
imperatives of its high-profile clientele.

(Top)
**Fin Chinese Restaurant,
Las Vegas (2006)**
YB took elements from
classical Chinese arts and
crafts and re-interpreted
them using cutting-edge
technology. The silvered
glass horse stands on a
'floating'/ stone plinth in a
reflective pool of water.
The textural feature behind
is made from custom-
made ceramic tiles by
artist Pascale Girardin.

(Centre)
**W Hotel, Times Square,
New York (2001)** Semi-
enclosed 'cabins' around
the perimeter of the lobby
break down the barrier
between private and public
space. The aesthetic of the
hotel is zen-like, imbued
with natural colours and
materials and offers a
series of striking visual
vignettes at every turn.

(Below)
**Lane Crawford, Pacific
Place, Hong Kong (2004)**
The company had become
somewhat moribund, and
looked to YP to develop
an identity for a younger,
more energetic audience.
The shopping experience
is a sensory and interactive
delight. The sneaker
department continually
revolves the merchandise
around hue-shifting
translucent panels.

(Far right)
**St Regis Hotel, San
Francisco (2006)** Situated
across the road from the
San Francisco Museum of
Modern Art, the concept
is based on the artistic
aspects of the location.
Original artworks are
displayed throughout
the public spaces. San
Francisco is America's
gateway to the Pacific;
a link between East
and West, and the
hotel contains many
eastern references.

Bibliography

3deluxe
3deluxe projects, Die Gestalten Verlag, 2002
www.3deluxe.de

24H Architecture
www.24h-architecture.com

Harry Allen
Wolff, Laetitia and Wang Xu (eds.), *Harry Allen
& Associates*, Design Focus series, 2000
www.harryallendesign.com

Ron Arad
Ron Arad, Barry Friedman Ltd, 2005
Ron Arad Talks to Matthew Collings, Phaidon Press,
2004
Sudjic, Deyan, *Ron Arad*, with graphics by Angus
Hyland, Pentagram, Laurence King Publishing, 1999
Ron Arad Associates: One off Three, with introductions
by Ettore Sottsass and Cedric Price, Artemis
Architectural Publications, 1993
www.ronarad.com

Antoni Arola
'Design Guide of Spain 06–07', *Experimenta*,
pp. 166–167
Premio Nacional de Diseño 2003, edited by Ministerio
de Ciencia y Tecnología and Barcelona Centro de Diseño
(BCD)
Zabalascoa, Anatxu, 'Perfil', *Experimenta*, no. 56
www.estudiarola.com

AV62
Wilhide, Elizabeth, *Design and Build Your Dream Home*,
Conran Octopus, 2006
Eiritz, Marta, *Lofts and Apartments*, Atrium, 2003
www.av62.com

Christian Biecher
Christian Biecher, foreword by Christian Lacroix,
coll. Design & Designers, Pyramyd, 2003
Michel, Florence and Constance Rubini, *Christian
Biecher: Architect and Designer*, Grégoire Gardette,
2002
www.biecher.com

Block Architecture
www.blockarchitecture.com

Giorgio Borruso
Blokland, Tessa, *Dress Code*, Frame Publications, 2006
Almanac of Architecture and Design 2005, Greenway
Communications, 2005
Store and Retail Spaces 7, ST Media Group
International
www.borrusodesign.com

Cassandra Complex
Van Schaik, Leon, *Design City Melbourne*, Wiley
Academy, 2006
Beaver, Robyn, *100 Top Houses from Down Under*,
The Images Publishing Group, 2005
Hyatt, Peter, *Great Glass Buildings*, The Images
Publishing Group, 2004
Michell, George, *New Australian Style 2 – Inner City
Living*, Thames & Hudson, 2003
www.cassandracomplex.com.au

Johnson Chou
Mostaedi, Arian, *Great Spaces: Flexible Homes*,
Link Books, 2006
Frank, Karen A. (ed.), 'Johnson Chou Architects' in
Food and Architecture, Wiley Academy, 2002
Del Valle, Cristina, *New Bars and Restaurants*, Harper
Design, 2004
Canizares, Ana Cristina G., *Home*, Loft Publications,
2002
www.johnsonchou.com

Antonio Citterio
Prestinenza Puglisi, Luigi, *Antonio Citterio*,
Edilstampa, 2005
Klein, Caroline, *Cool Shops Milan*, teNeues, 2005
Italy Builds, Arca Edizioni, 2005
Conran, Terence and Maz Fraser, *Designers on Design*,
Conran Octopus, 2004
Bassi, Alberto, *Antonio Citterio: Industrial Design*,
Electa, 2004
www.antonio-citterio.it

Claesson, Koivisto Rune
The Models, Garbor Palotai Publisher, 2005
Nine Houses, Sfera Publishing/Ricordi & Sfera Co., Ltd,
2003
Mårten Claesson, Eero Koivisto, Ola Rune: Furniture,
Totem Design Group, 2002
Claesson Koivisto Rune, GG, 2001
40 Architects Under 40, Taschen Books, 2000
www.claesson-koivisto-rune.se

Concrete
Concrete Architectural Associates, *Inspired*, 2005
www.concreteamsterdam.nl

Matali Crasset
Matali Crasset, daab, 2006
Williams, Gareth, *Matali Crasset – Design + Designer
006*, Pyramyd, 2003
www.matalicrasset.com

Interior Architecture Now

Eldridge Smerin
Chapman, Tony, *The Stirling Prize – Ten Years of Architecture and Innovation*, Merrell Publishers, 2006
Corcuera Aranguiz, Antonio, *Casas en la entré medianeras*, Monsa, 2005
The Architecture Foundation, *New Architects 2 – Guide to Britain's Best Young Architectural Practice*, Merrell Publishers, 2001
www.eldridgesmerin.com

Fantastic Design Works Incorporated
Tokyo Restaurant Design Collection, Japan Planning Association, 2006
Light Fever, Frame Publications, 2005
Takahashi, Masaaki, *Design City Tokyo*, Wiley Academy, 2004
Coates, Nigel, *Collidoscope: New Interior Design*, Laurence King Publishing, 2004
www.fantasticdesign.com

Gabellini Sheppard Associates
Meyers, Victoria, *Designing with Light*, Laurence King Publishing, 2006
Bingham, Neil, *The New Boutique: Fashion and Design*, Merrell Publishers, 2005
Curtis, Eleanor, *Fashion Retail*, John Wiley & Sons, 2004
Merkel, Jane, 'Top of the Rock Observatory', *Architectural Design*, May–June 2006, pp. 110–117
Vercelloni, Matteo, 'Silent Rooms/Absolute Spaces', *Interni*, December 1998, pp. 83–109
www.gabelliniassociates.com

Graft
Häuser, 2006, No. 5, pp. 148–154
Quest, 2005, No. 16, pp. 258–261
Bob International Magazine of Space Design, 2004, no. 006, pp. 6–27
www.usefulandagreeable.com/graft.html

Graven Images
Cameron, N., *Graven Images: Design in a Cold Climate*, Frame Monographs of Contemporary Interior Architects, Frame Publications, 2002
Graven Images, *Design Stories*, Graven Images, 2004
Flyett, P. and C. Mckay, *Re: Motion – New Movements in Scottish Architecture*, The Lighthouse, 2003
www.graven.co.uk

Eva Jiricna
Modernism, exhibition catalogue, Victoria and Albert Museum, London, 2006
V / Ex Terior: The Works of Eva Jiricna, Prostor, 2005
Manser, Jose, *The Joseph Shops: Eva Jiricna*, Phaidon Press, 1991
'Hotel Joseph', *Iconic Design Hotels*, Links International, 2005
www.ejal.com

Patrick Jouin
French Interior Architecture, ICI Consultants, 2006
Hudson, Jennifer, *1000 New Designs (and Where to Find Them)*, Laurence King Publishing, 2006
Architecture Now!, Volume IV, Taschen Books, 2006
Restaurant Design, daab, 2004
Patrick Jouin – Design and Designer, Pyramyd, 2004
www.patrickjouin.com

Klein Dytham architecture
Bullivant, Lucy, *Responsive Environments Architecture, Art & Design*, V&A Contemporary, 2006
Architecture Now!, Volume IV, Taschen Books, 2006
Wollhein, Ralf, *Patterns in Design, Art and Architecture*, Birkhauser, 2005
www.klein-dytham.com

Lazzarini Pickering Architetti
Interni, December 2000, no. 507
Frame, July 1998, no. 3
L'Architecture d'Aujourd'hui, February 1998, no. 315
www.lazzarinipickering.com

Lewis Tsurumaki Lewis Architects
Lewis.Tsurumaki.Lewis, *LTL: Opportunistic Architecture*, Princeton Architectural Press (release date: 2007)
Lewis.Tsurumaki.Lewis, *Situation Normal … Pamphlet Architecture #21*, Princeton Architectural Press, 1998
www.ltlwork.net

Lot-ek
Lot-ek: MDU (with essays by Aaron Betsky, Robert Kronenburg and Henry Urbach), DAP, 2003
Ian Luna (ed.), *New New York* (with an introduction by Joseph Giovannini), Rizzoli, 2003
Lot-ek Urbanscan, Princeton Architectural Press, 2002
Mobile: the art of portable architecture, Princeton Architectural Press, 2002
www.lot-ek.com

M41LH2
Ryder, Bethan, *New Bar + Club Design*, Laurence King Publishing, 2005
Hasanovic, Aisha, *100 of the World's Best Bars*, The Images Publishing Group, 2005
Canizares, Ana, *Chillout Spaces*, Tectum, 2004
Bahamon, Alejandro, *Chill Out*, Feierabend Verlag OHG
www.m41lh2.com

Norisada Maeda
New Domestic Interiors, Structure, 2005
Today's City Houses, Structure, 2005
Capturing Space, Harper Design International, 2004
Japan Modern, Periplus Editions, 2004
www.5a.biglobe.ne.jp/~norisada

Yasmine Mahmoudieh
'Hotel Design For the Future', *The Leading Hotels of the World*, May 2005
'Plane Talking', *Identity*, March 2005
'Five+ Sensotel: Sensory Hotel Exhibition', WGSN, March/April 2005
'Yasmine Mahmoudieh', *Interior*, May 2003
www.mahmoudieh.de

Maurice Mentjens
Blokland, Tessa, Dresscode, Frame Publications, 2006
Real Dutch Design 0607, BIS, 2006
Muto, Schiochi, *World Restaurants and Bars*, Shotenkenchiku-sha Publishing, 2005
Riewoldt, Otto, *Retail Design*, Laurence King Publishing, 2000
www.mauricementjens.com

Merkx + Girod Architekten
International Interiors Annual 2005, Rijksmuseum Amsterdam, 2005
1000 Architects, The Images Publishing Group, 2004
www.merkx-girod.nl

Morphosis
Frederic, Migayrou, *Morphosis: Continuities of the Incomplete*, Adagp, 2006
Mayne, Thom, *Fresh Morphosis – 1998–2004*, Rizzoli, 2006
Lee, Uje (ed.), C3 Korea 256, C3 Design Group, December 2005 (CAL, SCS)
Futagawa, Yoshio (ed.), GA Document Special Issue, *Competitions*. 87: Morphosis, August 2005
Mayne, Thom and Val Warke, *Morphosis*, Phaidon Press, 2003
Kipnis, Jeffrey and Todd Gannon, *Morphosis: Diamond Ranch High School*, The Monacelli Press, 2001
Lee, Uje (ed.), *New World Architect #7: Morphosis*, C3A, 2001
Bransburg, Pablo, *Casas Internaciona* 27: Morphosis, Kliczkowski, 2000
Lee, Uje (ed.), *C3 Korea 195*, C3 Design Group, November 1999
Vidler, Anthony, *Morphosis: Buildings and Projects 1993–1997*, Rizzoli, 1999
www.morphosis.net

Torsten Neeland
Brodbeck, Makus and Darius Ramazani (eds), *Rooms 40 Räume Berlin*, Avedition, 2005
Tom Dixon (ed.), *The International Yearbook 2004*, Laurence King, 2004
New Design, 2006, issue 40
Wallpaper, 2001, no. 9
www.torsten-neeland.co.uk

Fabio Novembre
Watson, Howard, *The Design Mix: Bars, Cocktails and Style*, John Wiley & Sons, 2006
Luna, Ian, *Retail, Architecture + Shopping*, Rizzoli, 2005
Cooper, Philip (ed.), *New Bar + Club Design*, Laurence King Publishing, 2005
Krauel, Jacobo (ed.), *Iconic Design Hotels*, Links International, 2005
Hasanovic, Aisha, *110 of the World's Best Bars*, The Images Publishing Group, 2005
Terragni, Emilia (ed.), *Spoon*, Phaidon Press, 2002
www.novembre.it

John Pawson
John Pawson Works, Phaidon Press, 2005
John Pawson: Themes and Projects, IVAM/Phaidon Press, 2002
John Pawson, Gustavo Gili, 1998
www.johnpawson.com

Pentagram
Yelavich, Susan (ed.), *Pentagram Profile*, 2004
Pentagram Book Five, The Monacelli Press, 1999
Hillman, David, *Pentagames*, Simon & Schuster, 1990
www.pentagram.com

plajer + franz studio
Blokland, Tessa, *Dresscode*, Frame Publications, 2006
'Racy Red and Smooth White', *Frame*, July 2006
'Architecture' *Quest*, January 2003
www.plajer-franz.de

Francesc Pons
www.estudifrancescpons.com

Pugh + Scarpa Architecture
Lan, Bruce (ed.), *Pugh + Scarpa*, China Architecture & Building Press, 2005
Losantos, Agata, *The Big Book of Interiors*, Collins Design, 2006
Ryker, Lori, *Off the Grid: Modern Houses + Alternative Energy*, Gibbs Smith, 2005
www.pugh-scarpa.com

Andrée Putman
Gerschel, Stéphane, *Putman Style*, Assouline, 2005
Andrée Putman, Pyramyd, 2003
Tasma-Anargyros, Sophie, *Andrée Putman*, Norma Editions, 1993
www.andreeputman.com

Muti Randolph
Frame, July/August 2006, no. 51
www.muti.cx

Karim Rashid
Rashid, Karim, *Design Your Self*, Regan Books, 2006
Karim, Rashid, Albrecht Bangert and Conway Lloyd Morgan, *Digipop*, Taschen Books, 2005
Bartolucci, Marisa, *Karim Rashid*, Chronicle Books, 2004
Rashid, Karim, *Karim Rashid: Evolution*, Universe, 2004
Rashid, Karim, *I Want to Change the World*, Universe, 2001
www.karimrashid.com

Francesc Rifé
Projects by Francesc Rifé, Gráficas Vernetta, 2005
www.rife-design.com

David Rockwell
Pleasure: The Architecture and Design of Rockwell Group, Universe, 2002
www.rockwellgroup.com

Fernando Salas
Casa Decor Book, 2005
Guide Hotels & Style, 2002
International Interiors 5, Calman & King Ltd, 1995
www.fernandosalas.com

Sevil Peach Gence Associates
Zelinsky, Marilyn, *The Inspired Workplace*, Rockport, 2004
Myerson, Jeremy and Philip Ross, *The 21st Century Office*, Laurence King Publishing, 2003
Duffy, Francis, *The New Office*, Conran Octopus, 1997
Jeska, Simone and Birgit Klauk, *Office Building – A Design Manual*, Birkhäuser
www.sevilpeach.com

Shubin + Donaldson
25 Houses Under 3000 Square Feet, Collins Design, 2006
Beach Houses, Feierabend Verlag, 2006
The 21st Century Office, Laurence King Publishing, 2003
Offices: Designer and Design, Loft, 2003
www.shubinanddonaldson.com

Philippe Starck
Tasma-Anargyros, Sophie, E. M. Cooper and E. Laville, *Starck by Starck*, Taschen Books, 2003
Lloyd-Morgan, Conway, *Philippe Starck*, Universe, 1999
Ryder, Bethan, *Restaurant Design*, Laurence King Publishing, 2004
www.philippe-starck.com

Seth Stein
Webb, Michael, *Art Invention House*, Rizzoli, 2005
Long, Kieran, New London Interiors, Merrell Publishers, 2004
Powell, Kenneth, *New Architecture in Britain*, Merrell Publishers, 2003
The House Book, Phaidon Press, 2001
www.sethstein.com

Tarruella and López
'Barcelona Architecture & Design', *Teneus*, 2004, p. 130
Sleeper, 2004, p. 88
Elle Deco, 2000, no. 65, p. 30
www.tarruellalopez.com

Adam D. Tihany
Tihany, Adam D. and Marci Sutin Levin, *Tihany Style: Hospitality Design*, Mondadori Electa, 2004
Tihany, Adam D., *Designing in Rome*, Edizioni Archivolto, 2003
Tihany Design, The Monacelli Press, 1999
www.tihanydesign.com

Marcel Wanders
Wanders, Marcel and Jennifer Hudson, *International Design Yearbook 2005*, Laurence King Publishing, 2005
Icon: the Official Guide to the London Design Festival 2005, Icon, 2005
White, Lisa, *View on Colour: Armour*, United, 2003
Voogel, M, *Dutch Interior Collections*, ten Hagen en Stam, 2000
www.marcelwanders.com

Wells Mackereth
The Architectural Foundation, *New Architects, a Guide to Britain's Best Young Architectural Practices*, Booth-Clibborn Editions, 1998.
Lond, Kieran, *New London Interiors*, Merrell Publishers, 2004
Field, Marcus and Mark Irving, *The Lofts*, Laurence King Publishing, 1999
www.wellsmackereth.com

Clive Wilkinson Architects
Chase, John Leighton, *LA 2000+: New Architecture in Los Angeles*, The Monacelli Press, 2006
Myerson, Jeremy and Philip Ross, *The 21st Century Office*, Laurence King Publishing, 2003
Chang, Jade, 'Behind the Glass Curtain', *Metropolis*, July 2006, pp. 136–147
'Honor Awards Interiors', *Architectural Record*, June 2006, pp. 175, 178–179
Zoo, Will Gompertz, 2001
www.clivewilkinson.com

Yabu Pushelberg
Cool Restaurants New York, teNeues
Ryder, Bethan, *Restaurant Design*, Laurence King Publishing, 2004
www.yabupushelberg.com

Index

Photo Credits

Åke E: Son Lindman (82–87, 102–103)
Roos Aldershoff (193 bottom, 195–197)
Courtesy Harry Allen & Associates (23 bottom right, 25)
Daici Ano (144–145, 146 bottom)
Davide Antonate (209)
Isaac Applebaum (75 bottom)
Courtesy Ron Arad Associates (27–33)
Tom Arben (71 top)
Susan Arechaga (43 bottom)
Luís Asín (310 bottom)
Farshid Assassi (202 left, 292 right)
Alejo Bagué (309 bottom–310 top, 312)
Patrick Bailer (297)
Roméo Balancourt (139 top)
Marc Ballogg (318 bottom)
Gabriele Basilico (76–77)
Jan Bitter (122–123)
Luc Boegely (47, 49 left)
Luc Boegely/Artedia (298)
Tom Bonner (290–292 left, 293–295)
Richard Bryant/ARCAID (131, 132 right, 134 top, 135, 302, 304, 307)
Hiepler Brunier (120–121)
Jordi Canosa (39)
John Casado (21)
Josep Casanova (42 top, 44 top)
Lluis Casals (280 bottom right)
Courtesy Cassandra Complex (68)
Benny Chan (59, 60 bottom, 62–63, 333–336)
Leon Chew (53–57)
Courtesy Concrete Architectural Associates (90, 91 bottom, 92 right, 93 bottom)
Geoffrey Cottenceau (97)
Matali Crasset Productions (96)
Richard Davies (100–101, 303, 305 bottom, 328–329 top)
Diephotodesigner.de (229–233)
Evan Dion (339, 342 top and middle)
Lyndon Douglas (104–105)
Thomas Duval (137–138. 139 bottom, 140, 141 bottom)
L'Espace S.A. (51)

Alberto Ferrero (210–215)
Rômulo Fialdini or Muti Randolph (253–257)
Joe Fletcher (343)
Klaus Frahm (205, 206)
Scott Frances (273)
William Furniss (50 top left)
Dennis Gilbert/VIEW (219 top)
Richard Glover/VIEW (217, 219 bottom, 220–221 bottom)
John Gollings (65–67, 69 top)
Janos Grapow (316 left)
Courtesy Graven Images (128)
Patrick Gries (95 top, 98)
Courtesy Guerlain (248–249)
Hage (24)
Roland Halbe/artur (203)
Bruno Helbling (208 top)
Richard van Herckenrode (43 top, 45)
Heinrich Hermes (208 bottom)
Keith Hunter (126–127 top, 129)
Industrial & Corporate Profiles (150 right)
Bert Janssen (190 right)
Jean François Jaussaud (261 top, 263)
Courtesy Eva Jiricna Architects (133 bottom)
David M Joseph (262 top, 340–341)
David M Joseph and The Rockwell Group (276 bottom, 277 top)
Jun Kawasjima (109 bottom left)
Kessler (208 middle)
Katsuhisa Kida (143, 147)
Jody Kivort (224)
Nikolas Koenig (301)
Luc Kramer (92)
Theo Krijgsman (192 top)
Kim van der Laden (89 top, 93 top)
Eric Laignol (136, 141 top)
André Lichtenberg (321 top)
Linus Lintner (185)
Courtesy Lot-ek (162 top)
Courtesy Yasmine Mahmoudieh (181–184)
Gilles Martin-Raget (150 left)
Andrea Martiradonna (315, 316 right)
Peter Mauss/ESTO (225 top)
Renzo Mazzolini (125, 127 bottom)
James Merrell (330 top)

Christian Michel/VIEW (218)
Nina Miralbell/Toni Lladó of Santa & Cole (38 bottom)
Keisuke Miyamoto (108)
Arash Moallemi (262 bottom)
Jean-Marie Monthiers (48, 49 right)
André Morain – Fondation de France (95 bottom)
Michael Moran (155–159)
Courtesy Morphosis (199)
Courtesy M. W. Moss Ltd (23 top)
Jeroen Musch (89 bottom)
Nacasa & Partners (22, 107, 108 top and bottom right, 110–111, 173, 174–175, 176 bottom–177, 342 bottom)
Ivan Nemec (134)
Daniël Nicolas (322 bottom)
Sam Nugroho (319 bottom)
Gerry O'Leary (50 top right)
Brian Park (259)
Jordi Pareto (311 top)
Courtesy Pentagram (223 top)
Keith Perry (330 bottom)
Matteo Piazza (149, 151–153)
Eugeni Pons (34–37, 38 top, 42, 265–271, 308 top, 311 bottom)
Inga Powilleit – styling Tatjana Quox (321 bottom–322 top, 325 bottom)
Matti Pyykkö (167 bottom–168, 169 bottom, 170–171)
Matti Pyykkö/Janne Suhonen (167 top)
Emanuel Raab (9–12 top & bottom left, 13)
Francesco Radino (132 left)
Paul Raeside (327)
Marvin Rand (240–245)
Ed Reeve (226)
Christian Richters (15–19)
Ricky Ridecos (118–119)
Courtesy The Rockwell Group (276 bottom)
Jordi Sarra (280 bottom left)
Phil Sayer (223 bottom)
Eric Ian Schaetzke (22 bottom left)
Arjen Schmitz (187–190 left, 191)
Rudi Schmutz (207)
Volker Seding (71 bottom–75 top)
Eva Serrats (41 bottom)

Deidi von Shaewen (246–247, 250–251)
Shin Photowork (178 left)
Shinozawa Archi Photo (176, 178 right–179)
Yoshio Shiratori (50 bottom)
Imanol Sistiaga (45 bottom)
Kolin Smith (260)
Tim Soar (225 bottom)
Raimon Solà (234–239)
Uwe Spoering (99)
Wolfgang Stahl (12 bottom right)
Courtesy Philippe Starck (299 bottom–300 top left)
Courtesy Seth Stein (305 top, 306)
Morley von Sternberg/ARCAID (299 top)
Timothy Street-Porter (300 right)
Timothy Street-Porter and The Rockwell Group (277 bottom)
Janne Suhonen (169 top)
Kozo Takayama (146 top)
Ottavio Tomasini (324)
Leo Torri (78–81)
Gary Turnball (286–289 top)
George Turberg (323)
Nick Turner (227)
Tom Vack (261 bottom)
Thomas Vagner (281)
Rafael Vargas (279–280 top, 282 top–283, 313)
Marc Vaughn (60 top, 61)
Colin Vincent (91 top)
Peter Vitale (20)
Pieter Vlamings (194)
Deidi von Shaewen (246–247, 250–251)
Courtesy Marcel Wanders Studio (325 top)
Paul Warchol (112–117, 161, 162 bottom, 163, 164 bottom–165, 314, 318 top)
Paul Warchol and The Rockwell Group (274–275)
Michael Weber (317, 319 top)
Courtesy Wells Meckereth (329 bottom, 330 middle, 331)
Felix Wey (287 bottom)
Courtesy Whitney Museum (164 top)
Adrian Wilson (337)
Miro Zagnoli (285)
Kim Zwarts (200–201, 202 right)